WILD BRITAIN

A TRAVELER'S AND NATURALIST'S GUIDE

DOUGLAS BOTTING

PRENTICE HALL
NEW YORK

Published in the United States
and Canada in 1989 by
Prentice Hall Trade Division
A division of Simon & Schuster Inc.
One Gulf & Western Plaza
New York, New York 10023

Designed and produced by
Sheldrake Press Ltd
188 Cavendish Road
London SW12 0DA

ISBN 0-13-959560-0

Printed in Italy by Imago Publishing

EDITOR: SIMON RIGGE
Picture Editor: Karin B. Hills
Art Direction and Book Design:
Bob Hook & Ivor Claydon
Assistant Editors: Sarah Bevan, Chris Schüler
Researcher: Dominic Cotton
Editorial Assistants: Fenella Dick, Joan Lee,
Sally Weatherill
Production Manager: Hugh Allan
Production Assistant: Helen Seccombe
Maps: Oxford Cartographers
Line illustrations: Syd Lewis

THE AUTHOR

DOUGLAS BOTTING was born in London
and educated at Oxford. He has travelled to
Brazil, South Yemen, the Sahara, Arctic
Siberia, and to many European wild places
including the reed marshes of the Danube delta.
   Douglas Botting's travel books include *One
Chilly Siberian Morning*, *Wilderness Europe*
and *Rio de Janeiro*. He has also written a
biography of the great naturalist and explorer
Alexander von Humboldt, entitled *Humboldt
and the Cosmos*. Douglas Botting is General
Editor of the Traveler's and Naturalist's
Guide series.

CONTRIBUTORS

NEIL FAIRBAIRN, who contributed many of
the fact packs and smaller exploration zones
throughout the book, is a freelance writer and
bassoon player. His books include *A Traveller's
Guide To The Kingdoms of Arthur*.

FERDIE McDONALD, who made extensive
contributions to the chapter on Lowland
Scotland, is a freelance writer specialising in
travel and guide books.

DAVID SAUNDERS, who made extensive
contributions to the chapter on Wales, is
director of the Dyfed Wildlife Trust. Formerly
Warden of Skomer Island and organiser of
Operation Seafarer, he has written many bird
books.

CONSULTANTS

JOHN BURTON is a natural history and
wildlife conservation writer and consultant.
Formerly secretary of the Fauna and Flora
Preservation Society, he is the co-founder with
Douglas Botting of the Traveler's and
Naturalist's Guide series.

DAVID BLACK is a writer and editor who has
worked on many nature books including Gerald
and Lee Durrell's *Practical Guide For The
Amateur Naturalist*.

ALLAN MARLES is a map consultant with
many years' experience with the Ordnance
Survey.

For a full list of credits and acknowledgements
see page 224.

CONTENTS

This book is dedicated to the memory of my father
Leslie William Botting
who loved the countryside of Britain and all its wild creatures

ABOUT THE SERIES

What would the world be, once bereft
Of wet and of wilderness? Let them be
  left,
O let them be left, wildness and wet;
Long live the weeds and the wilderness
  yet.

Gerard Manley Hopkins: Inversnaid

These books are about those embattled refuges of wildness and wet, the wild places of Europe. But where, in this most densely-populated sub-continent, do we find a truly wild place? Ever since our Cro-Magnon ancestors began their forays into the virgin forests of Europe 40,000 years ago, the land and its creatures have been in retreat before *Homo sapiens*. Forests have been cleared, marshes drained and rivers straightened. Even some of those landscapes that appear primordial are in fact the result of human activity. Heather-covered moorland in North Yorkshire and parched Andalucian desert have this in common; both were once covered by great forests which ancient settlers knocked flat.

What then remains that can be called wild? There are still a few areas in Europe that are untouched by man – places generally so unwelcoming either in terrain or in climate that man has not wanted to touch them at all – and these are indisputably wild.

For some people, wildness suggests conflict with nature: a wild place is a part of the planet so savage and desolate that you risk your life whenever you venture into it. This is in part true but would limit the eligible places to the most impenetrable bog or highest mountain tops in the worst winter weather, a rather restricted view. Another much broader definition considers a wild place to be a part of the planet where living things can find a natural refuge from the influence of modern industrial society. By this definition a wild place is for wild life as well as that portmanteau figure referred to in these pages as the wild traveller: the hillwalker, backpacker, bird watcher,

nature lover, explorer, nomad, loner, mystic, masochist, afficionado of the great outdoors, or permutations of all these things.

This is the definition we have observed in selecting the wild places described in these books. Choosing them has not been easy. Even so, we hope the criterion has proved rigid enough to exclude purely pretty (though popular) countryside, and flexible enough to include the greener, gentler wild places, of great natural historical interest perhaps, as well as the starker, more savage ones where the wild explorer comes into their own.

These are not guide books in the conventional sense, for to describe every neck of the woods and twist of the trail throughout Europe would require a library of volumes. Nor are these books addressed to the technical specialist – the caver, diver, rock climber and cross-country skier, the orchid-hunter, lepidopterist and beetlemaniac, for such experts will have reference data of their own. They are books intended for the general outdoor traveller – including the expert outside of his field of expertise (the orchid-hunter in a cave, the diver on a mountain top) – who wishes to scrutinize the range of wild places on offer in Europe, to learn a little more about them and to set about exploring them off the beaten track.

One of the great consolations in the preparation of these books has been to find that after 40,000 years of hunting, clearing, draining and ploughing Cro-Magnon and their descendants have left so much of Europe that can still be defined as wild.

Douglas Botting

4

WILD BRITAIN:
AN INTRODUCTION

Great Britain boasts of the most varied landscapes and most beautiful coastline in the world. Its wild places embrace a multitude of different terrains and habitats, all the way from the underwater world beneath the sea to the Arctic tundra of the mountain tops via sand dunes, seashore, grassland, moorland, forest and fen, island and tor, bog and lake, waterfall and cave, down and dale – the variety is endless. Few of these wild and empty spots are truly primordial in the sense that parts of the Amazon rain forest or Arctic Siberia are still primordial, meaning unaltered by human activity. But by all but this purest of definitions, there are many parts of Britain that are still wild.

Some of the wild places of Britain – like the bird rock of Handa, one mile long by half a mile wide – are tiny. Others – like the Cairngorms, which cover 160 square miles of mountain wilderness – are huge by British standards. Some have survived to the present day because they have been the hunting grounds of the landed aristocracy. Others have survived because they are out-and-out badlands and have thus been spared the plough and the housing estate – the great bog wastes of Scotland's Flow Country for instance although they are now fast disappearing beneath conifers. A few wild places – like Wicken Fen in Cambridgeshire – have survived as a result of historical accident. Very many have been saved as oases of natural habitat in a wasteland of agricultural and urban development and commercial afforestation because of the successful rearguard action of conservationists, aghast at the accelerated destruction of the natural environment of the British Isles, especially since the end of the Second World War.

A measure of the scale of the havoc can be gained from the statistics of a typical case like Worcestershire, a rural county in lowland England with few pretensions to wilderness status: 30 per cent of ancient woodlands destroyed, 50 per cent of the pools, 95 per cent of the marshes and bogs, 99 per cent of the pastures and all their flowers and herbs, and 2,500 miles of hedges – a microcosm of Armageddon in the British countryside. The national picture is as bad or worse.

Lowland England has taken the worst of the bashing. The few wild places cling to the extremities, while the farmed, suburban countryside claims the middle ground all the way from Dover to north of Derby, where the Peak marks the beginning of upland Britain, the stronghold of the British wilds.

Yet if you take to the air over England, the predominance of countryside is astonishing; an apparently limitless carpet of greenery rolls over the landscape and sems to engulf even the most obtrusive conurbation. This greenery is mostly cultivated land, however. In such a landscape the wild places of southern and central England are simply scattered outposts. By contrast, Scotland and Wales present a reverse image of the English scene, for there it is civilization that holds the outposts in a landscape that is still largely wild – though no longer primordial.

In compiling this book the difficulty has generally been deciding what to leave out rather than what to include. Very small places I have excluded unless they are very isolated (like the Monach Isles), very unique (like Wicken Fen) or both (like North Rona) – or part of a series making up a greater whole (like the bird reserves of the East Anglian coast). On the other hand, very large places are not included merely because they are very large, which explains why the great expanse of the Monadhliath Mountains in the Grampian Highlands of Scotland cannot be found in these pages. I have also excluded places of purely natural historical interest, where the human presence is too intrusive (as in the major bird stations at Dungeness and

5

Sandwich Bay, and most harbour estuaries and country parks), but I have included them where it is impermanent or seasonally adjusted (as on the North Norfolk Marshes, which become deserted and bitterly wild in winter). Similarly, it goes without saying, places of no outstanding wildlife interest are not excluded for that reason if their wilderness quality is self-evident (some of Dartmoor and the Peak, and places like Glen Coe fall into this category).

Of all the world's wild places, those of Great Britain are perhaps the least typical. Some of them, especially in the Scottish Highlands, are pure wilderness. But many of them, particularly in England, are highly organized, thoroughly mapped, exhaustively studied and minutely described, with waymarked paths and a network of elaborately evolved long-distance tracks. As a consequence, in the peak holiday season it may be difficult to get away from it all – or them all – even in the furthest back of the British beyond. Even a remote North Highland Peak like Stac Polly will have an approach trail blazed across the wild peat moors by the sheer weight of back-packing feet in the busy season, and walkers are being actively discouraged from using some of the most popular long-distance paths like the Lyke Wake Walk over the North York Moors because the ground is being worn away by sheer over-use. At Loch Garten in the Scottish Highlands the number of people who have come to see the ospreys now exceeds a million; in the Peak District National Park the annual number of visits has reached 20 million.

It could be argued that I am helping to make this situation worse by publicizing the wild places in this book. I can only answer that part of my aim has been to instill a respect and love for such places among a wider public, and if this happens it can only be to the advantage of the

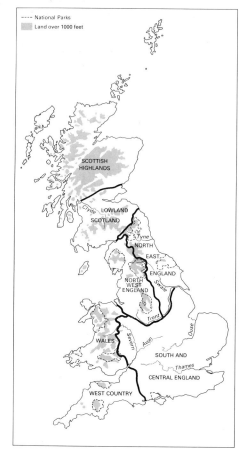

wilderness areas and nature reserves of Britain. Treat these places with the respect they deserve as a precious natural heritage. Follow the Country Code. Observe the rights-of-way. Remember the code of conduct in the sensitive ecosystems of the nature reserves: 'Take nothing but photographs. Leave nothing but footprints. Kill nothing but time.' And enjoy yourself.

THE KEY TO BRITAIN'S WILD PLACES

THE SHAPE OF THE WILD

Britain (here meaning England, Scotland and Wales) can be said to consist of a semicircle of islands (700 off Scotland alone) and 7,000 miles (11,200 kilometres) of coastline of immense variety and beauty, enclosing a land roughly divided in two by a diagonal line that runs from the Blackdown Hills in the south-west to the North York Moors in the north-east. Generally speaking, the country to the north and west of this line is Highland Britain, and the country to the south and east of it is Lowland Britain.

Wild places are few and far between in Lowland Britain, and for the most part occupy the periphery where for one reason or another modern farming and development – the scourge of wild places – cannot reach. Our few lowland wild places include parts of the coast (such as North Norfolk), some of the islands, and the oases of woodland (such as the New Forest), wetland (such as Wicken Fen) and heath (such as Purbeck and Breckland).

It is in the most rugged, bleaker, less easily farmed upland country of Highland Britain that most of the wild places lie: the moorland plateaux of the West Country (Dartmoor, Exmoor and Bodmin Moor); the high fells and moors of the North Country (either strung out along the central spine of the Pennines, like the Peak District, Yorkshire Dales and Upper Teesdale, rising alongside it, like the North York Moors, Lake District and Cheviot Hills of Northumberland; the great upland mass that occupies nearly all of Wales (Brecon Beacons, the Cambrian Mountains and Snowdonia); and, to the north, the Scottish Highland and Islands, separated from Lowland Scotland by the Highland Boundary Fault, split in two halves (the Grampians and the North-West Highlands) by the Great Glen and altogether forming the highest and most extensive wilderness area in the British Isles.

Throughout this wide spectrum of landscape types between seashore and mountain top, certain broadly distinct habitats recur. Each kind of habitat displays roughly similar land forms and range of wildlife species, allowing for regional variations from south to north. The main habitats of wild Britain are:

Coastlands and Islands: *cliffs* (e.g. those along the coast of Cornwall, Yorkshire, Shetland and Orkney). Cliff nesting birds like gulls, auks, fulmars and cormorants. Salt and wind tolerant plants like thrift, spring squill and samphire. *Dunes* (e.g. Braunton Burrows, Newborough Warren, Ainsdale and Culbin Sands). Many butterflies and flowers, sea holly and sea bindweed on the foredunes, marsh helleborine and the rare natterjack toad in the dune slacks, with marram grass binding the sands. *Spits and sand bars* (massive coastal sediment features, e.g. Chesil Bar, the spits of Blakeney Point, Spurn Head and Gibraltar Point). Notable for wide range of plants and nesting birds, especially terns. Also seal breeding colonies. *Salt marshes and mud flats* (in sheltered estuaries, bays and sea lochs, e.g. the North Kent Marshes, the Wash, Humber, Morecambe Bay, Solway Firth, Moray and Cromarty Firths). Salt-tolerant plants like eelgrass, colourful sea lavender, sea aster and sea pink. Important feeding ground for thousands of wintering waders and wildfowl which feed on the salt-marsh plants or the masses of mud-flat invertebrates.

Woodlands: Woods cover seven per cent of Britain, but 80 per cent of that is commercial conifer plantation. Hardly any ancient woods left, but notable relics of ancient broadleaved forest include Anses Wood and Mark Ash Wood in the New Forest and the woods on the cliffs of the Lower Wye. Rich ground flora of classic woodland flowers, and woodland birds, insects and fungi. Ancient natural pinewoods – Caledonian forests – survive only in scattered areas of northern Scotland such as Rothiemuchus, Black Wood of Rannoch, Loch Maree and Glen Affric. Understorey of juniper, cowberry and bilberry, crossbill and capercaillie, pine marten, wild cat and red squirrel.

Lowland grassland and heaths: open, often man-made (and rabbit-made!) spaces dominated by grasses, heathers and other dwarf shrubs, generally growing on sandy, chalky or limestone soils, mostly in Southern England. Notable for their distinctive flora and specialised fauna, including all six British reptiles. *Dry lowland heath* (e.g. pacts of the New Forest and the Isle of Purbeck). Specialist flora and fauna, including Dartford warbler and hobby falcon, sand lizard and spider-hunting wasp – all under siege from pasture, plantation and development. Few *chalk grasslands* in Britain (e.g. the downs of Wiltshire, Sussex and

Kent) can be now described as wild, and most are much frequented and under threat. The *limestone country* (e.g. the Mendips and the Derbyshire and Yorkshire Dales) often combines spectacular karst landscape with brilliant richness of flora. The *Breckland* in East Anglia is a large, sandy area of heath and grassland of a type virtually unique in Britain. Very few unimproved natural grassland; traditional meadows and pastures survive in the lowlands.

Freshwater wetlands: in addition to the *lakes, rivers and streams*, there are the *marshes, broads and fens* (e.g. Insh Marshes, the Somerset Levels, the Norfolk Broads and surviving fens such as Wicken and Woodwalton). Lush vegetation and a myriad of wetland birds and insects: bittern, reed bunting and bearded tit, many dragonflies and rare butterflies like the swallowtail.

Uplands: hills, moors and mountains above 800 feet (240 metres). The most extensive land habitat in Britain, and generally the wildest comprising one eighth of England and Wales and nearly two thirds of Scotland. Noteworthy habitat types include *wet upland moor* (e.g. the great uncultivated peat moors of Dartmoor, the Peak, the North Pennines, North York Moors, Upland Wales, Rannoch and the Flow Country). Heather, bilberry and bracken. Red grouse, ring ouzel, merlin and hen harrier. Bogs and mires, with cotton grass, orchids and insectivorous plants. Very high up you come to the *tundra and arctic-alpine zone* (e.g. Ben Lawers, the Cairngorms and Upper Teesdale). Notable for their cold, for relict plants from Britain's glacial past (e.g. spring gentian) and specialist fauna which includes the dotterel, snow bunting, ptarmigan and mountain hare.

PROTECTED WILD PLACES

A number of our wild places enjoy some sort of official status and some measure of protection. Some lie within the boundaries of the National Parks, of which there are ten in England and Wales (but none as yet in Scotland), or are National Nature Reserves (NNRs), or form smaller reserves and wildlife sanctuaries run by the Royal Society for the Protection of Birds and the county naturalists' trusts of the Royal Society for Nature Conservation and other conservation bodies. There are more than 40 areas of Outstanding Natural Beauty (AONB) and Heritage Coast in England and Wales, and

about the same number of National Scenic Areas in Scotland. There are also the areas of National Trust land, Sites of Special Scientific Interest (SSSIs) and Forest Parks. Many other wild places, including some of the largest and wildest – like the huge estates and deer forests of the Scottish Highlands – are private property and enjoy no such status or protection, though this does not necessarily mean they are at greater risk.

WHEN TO VISIT BRITAIN'S WILD PLACES

Season and weather greatly affect wild places. Summer obviously offers the warmest weather, the longest day and easiest going; but it also draws the biggest crowds, so that even the remotest places can be overrun, and accommodation is scarce and expensive. Winter has its enthusiasts, for many places are transformed into true wildernesses with their own special beauty and challenge, especially on the high moors and hills under snow; but in winter's low temperatures, icy conditions and short days the going can be tough and sometimes dangerous – so beginners take care. Spring and autumn enjoy relatively settled, gentler weather, intense wildlife activity, few crowds and ample accommodation.

The rhythm of the seasons dictates the natural history calendar: winter for overwintering waders, wildfowl and other birds; spring and early summer for migrating birds, nesting birds, flowering plants and pupping seals; autumn for migrating birds and woodland leaves, berries and fungi. Overall, early summer and early autumn seem to offer most to the average wild traveller – but bear in mind that spring comes later and autumn earlier the more northerly the latitude and the higher the altitude to which you venture.

THE RULES OF THE WILD

The wild traveller should always be prepared for sudden changes in the unpredictable British weather. Mist can come down suddenly (notoriously on Dartmoor). Rivers can rise rapidly in spate (as in the West Highlands). Clouds can roll over and temperatures drop on the high mountains, where the wind chill factor may be crucial to survival. Winter can turn the green slopes of summer into Yukon blizzard country. So always try and take a weather check. Always take appropriate footwear and clothing, food and necessary gear. Always take the right map and know how to read it in conjunction with a compass. Observe the Mountain Code. Learn the first principles in emergencies, and what to do if you get lost.

The Mountain Code: learn the use of map and compass. Know the weather signs and local forecast. Plan a route within your capabilities and leave time to get down before dark. Know simple first aid and the symptoms of exposure. Know the mountain distress signals (to give a signal for help, give six blasts on a whistle and/ or six winks with a torch. Wait 1 minute. Repeat. To answer a signal for help, give three blasts on a whistle and/or three winks with a torch. Repeat. Take a bearing on the signal and move towards it while continuing to signal). Never go alone. Leave written word of your route and estimated time of return, and report when you get back. Take warm weatherproof clothing and survival bag. Take map and compass, torch and food. Wear climbing boots. Keep alert all day. Be prepared to turn back if the weather becomes bad or if any member of your party is becoming slow or exhausted. *If there is snow on the hills* – always have an ice-axe for each person. Carry a climbing rope. Know the correct use of ropes and ice-axe. Learn to recognize dangerous snow slopes. Lack of space precludes a detailed description of equipment and techniques recommended for travellers in wild places. If in doubt refer to one of the many manuals of this subject.

The Country Code: while you are in the countryside you should observe the general code of behaviour drawn up by the Countryside Commission.

Enjoy the countryside and respect its life and work. Guard against all risk of fire. Fasten all gates. Keep your dogs under close control. Keep to public footpaths across farmland. Use gates and stiles to cross fences, hedges and wall. Leave livestock, crops and machinery alone. Take your litter home. Help to keep all water clean. Protect wildlife, plants and trees. Take special care on country roads. Make no unnecessary noise.

TO THE READER

Eagle symbols: the eagle symbols used at the head of some entries in this book indicate the wildness quality of the place to which they refer. This is based on a number of factors, including remoteness, ruggedness, spaciousness, uniqueness, wildlife interest and the author's subjective reactions. Three eagles is the highest rating, no eagles the lowest.

Grid references: occasionally a grid reference is given if the location of a wild place is otherwise difficult to pin-point. The reference is based on the standard Ordnance Survey national grid system.

Updating: while everything possible has been done to ensure the accuracy of the facts in this book, information does gradually become outdated in our ever-changing countryside. For this reason we would welcome readers' updates, corrections and comments for incorporation in subsequent revised editions. Please write to Douglas Botting, Wild Britain, Sheldrake Press, 188 Cavendish Road, London SW12 0DA.

Non-liability: both author and publishers have gone to great pains to point out the hazards that may confront the traveller in certain places described in WILD BRITAIN. We cannot under any circumstances accept any liability for any mishap, loss or injury sustained by any person venturing into any of the wild places listed in this book.

CHAPTER 1

The West Country

A few years ago an old acquaintance of mine, the Irish writer Brendan Lehane, spent part of the summer in a remote wooded valley on the edge of the Brendon Hills on Exmoor, as an experiment in post-Armageddon Stone Age living. He brought nothing with him to his valley but a goat, a few hens, a sack of oats, a hammer, an axe, a bucket, two mugs and a wife.

For two months he and his wife lived on what they could squeeze out of their livestock and forage from the surrounding woods and stream. They drank dandelion coffee and buttercup tea; sought solace in whortleberry wine and herb cigarettes; filled their bellies with beech-mast cake, roast squirrel, fried grasshoppers and boiled bogweed; washed in homemade sorrel soap and lit their tumbledown hut with the light from a bulrush lamp. They lost weight, looked farouche, grew smelly and slept long. If their green valley had seemed a lush corner of rural England when they arrived, it had become like a wild neck of the New Guinea jungle by the time they left.

The lessons they learned had nothing to do with noble savages or the virtues of self-sufficiency, but with the modern civilized world to which they returned. The first town they came to seemed hideously vulgar and brash, the first restaurant meal unbelievably sweet and cloying, the first office dwellers grotesque caricatures of the consumer society. 'We found the world took some getting back to,' Brendan reported. 'We were thinking of the other side of the hill, and of the peace

The tors of Devon and Cornwall were shaped by the action of wind and water, as all good materialists know, yet few see them for the first time without a disquieting sense of some supernatural force

and freedom from disturbance, the closeness to nature, of putting food, if not in the right place, in a less wrong one; and of a few specially nice moments under the oak trees and stars.' A classic wilderness withdrawal syndrome.

Wilderness is something the West Country has in reasonable proportion. By the West Country I mean the long south-west peninsula of England which juts into the Atlantic west of a line from Bristol to Bournemouth and comprises the counties of Somerset and Avon, Devon, Cornwall and Dorset. This is a very distinctive region, at one and the same time wild and gentle, rugged and lush. Climatically, because of its southerly latitude and warmish sea, it is the most favoured corner of the kingdom; palm trees and sub-tropical plants flourish on the Cornish and Devon Rivieras, and daffodils bloom in mid-winter on the off-shore Isles of Scilly.

Yet there can be few places where the elements rage more violently than along the great Atlantic-facing cliff frontier of Cornwall and North Devon, where gale-swept seas batter the

Some of the small wild flowers that thrive on damp or marshy ground are (from left to right) the bog pimpernel, the ivy-leaved bellflower, both low delicate creepers, and the sturdier bog violet

granite battlements of the West Country with a thud that makes the earth tremble; and no wilder place anywhere in southern Britain than the bleak upland moorland of Dartmoor, with its sudden mists, its quaking bogs, its vast, unpeopled horizons.

Dartmoor is the largest and highest of a series of granite bosses which, ranged like the knuckles of a clenched fist, form the exposed tops of a gigantic rock-mass, or batholith, underlying the West Country – the others being Bodmin Moor, St Austell, Carnmenellis, Land's End and the Isles of Scilly, which many people think were the legendary, long-drowned Cornish kingdom of Lyonesse, and some feel still are.

Long before Brendan and his wife fled West from the pressures of twentieth-century living, mainland Britain's granite fastness was a place of refuge. The Celts sought safety there from the Roman invaders, and the Romanized Britons in turn fled here from the incoming Saxons. It was one such Romano-British chieftain whose exploits, obscured by the mists of this chaotic transitional period and embroidered by later monastic chroniclers, formed the basis of the legend of King Arthur.

The West Country was a cradle of human habitation – and an arena for human conflict – long before Arthurian times, however. Prehistoric peoples left their barrows, hut circles and standing stones on the moors and high places. At Cranbrook, a Dartmoor hilltop more than 1,100 feet (335 metres) above sea level, stands an unfinished hill fort built by Iron Age people, Celts from Brittany and northern France who reinforced this natural strongpoint with ditches, banks and a stone-faced rampart. I first saw this fort by moonlight, when clouds were scudding across the pock-marked face of the moon before a warm, wet southwest wind. Far below this desperate, ancient place I could hear a river gurgling off the moor towards the edge of darkness and the world, and as I stood there a sudden scream echoed through the night – bird or beast, fox or owl, man or phantom of times and peoples past, I never knew.

Like the refugees of times past, the wild places of the West Country hold out on the high ground, the moors and hills of the interior, and the remoter stretches of the sea coast where the islands, estuaries, salt flats, sand dunes and relic heaths and woods form some of the region's finest wildlife sanctuaries and nature reserves.

GETTING THERE

By air: regular scheduled services fly to airports at Bristol, Exeter, Bournemouth, Plymouth, Newquay and the Isles of Scilly (which also has a helicopter service from Penzance).

By sea: visitors from the Continent can travel direct to the West Country on Sealink Ferries between Cherbourg and Poole, Weymouth, Portsmouth or Southampton; and on Brittany Ferries between Roscoff and Plymouth, or between St Malo and Portsmouth. A regular ferry service also operates between Penzance and the Isles of Scilly. (For details see ISLE OF SCILLY, p.36).

By train: the main towns in the West Country are served by fast, direct and regular train services from London, the North and Midlands throughout the year. Inter-City 125 trains run from London on a north-about route to Swindon, Bath, Bristol and Weston-super-Mare, and on a south-about route to Taunton, Exeter, Plymouth and Penzance. Inter-City 125 trains also run to the West Country on a cross-country route from Scotland, the North-East and Midlands. Sleeper services to Devon and Cornwall are available on trains from London, and also on trains to Bristol from Glasgow and Edinburgh. Motorail services operate to key West Country locations, and branch lines run local services to many of the smaller towns. For details contact British Rail or nearest travel centre.

By bus: National Express operate a network of rapid services to many parts of the West Country from all over Britain. Luxury Rapide provide de luxe services from London to more than 30 West Country towns. For details contact nearest National Express travel agent or National Bus Company office.

WHERE TO STAY

The West Country has a multitude of accommodation to choose from, ranging from grand luxe hotels to farmers' barns where you can roll out your sleeping bag. Visitors are advised to get hold of the relevant accommodation guides published annually by the West Country Tourist Board, Trinity Court, Southernhay East, Exeter EX1 1QS, T:0392 211171, including the following: *Where to Stay in the West Country* (hotels, guest houses, self-catering or vacation homes, camping and caravan or motor-home sites), *Stay at an Inn*, *Farm Holidays*, *Camping and Caravan Parks* and the two out-of-season bargain-break accommodation guides, *Spring into Summer* and *Go West Country*. The Tourist Information Centre network can help you find and reserve accommodation. A list of Tourist Information Centres is available from the West Country Tourist Board.

ACTIVITIES

Walking: the West Country offers some marvellous walking in wild or wildish places. Virtually the entire coastline is circumambulated by the SOUTH WEST WAY, the longest footpath in Britain; and another long-distance footpath, the TWO MOORS WAY, links Dartmoor and Exmoor.

Climbing: some rock climbing is possible on Dartmoor, and there is spectacular sea-cliff climbing at all grades on the Cornish and Dorset coast. Information from British Mountaineering Council.

Riding: the riding and pony trekking is excellent on Dartmoor, Exmoor and Bodmin Moor. For a list of riding centres, contact the West Country Tourist Board.

Fishing: the West Country also provides some of the best sea, game and coarse fishing in Britain, from the wild trout of Exmoor to the mighty porbeagle shark off the Cornwall coast. For details, get *Fishing in England's West Country* from the West Country Tourist Board.

Dartmoor

365 square miles (945sq km) of high granite moorland in South Devon National Park

It was a lovely summer's day on old Dartmoor and the mortar bombs were falling all around me in tight little smokey groups. *Ping*, crump! went the bombs. *Pong*, crump! The rest of my squad were lying flat on their tummies in shallow hollows, tightly clutching their steel helmets to their heads. But in those days I suffered from a patho-logical lack of physical fear, so I continued to stand and stare about me, not so much out of bravado as indifference. What an amazing place, I thought to myself – *such* horizons, *such* space, *such* a huge blue bell-jar of a sky.

Then a voice shouted from a hollow in the hill: 'Get down, you fool! Can't you see this place is bloody dangerous?' A blow on the back of my helmet brought me to my senses. Clubbed to the ground by a pick-axe handle wielded by an irate infantry major, I rubbed my nose in the sour peaty soil. 'What are you?' the Major, a Korean War veteran, hissed in my ear, 'Some kind of nut? Anyone would think you were only here for the view!'

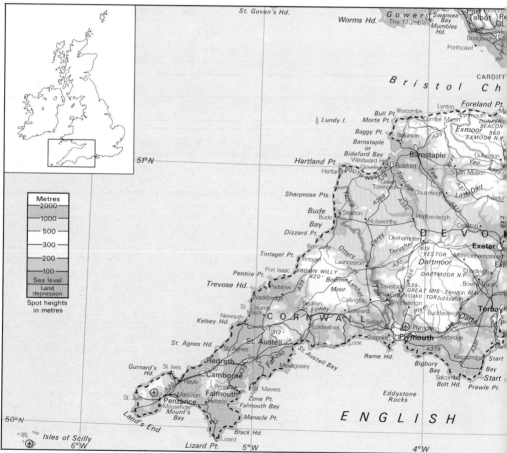

It was my first impression of Dartmoor, and my most vivid, for I was there at an impressionable age – one of a squad of infantry and commando officer cadets on a battle course at Okehampton Camp, where the army had exercised a hotly debated presence on the moor since World War Two. Our days on the highest, wildest land in England south of the Pennines brought saturating rain, obliterating mist, towering cloudscapes and a saucy sun gleaming brazenly out of a pellucid, rain-rinsed sky. There were no trees to shade us, precious few bushes to provide shelter from the wind that slithered over the long curving granite scarp of Corn Ridge. We squelched back and forth across an amphitheatre of blanket bog and waded knee deep down the icy, scurrying streams that fanned out like the veins of a leaf. Now and then we holed up for a smoke and a corned beef sandwich inside the stone ruins of a Bronze Age hut, where once people just like us, looking out on a view just like this, had contemplated mortality and the infinite in a fug of peat smoke and steaming cow dung. At the end of the day we yomped home across the wilderness in Indian file while the sunset flickered and flared behind the primordial silhouettes of the blackened tors, like a herd of grazing dragons, and every so often someone behind a rock or a megalith took a pot at us.

I returned to Dartmoor in later years, and in time learned more about the place than I had ever obtained from behind the view of a gun. Dartmoor is a kind of island continent in microcosm. Its shape is roughly like Antarctica, its pattern of human settlement roughly like that of Australia: a narrow fringe round the circumference of a largely desert interior (of bog and granite moor in the case of Dartmoor). Like Australia, Dartmoor has had its penal colony of convicts, its military comings and goings, its early pioneers, its diggers, mineral claims and mining camps, even its aborigines (Bronze Age Beaker Folk, who vanished long ago). Like the macro island continents of Australia and Antarctica, the micro one of Dartmoor is largely undeveloped because it is still for the most part a wilderness.

Granite is the key to Dartmoor. The broad, rolling uplands of the moor are the highest landmass in Britain south of the Peak District, averaging 1,200 feet (365 metres) above sea level and reaching 2,038 feet (621 metres) at High Willhays, the highest point, and 2,030 feet (619 metres) at Yes Tor. Yet the land surface was once very much higher, rising perhaps to alpine heights. Nearly 300 million years of erosion – the physical and chemical interaction of rock with rain and frost – have reduced the granite mass to its present level and fashioned the unusual landscape we see today. The most noticeable features in the Dartmoor landscape – the fantastic rock-

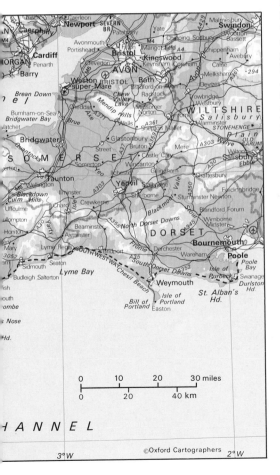

15

piles, or tors, which crown many of the hilltops on the central moor – are embattled survivors of this continuing process of attrition, the exposed tips of the underlying granite range from which the covering of softer rock has been worn away.

Up to 170 tors have been recorded on Dartmoor, and some 30 are marked on the map, including the best known ones: Hound Tor, Hay Tor, Yes Tor, and Great Mis Tor. They top almost every horizon, these still, brooding, apocalyptic rock towers. Cracked by their natural jointing, they look from a distance like man-made edifices, ancient Inca citadels of massive hewn stone on the bleak *paramo* of the high Andes.

The tors differ greatly in size and appearance. Blackingstone Rock (near Moretonhampstead) is shaped like a dome, Shape Tor (near Merrivale) like a series of steeples, Hound Tor like a castle keep with battlements; Bowerman's Nose (near Manaton) like a pile of children's building blocks. The topmost boulders of these tors have been worn round and smooth by the natural process of weathering, and circular rainfilled hollows, called rock basins, like primordial wash bowls and hip baths, have been gouged into their flat tops by the action of freezing water.

Erosion debris, in the form of boulders and large stones called clitter, lies thickly strewn down the slopes beneath the tors, most notably at Hen Tor, near Shaugh Prior. In some parts of high Dartmoor the granite has undergone even greater deterioration and weathered into a gravelly subsoil called growan. The relative ease with which granite can be rotted accounts for the rolling landscape of the uplands, the gentle slopes, the wide shallow valleys.

Water is the other major factor in the shape and life of the moor. The nearness to the sea, the moist south-westerly winds and the highness of the ground ensure a heavy annual rainfall and a prevalence of saturating mist and hill fog. Most of the interior of Dartmoor is made up of two high plateaux, separated by the two main east–west roads that cross like a pair of scissors at Two Bridges. Blanket bog,

consisting of peat 10–13 feet (3–4 metres) thick in places, covers much of the plateaux and acts as a vast sponge-like reservoir where most of the major rivers of Devon, radiating outwards like the spokes of a wheel, have their source: the Teign, the Taw, the Okement (headwater of the Torridge), the Tavy, Meavy, Plym, Yeam, Erme, Avon, Dart and others.

Since Dartmoor is tilted to the south, like most of the south-west peninsula, all but two of these rivers flow southward. In prolonged periods of heavy rain there is a spectacular surface run-off from the granite and saturated peat, and the rivers flood and rise with great rapidity. At other times the rivers flow placidly down their shallow wooded valleys till they reach the edge of the granite country.

Here their passage undergoes a dramatic change, for different kinds of rock have been weathered into steeper scarps, deep narrow ravines where the rivers plunge precipitately off the Dartmoor plateaux. At Lustleigh Cleave, Tavy Cleave and Becka Falls, the rivers tumble off the plateau edge in cascades and waterfalls. At the western rim of Dartmoor, the River Lydd plummets into a deep, heavily pot-holed gorge, where it is shortly joined by an exquisitely beautiful tributary waterfall, a 100-foot – (30-metre) – high skein of tumbling white water known locally as the White Lady. They are lovely places, these Dartmoor streams, water-loud, lush-green and dapple-shaded in summer, haunt of herons stalking in the pools, dippers bobbing on the rocks, dragonflies darting across the shallows – a far cry from the bleak and windswept heaths and bogs of the central moors.

The Dartmoor bogs are not everyone's idea of pretty country. Some quake underfoot, some tremble, most can be crossed on foot without sinking further than your knees. Only one is positively dangerous and that is Fox Tor Mire on the southern plateau to the south-east of the disued tin works at Whiteworks. The only prisoner never to have been recaptured after escaping from Dartmoor Prison was last seen heading for Fox Tor Mire. There is no firm ground to be felt under this treacherous bog and any walker, or even rider, crossing the moor in its vicinity would do well to give it a wide berth. It was Fox Tor Mire which Arthur Conan Doyle used under the fictitious name of Grimpen Mire for one of the more fearful locations in his Sherlock Holmes story, *The Hound of the Baskervilles* – a trackless waste covered in mist where a man could disappear for ever without trace.

Most of the upland bog on Dartmoor would be more accurately described as wet heath. It is a land of silence and nowhere, a place for the lover of solitude and the wilds, the seeker of far horizons. Here a raven may address a croak to you, a curlew a babble, a buzzard a pealing cry. Otherwise you are as on your own, as circumscribed by the continuous skyline as any hitch-hiker in the Gobi.

The bogs are no place for man or beast and few traces of either are ever found in their acid soil, either present or past. But firm open moorland rings the blanket bog of the Dartmoor uplands and rolls away from tor to tor. This was the country of old men, a world of rock, a land of stone – the natural habitat of Stone Age folk and their Bronze Age successors. Few parts of Britain are so thickly littered with monuments of the past. Dolmens, menhirs, cists and cairns, hut circles, stone circles and stone rows, field systems and hill forts. They are everywhere, these testimonies of prehistoric life: 2,000 buildings and several hundred tombs, the earliest dating from about 3000BC.

Relics of the past dominate the moor: no visitor can miss them. More elusive is the wildlife of the moor. Dartmoor is a wild and open place but it is not the Serengeti. There are no red deer here. With luck the casual walker will see a few wild ponies – the tough little native ponies that graze the high moor – and a wheeling buzzard or two, for this is good buzzard country; he may hear a skylark soaring and the loud babbling cry of the curlew; he may spy the bright green patch of sphagnum moss which is the telltale sign of bog beneath; he will be only too aware of miles of rock-strewn turf, heather and bracken stretching endlessly before

him; but not, at first glance, much more.

The granite tors are virtually lifeless, though their clitter slopes, which are difficult to graze, may shelter a rich growth of plants, including several important relic woods. The wet acid soil, low temperatures and wind exposure of the great blanket bogs of the plateaux severely restrict the range of living things.

The plant cover is dominated by common bog mosses, cottongrass and rushes, and the bird life is limited to ravens, buzzards, carrion crows, a few snipe, a few curlew, and skylark and meadow pipit in the summer. Over the long, rolling expanses of grass and heather moor that stretch away from the central bog country flit stonechats, whinchats and wheatears, and golden plover, dunlin and a few red grouse nest in the remoter reaches.

Numerous woodlands crowd around the edge of the moor and in the river valleys. But there are some, like Wistman's Wood, Black Tor Copse and Pile's Wood, which are high-level woods of dwarf pedunculate oak where relic fragments of the indigenous woodland of the moor, many hundreds of years old, survive in windswept conditions of extreme severity on very steep clitter slopes. Wistman's, an NCC reserve, is the most celebrated and least understood of high Dartmoor's woodland pockets. The trees grow in an almost impenetrably tangled copse among massive boulders on a precipitous clitter slope which is extremely difficult to negotiate. They are unbelievably gnarled and contorted: the effect, in all probability, of the relentless wind. The very moist, unpolluted air has encouraged an extraordinarily thick epiphytic growth of mosses, lichens and ferns on the trunks and boughs of the trees, so that the wood looks more like the beard-moss forest high up on the slopes of Mount Kilimanjaro than a hillside on Dartmoor.

'It is a wonderful place, the moor,' recorded Sherlock Holmes' sidekick, Dr Watson, in *The Hound of the Baskervilles*. 'You never tire of the moor. You cannot think of the wonderful secrets which it contains. It is so vast, and so barren, and so mysterious.'

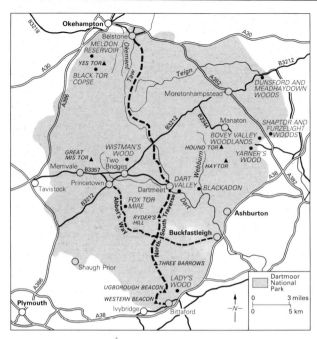

BEFORE YOU GO

Map: OS 1:25,000 Outdoor Leisure Map No. 28.

Guidebooks: contact the Dartmoor National Park Department, Parke, Haytor Road, Bovey Tracey, Devon TQ13 9JQ, T:0626 832093. Get from them *The Dartmoor Visitor* (free information digest published annually) and *Walks in The Dartmoor National Park* by Elizabeth Prince (4 illustrated booklets). The Countryside Commission guide is *Dartmoor National Park* edited by John Weir (Webb and Bower).

GETTING THERE

By car: the M5 feeds into the A30 and A38, the main ringroads around Dartmoor. Most roads on Dartmoor itself are narrow, winding, hilly and open to wandering animals; traffic can be heavy in summer. Green signposts indicate national through roads suitable for all kinds of

18

traffic; black signposts A or B class roads, suitable for most types of vehicles; blue signposts medium-sized vehicles only; brown signposts cars only; and white indicate most difficult roads, suitable for local access only. It is illegal to drive more than 15yds (13.5m) off the road on to common land.

By train: nearest main line stations are Exeter (St David's), Newton Abbot and Plymouth.

By bus: National Express terminals at Exeter and Plymouth, also at Ashburton and Okehampton on the edge of Dartmoor.

WHERE TO STAY

Plentiful and various accommodation – large and small hotels, guest houses, inns, bed and breakfast, farmhouses, etc. – exists in towns and villages in and around the park. For details consult the standard national

accommodation guides or contact the West Country Tourist Board, Trinity Court, Southernhay East, Exeter, Devon, T:0392 76351.

Youth hostels: the YHA has 3 small hostels inside the park – Steps Bridge (closed Tuesday), Bellever (closed Monday), Gidleigh (closed Thursday) – and 4 larger ones not far away outside. Details from YHA, Belmont Place, Devonport Road, Stoke, Plymouth PL3 4DW.

Outdoor living: Dartmoor offers superb opportunities for camping and caravanning. The *Dartmoor Visitor* carries details of nearly 30 sites. Parking on the side of the road (or off it) is not allowed. You can camp on enclosed land with the landowner's permission, and anywhere on the open moor provided it is out of sight of houses or roads.

ACCESS AND CLOSURES

Nature reserves: there are 10 nature reserves within the park boundaries: **Blackadon**, DTNC Reserve: wooded valley slope and moorland. Open to the public. **Black Tor Copse**, Duchy of Cornwall/NCC Reserve: dwarf high woodland near Dartmoor's highest point. Open to the public. **Bovey Valley Woodlands**, NCC Reserve: old coppiced woodland and valley bog. Permit required off rights of way. **Dart Valley**, DNPA/DTNC Reserve: heath and woodland in one of Dartmoor's most attractive valleys. Open to the public. **Dunsford and Meadhaydown Woods**, DTNC Reserve: mixed valley woodland. Open to the public. **Lady's Wood**, DTNC Reserve: coppiced woodland. Open to the public. **Meldon Reservoir**, DTNC Reserve: sanctuary area in moorland reservoir. Permit

only. **Shapton and Furzelight Woods**, WDT Reserve: mixed woodland. Open to the public.
Wistman's Wood, Duchy of Cornwall/NCC Reserve: dwarfed moorland oakwood. Permit may be required.
Yarner's Wood, NCC Reserve: oak woodland with wood warblers, holly blue and white admiral butterflies. Permit required off marked trails. For further information enquire at any National Park Information Centre.
Army firing ranges: the army uses 3 live ammunition firing ranges inside a large training area on the northern part of the moor. Extreme care must be taken in the vicinity – fatal accidents still occur. Firing range perimeters are marked by a series of red and white posts and by noticeboards on the main approaches. Entry is forbidden when warning signals (red flags by day and red light by night) are shown.

ACTIVITIES
Walking: the park authorities

Hay Tor, protruding from a morass of bog cotton is one of Dartmoor's most distinctive granite landmarks

organize a full range of guided walks: full details in *The Dartmoor Visitor*.

The 25-mile (40-km) North to South Traverse takes experienced walkers about 14 hours across rough and boggy moorland. It begins at Belstone, just south of Okehampton, and roughly follows high ground along the line of the East Dart River, via Postbridge and Dartmeet. At Dartmeet the walk leaves the river and heads south via Ryder's Hill, Three Barrows, Ugborough Beacon and Western Beacon, to journey's end at Bittaford. Another classic long walk, the Two Moors Way, is dealt with later in this chapter (p.23).
Field studies: the following offer Dartmoor-based courses:
Dartmoor Field Studies Centre, Haytor Road, Bovey Tracey. **Dartmoor Expedition Centre,** Warden (John Earle), Widdecombe-in-the-Moor, Newton Abbot. **Landscape Overview,** Director (Bud Young), 26 Cross Street, Moretonhampstead.

PRECAUTIONS FOR WALKERS

Rights of Way: bridle paths for riders and walkers are marked by blue spots, footpaths for walkers by yellow spots.
Kit: the moor is often wet and slippery, so rubber boots – ideally classic Wellingtons – or very strong shoes and waterproof clothing is essential. Take a sweater even in summer – cloud and wind can drastically lower the temperature. Take a map and compass and be sure you know how to use them. **Weather:** can change rapidly – you can easily get lost in heavy mists. If you are overtaken by mist while crossing trackless moorland, do not go on but retrace your steps. Beware of rivers flooding during heavy rain. If in doubt phone for a weather forecast on 0392 8091 (Exeter), 0803 8091 (Torquay) or 0752 8091 (Plymouth). **Emergencies:** lone walkers should leave a note of their route and estimated return time. If someone fails to return and there is genuine cause for concern, dial 999 for the police who will alert the Dartmoor Rescue Group. If you suffer a cut, wash the wound with sphagnum moss to guard against infection.
Animals: if you see sheep grazing, put your dog on a leash, especially in lambing time. Dogs that attack sheep may be shot. Keep your distance from moorland ponies: they can bite and kick. Do not feed ponies on or near the road: they will see cars as a source of food and may pay with their lives.

Exmoor

*265 square miles (686sq km) of Devon
and Somerset moorland
National Park*

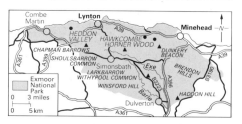

The Exmoor National Park takes in the whole of the main moorland plateau once occupied by the old Royal Forest of Exmoor in the west and centre, together with much of the reclaimed Brendon Hills to the east, the whole of the 29-mile (46-kilometre) stretch of sea coast between Minehead and Combe Martin to the north, and the whole of the high ridge that runs from Dulverton to Shoulsbarrow Common in the south. Though Exmoor has no mountains, much of it lies at 1,200 to 1,500 feet (365 to 457 metres) above sea level. From the highest point at Dunkery Beacon, 1,706 feet (520 metres) above sea level, one looks out over a broad, level land of heather, bracken and peat bogs, sloping gently to the heads of deep valleys and set amid a patchwork of beech-hedged pasture.

The core of Exmoor is the old Royal Forest around Simonsbath, once an exclusive hunting ground for the Norman kings. The area is now largely grass moorland, covered in purple moor grass or flying bent, so called because in spring it turns purple and in winter its leaves are snapped by the frost and fly about in the wind. On higher grassland areas, like the desolate wilderness called the Chains, stretches of deer sedge and peat bog three feet (one metre) deep blanket the sodden ground, brightened here and there by cottongrass, bog asphodel and heath spotted-orchid. This high land is the source of many of Exmoor's rivers, and more than 70 inches (178 centimetres) of rain can fall in a year.

Bordering the 'forest' stretches the open heather moor, a low, dense scrub of ling, bell-heather, bracken, whortleberry, bristle bent and gorse. Though it may not look it, this is a largely man-made habitat,

for grazing and burning cleared the thin tree cover long ago. The heath now occurs as islands within areas of reclamation and forestry. In high summer it presents a marvellous sight, especially on the coastal downs, where the western gorse glows bright yellow and the purple-pink mass of the ling in full bloom is interwoven with the deep purple of the bell heather, and the air is loud with the growling of honey bees.

The upland moors are the haunt of the shaggy-haired Exmoor pony, a tough and agile breed closely related to the wild horses which survived the last Ice Age. Other creatures of the open uplands are the grass snake, adder, common lizard and slow worm, and the birds of prey: the buzzards wheeling majestically with their four-foot wings held stiff and motionless on the thermals that rise from the heath; the kestrels hovering as they quarter the ground for prey; the sparrowhawks in low scurrying flight; a few rare peregrine falcons and the even rarer merlin.

The woodland of Exmoor is confined to the coastal downs and to the 'cleaves', the steep-sided valleys where the streams cut their way to the sea. These are the richest habitat for wildlife on Exmoor and some of the ancient oak woodlands, such as those at Horner Wood, Hawkcombe and the Heddon Valley, which may date back several thousand years, are now nature reserves or Sites of Special Scientific Interest. The red deer of the valley woods are the largest herd outside Scotland and number some 500 to 800 head, direct descendants of the deer that roamed these parts in prehistoric times. At the autumn rut in October the mating stags can be heard bellowing and rattling their horns in fearsome (though rarely lethal) combat. They are wild and elusive creatures: the

20

best times to look out for them are early morning and late evening, when they come out into the open to graze; on open moorland in early summer when the young grass makes good grazing; or on farmland or the fringes of the moor in winter.

The very beautiful, very pure, swiftly flowing streams which cascade down through the valley woods support their own characteristic wildlife: plants like spearwort, fool's watercress, water forget-me-not and water mint; birds like the dipper, grey wagtail, kingfisher, mallard and heron; insects like the caddisfly, mayfly, stonefly, beautiful demoiselle (damselfly) and black and lemon-yellow, golden-ringed dragonfly.

Salmon run up the Exe, Barle and East Lyn rivers and can sometimes be seen in late spring at the numerous small falls leaping their way upstream to their spawning grounds. Sea trout occasionally appear in the tributaries of the Taw, and rainbow trout, brown trout and grayling are common in the larger streams. But otters are scarcer and less seldom seen than in the days of Tarka.

The sea forms Exmoor's northern boundary – nearly 30 miles (48 kilometers) of the highest coastline in England, mostly hog-backed cliffs of long convex slopes reaching almost down to the sea, sometimes descending more than 1,200 feet (365 metres) over a horizontal distance of a mile or so (between Foreland and Porlock Weir), with a few vertical cliff faces falling as much as 800 feet (245 metres) sheer into the water, as at Great Hangman.

In the more sheltered parts, coastal woods of gnarled and stunted oaks grow right down to the beach and here you can see an unusual mixture of sea and woodland birds – woodpeckers and oystercatchers, fulmars and jays – and sometimes even a red deer on the beach. At Porlock Bay a massive pebble beach has trapped marshes and pools where migrating birds can rest and feed. Elsewhere the cliffs are the domain of guillemot and razorbill, cormorant and shag, kittiwake, fulmar, gannet, rave and jackdaw.

The Somerset and North Devon Coastal Path (part of the South West Way) picks its way along this coast. This is dealt with in more detail later in this chapter.

BIRD WATCHER'S CHECKLIST

The high moor in winter is the preserve of the curlew and the raven, although occasional visitors include the hen harrier, short-eared owl, golden plover, woodcock, common sandpiper, fieldfare and redwing. Spring brings the wheatears and ring ouzels from Africa, and later tree pipits, grasshopper warblers, skylarks, cuckoos, stonechats and whinchats (for which Exmoor is a national stronghold). Wren, dunnock, whitethroat, willow warbler and yellowhammer breed on parts of the moor where grass and heather grow together. Black grouse and red grouse also breed on the open moor, though neither is common.

BEFORE YOU GO
Maps: OS 1:50,000 Landranger Series Map Nos. 180 and 181.
Guidebooks: contact the Exmoor National Park Authority (NPA) at Exmoor House, Dulverton, Somerset, T:0398 23665, and get from them *The Exmoor Visitor:* free annual guide to transport, accommodation, information centres, ranger services, driving, walking, riding and fishing on Exmoor.
The Countryside Commission Guide is *Exmoor National Park* by Glyn Court (Webb and Bower).

GETTING THERE
Most visitors will approach Exmoor via Taunton; from here the A361 runs along the park's southern boundary, and the A358 cuts north to the coast where it joins the A39.

ACTIVITIES
Although Exmoor is a national park, land is privately owned. You can go almost anywhere, but this is a traditional privilege, not a statutory right. For everybody's sake, observe the Country Code.
Walking: there are 600 miles (960km) of public footpaths and bridle paths on Exmoor, from gentle to rugged. Most are signposted and many waymarked with coloured squares and arrows. The NPA publish a first-class series of detailed guides, *Waymarked Walks*, in 3 volumes, including some non-waymarked walks

on the remoter parts of the moor.

Walkers wishing to blaze their own trails should use the OS 1:10,000 Pathfinder Series Map Nos. SS 63–73, SS 64–74, SS82–92, SS 83–93, SS 84–94, ST 03–31 and ST 04–14. There are 7 basic routes which open up the whole of Exmoor: the coast; Dunkery and the Brendon plateau; the Exmoor Forest east of the Lynton–Simonsbath road (including Badgworthy and the Doone country); the Exmoor Forest west of the Lynton–Simonstown road (including the Chains); the Exe valley; the Barle valley; and the southern ridge from Dulverton to Shoulsbarrow Common.

The NPA offers a series of guided walks (including special interest walks – birds, archaeology, local history) led by local experts in spring and summer. For details see *The Exmoor Visitor*.

Two long-distance paths traverse the whole of Exmoor along part of their route: east to west along the SOMERSET AND NORTH DEVON COAST PATH (part of the South West Way) – for details, see p.30; and north to south along the TWO MOORS WAY linking Dartmoor and Exmoor. Two other long walks are confined to Exmoor itself: the 'Roof of Exmoor', which traverses the main ridge of Exmoor between Chapman Barrows and Dunkery Beacon; and the 'Perambulation', which is a circumnavigation of the former Royal Forest boundary (may not be marked on OS map so follow co-extensive Exmoor parish boundary).

From the summit of Little Hangman in North Devon you look along the line of the South West Way to Great Hangman

Another shorter but popular walk is the 'Doone Valley Trail' from Lorna Doone Farm, Malmsmead, along Badgworthy Water to Hoccombe Combe.

The Two Moors Way

A long walk of 102 miles (163km) crossing Devon south to north (or vice versa) via both the Dartmoor and Exmoor National Parks

From Ivybridge at the southern boundary of Dartmoor in South Devon the Way heads north over Dartmoor to Drewsteignton on the northern boundary. From there it follows roads and paths across farmland and countryside to West Anstey on the southern boundary of Exmoor to Lynmouth on the North Devon coast, where it links up with the SOUTH WEST WAY (p.26).

Before you go:
OS Landranger Series Map Nos. 202, 191, 181, 180.

Further information: for full details, including outline description of route, sketch maps, bad weather alternatives, transport, overnight camping sites and accommodation known to welcome ramblers, see official guide, *Two Moors Way* by H. Rowett (available from J.R. Turner, Coppins, The Poplars, Pinhoe, Exeter, Devon EX4 5HH or Ramblers' Association National Office).

Bodmin Moor

80 square miles (207sq km) of granite upland, averaging 800ft (245m) above sea level, between Dartmoor and the Atlantic in north-western Cornwall A O N B

A lonely landscape of rolling moors, craggy tors, clitter slopes and barren peat bogs (the source of the river Camel and Fowey), the moor is remarkable for the stone relics of its ancient peoples. Good, undemanding walking across big open country, with wide unrestricted views, especially from Brown Willy (1,375ft, 419m) and Rough Tor (1,312ft, 400m) – the highest points in Cornwall. Orchids, insect-eating sundews, bog bean and other wetland plants. Wintering wildfowl and waders at the remote and mysterious Dozmary Pool. **Where to stay:** nearest town for accommodation and information is Bodmin. **Access:** open all year. Best general base is Launceston (Tourist Office T:0566 2321) or, for northern moor only, Camelford (Tourist Office T:0840 212954). Best starting point for southern moor only is village of Pensilva, with path north to Minions, Cheeswring and Twelve Men's Moor. **Facilities:** the Ramblers' Association sponsor guided walks. Naturalists' field trips arranged by Bodmin Moor Nature Observatory, Ninestones Farm, Liskeard, Cornwall, T:0579 20455.

23

The Mendip Hills

From the Welsh *myndd*, a hill

84 square miles (218 sq km) of limestone hills rising steeply to over 1,000ft (305m) and stretching from the Bristol Channel into the middle of Somerset. AONB containing several important nature reserves and areas of NT land

The Mendips (or Mendip to the expert) are not wild in the way that Dartmoor can be wild, but they are liberating. The wind from the sea blows sweetly over its open heaths and moors, and although the hills are not high, they rise sheer out of the Somerset Levels in a massive, unbroken wall. From the sandstone outcrop of Black Down, at 1,067ft (325m) the highest point in the Mendip Hills, one can look out over half the West Country to Wales, the Brecon Beacons and the Black Mountains.

The key to this landscape is the relationship between rock and rain. There are no surface streams in the Mendips. Rainwater drains through the limestone, dissolving the rock by chemical action and creating a vast underground cave system. On the surface, collapses and closed depressions give the landscape a pock-marked appearance.

Mendip supports an unusual range of natural habitats, each with its own particular population of plant and animal life. The intrinsic richness of the limestone flora and fauna of Mendip is further enriched by its nearness to the wetland area of the Somerset Levels.

The broad leaved woodlands of oak and ash, some of them dating back to the original woodland cover of the region, lie mainly on the slopes of Mendip, and in spring they are full of bird song and wild flowers (including uncommon ones such as herb Paris).

Grassland covers the limestone plateau, and heathland thrives on the sandstone outcrops like Black Down. The cliffs of Cheddar and Ebbor Gorges, and their related cave systems, harbour a special range of animals, plants and small organisms, including the rare horseshoe bat and a unique micro-organism in Wookey Hole which is part fungus and part algae.

Before you go: OS Landranger Series Map No. 182 Weston and Bridgewater (for main routes). 1:25,000 Pathfinder Series for foot and bridle paths: Map Nos. ST 25/35 Brent Knoll; ST 44/54 Wells and Wedmore; ST 45/55 Cheddar: ST 46/56 Yatton and Chew Magna. *Mendip – A New Study* by Robin Atthill (David & Charles 1976) gives a good general overview. **Getting there:** A38 from Bristol; A368 from Bath; A370 from Weston-super-Mare; A371 from Wells. The roads across Mendip are B roads or less. They are narrow – too narrow for comfort for caravans and motor homes – and parking is difficult except in villages or areas specified on map. Rural car parks are preferable as they are near best walks and best views. **Where to stay:** most accommodation is in the Mendip towns of Wells and Cheddar, or further afield in Weston-super-Mare, though bed and breakfast and farmhouse accommodation is more widely scattered. Caravan sites and motor home

parks are concentrated near Weston, Brean and along A371 near Cheddar. **Access:** free access to Mendip as a whole at all times, but no access to army range (paratroop dropping zone) shown on map in central Mendip. Most nature reserves and Sites of Special Scientific Interest are open to public subject to local regulations. A warden service consisting of full-time warden and volunteers can help and advise visitors: office at Charterhouse Outdoor Activity Centre (T:0761 62338).

The Somerset Levels and West Sedgemoor

220 square miles (570sq km) of low-lying, marshy land in the flood plain of the Rivers Parrett, Brue and Axe. One of the most important surviving wetland areas in Britain.

Occupying a rough square between Weston-super-Mare, Glastonbury, Taunton and Bridgewater, the Somerset Levels are not a wilderness, nor even a nature reserve or conservation area, but populated farming land which is subject to widespread annual flooding. Once a marsh, now a partly-drained fen, the area is divided into two distinct parts: the Levels, a 5–6-mile (8–10-km) belt of slightly raised land along the coast) and the Moors (low-lying river valleys further inland). Because the Levels are higher than the Moors, the rivers have difficulty discharging through them into the Bristol Channel, so that in periods of heavy rain the rivers frequently burst their banks and flood the surrounding meadows over a wide area. The winter flooding and the resulting high summer water table provide a special wetland habitat for a wide variety of birds, plants and animals.

In winter huge flocks of waders (whimbrel, snipe, dunlin, ruff, golden plover, lapwing) and wildfowl (Bewick's swan, mallard, teal, widgeon, shoveler) feed on the abundant supply of invertebrates and plant seeds. Some of these birds (redshank, snipe, curlew, lapwing) stay to breed in summer, when the floods have subsided and the meadows glow with brilliant spreads of wild flowers.

Plants of the Somerset Levels include orchids (marsh, fragrant, frog and green-winged), bog myrtle and bog pimpernel, devil's bit, scabious and adder's tongue fern, and uncommon plants like bladderwort, marsh pea and marsh fern. An extensive network of willow-lined drainage ditches called rhynes provide an undisturbed aquatic environment for water plants like frog-bit, water dropwort, water violet and the flowering rush, for an abundance of fish and invertebrates, and above all for the otter, whose main stronghold in England is here.

Several nature reserves serve as enclaves of unspoiled Somerset Level wetland habitat. The most notable of these is the RSPB reserve at West Sedgemoor. The reserve consists of 740 acres (300 ha) of wet grazing meadows, criss-crossed by drainage ditches and bordered by woods, within a bigger complex of the Somerset Levels covering 3,000 acres (1,215 ha). The

Britain's best-loved wild mammal, the otter, is seriously threatened by the pollution of its habitats

West Sedgemoor reserve is one of the major breeding sites in south-west England for waders (black-tailed godwit, curlew, lapwing, redshank, snipe) and the most important site in Britain for whimbrel on spring migration. Large flocks of lapwing winter here, and redwing and fieldfare may be seen in the daylight hours. There is a heronry, and roe deer also inhabit the reserve. Wetland plants include marsh marigold, marsh orchid, water violet and ragged robin.

Like other wetland areas in Europe, the Somerset Levels are threatened by agricultural improvement and drainage schemes which would wipe out much of their wealth of flora and fauna.

Where to stay: hotel and bed and breakfast accommodation is available in Taunton and Bridgewater. **Access:** the West Sedgemoor Reserve lies to north of A378 Langport to Taunton road, near village of Fivehead. Open all year. Also worth visiting are the STNC reserves at Catcott, Tealham Moor and Westhay Moor (entry by permit only), the

'The loneliness of Mendip is a real loneliness . . . One is caught as it were in an empty space, a featureless desolation, a solitude that is like no other solitude.'
Edward Hutton:
Highways and
Byways in Somerset

NCC reserve at Shapwick Heath (permit only), and the AWT reserve at Weston Moor in the Gordano valley (an oasis for reed-nesting birds and many kinds of insects, permit only). **Further information:** contact Warden (John Humphreys), Hadleigh, White Street, North Curry, nr Taunton, Somerset, T:0823 490679.

The South West Way

Officially known as the South West Peninsula Coast Path, this is the longest official footpath in Britain, running for approximately 560 miles (896 kilometres) from Minehead in Somerset to Shell Bay in Sortset. It encompasses some of the most magnificent coastal scenery in Europe, and in places it is as wild and weatherbeaten as anywhere in the British Isles.

I lived on the South West Way once, in a lonely stone farmhouse, a converted medieval barn, high up by the great chalk cliffs of St Alban's Head on the coast of a part of Dorset called the Isle of Purbeck. It was not known as the South West Way then, for that was still a dream in the minds of its creators. But the path had been there a long time, an old coastguard track that teetered airily along the edge of the cliffs, bearing east to Swanage and the sunrise in one direction, and west to Weymouth, Cornwall and the wild Atlantic in the other. From the top of these cliffs, more than 300 feet (92 metres) above the sea, I could look out over a vast, dappled sea to the horizon, and almost vertically down on to the decks of boats passing below. The voices of the people on board, raised above the clamour of the engine and the sea, came up to me clear and sharp on my lofty eminence. 'Look up there!' came the cry. 'There's a dwarf on the top of those cliffs. Doesn't he look *titchy!*'

It was over these cliffs that the weather came: thick white mists that rolled in from the sea and overwhelmed the house as if it was an alpine eyrie; equinoctial gales that shrieked over the headland, tugging at the roof slates and battering at the window panes; rain, rainbows, and opalescent moon; scream of gulls, wail of foghorn, deep throb of a big ship's diesels – they all came over these cliffs.

On paper at least this could not properly pass as a wild place. A fine-weather track wound inland to a village with a general store and a pub. Arable fields reached down to a dry-stone wall enclosing a garden

that grew nothing but chives as thick as a lawn. But a combination of circumstances – of season and weather, health and amenities – made even this little corner of the Dorset coast seem as isolated and austere as a Hebridean croft in mid-winter. There was no electricity in the house, only a pot-bellied iron stove, candles and a couple of hurricane lamps. All through the winter months the farmhouse had been deserted and its ancient stone walls had grown as chill and clammy as a tomb; in the flickering candlelight the bare stone glistened with moisture like a cave.

The pocket diary I had brought with me from London indicated that winter was over and spring had begun by the time I arrived. But the season was so retarded that none of the illiterates with whom I shared this simple abode paid any attention to such mathematical niceties. At the beginning of winter the empty house had been taken over by various creatures with varying number of legs – 4, 6, 8, 100, 1,000, or no legs at all. Now, though spring had officially begun, all these various slithering, skulking, crawling things were still obstinately asleep in tight little balls and coils and spirals all over the house. Just to open a drawer was an adventure. In a linen cupboard I discovered a solitary mouse out for the count in a perfectly rounded nest fashioned out of a finely shredded *Farmer's Weekly*. Under a wooden fruit box by the scullery door I found a dormant adder as neatly coiled as a liquorice catherine wheel, an exquisite creature which did not move except to raise a glittering eye and stare fixedly back at me.

I was the only creature with two legs, and they were the biggest in the place, but before long they let me down. In the cold and damp I soon succumbed to a bronchial influenza and lay shivering and sweating on a mattress on the floor by the stove, a candle on one side of me and an axe on the other. When the fire sank low I feebly raised the axe and let it fall with its own weight on to a pile of old orange crates, and with this wood I fed the fire. All through the night I could hear the melancholy bray of the lighthouse foghorn. All through the day

The sheer millstone grit cliffs at Hartland Quay on the North Devon Coast Path overlook the site of a vanished quay financed by Elizabethan seafarers Raleigh, Drake and Hawkins

I could watch the mad March hares, like surreal creatures of delirium, cross and recross my line of vision as they boxed each other across the lawn of chives. I never knew who won. I never cared. I couldn't tell one March hare from another.

Then one morning the sun came up and stayed out, and I got up and went out – into the sunlight, on to the hill. I was better. And it was spring. The first butterfly spreading its wings in the shelter of a sunny wall. A skylark ascending. The first migrant birds, wheatears among them, flitting across the downland from the Channel cliff. The mouse had gone from the linen cupboard, the snake from under the fruit box. I walked out to the coast path along the cliffs, the sea a blinding silver, a soft warm wind sidling in from the south west. On the rock ledges below me kittiwakes were shrieking like fishwives in their bird-slum tenements, and fulmars were soaring and gliding over the waves and hovering in the wind-sheer off the cliff edge. No, not a wild place, perhaps, I reckoned, but a heck of a place to be.

For these West Country cliffs – in some parts 600 feet (185 metres) or more above the thunderous sea – are a frontier, where the elements of earth, air and water are locked in perpetual conflict. Once there was a fourth element, fire, the fiery molten lava forced up from the magma of the inner earth to form the igneous rocks of the great Atlantic-facing cliffs of Cornwall and north Devon. Sea and weather claw and pound at these rocks, gouging out sandy coves, rock arches and long spines of rock jutting out to sea. To walk the South West Way along such a spectacular and varied coast you must pick your way from headland to headland, from cliff to valley, stream, waterfall, rock pool, beach, river, estuary, mud flat, back to cliff, plateau, heath and moor, wood and pasture – all the time within sight and sound and smell and feel and even, when the salt spray blows in on the wind, taste of the open, restless sea.

It can be glorious walking, through an exceptional range of habitats, and wildlife of one sort or another is with you most of the way. Grey seals haul out on the rocks and breed in the secluded coves. Seabirds teem on the cliffs, waders and wildfowl on the tidal estuaries.

The wind is a dominant element here. Trees grow horizontally because of it, and the rocky shore is littered with shipwrecks. Other ruins mark the passage of humankind: Iron Age camps and Bronze Age burial sites on the headlands, the melancholy remains of the Cornish tin and copper mines on the cliffs. Slowly these monuments to mortality are weathered away by the wind and the waves. Walking this magnificent coast you become part of the elemental conflict and the ebb and flow of life on England's south-west frontier, and for a day or a week or a month you can become a frontiersman in your own right.

I have traversed the South West Way three ways in its entirety, always in the same direction: anti- or counter-clockwise from the Bristol to the English Channel. But I fear I would not qualify for any medal for this apparent feat of derring-do, still less the certificate awarded by the South West Way Association to anyone who has walked the 560 miles of this path from end to end.

The first way I followed the Way was in an old Auster Husky monoplane, which toiled in and out along the outline of the coast at the minimum legal altitude of 500

SIGNS OF DISTRESS AT SEA
If you see any of these signs out at sea, dial 999 and inform the Coastguard:
Rocket, parachute flare or hand flare showing red light
Rocket or shell throwing red stars one at a time at short intervals
Smoke signal with orange smoke
Any signal reproducing the words SOS or MAYDAY (from the French *m'aidez*)
Continuous sound from a fog horn
Flames on a vessel from a burning tar barrel
Square flag with a ball below it
Red ensign upside down
Red ensign made fast to upper part of rigging
International distress code signal NC (blue and white chequered flag with 16 squares above a flag striped horizontally – blue, white, red, white, blue)
Clothing fixed to an oar
Human figure slowly raising and lowering outstretched arms
Any obvious disaster.

feet or about 150 metres – a wonderful way to see the south-western shore in its geographical context. The second way was in a mahogany-and-brass Owl class sail-and-motor cruiser that had been built on the Clyde in the 1930s and butted the sea and the weather like a tank. The third way was in an ex-army signals truck converted to provide rather tight living quarters for four men and two women on a conservation study of the whole coastline.

The immense panoramic blur left in my mind by these protracted ventures leaves me in no doubt that this is one of the most magnificent wild coasts in the world.

BEFORE YOU GO

Maps: as on any serious walk, you should set out equipped with the relevant maps. These are: OS 1:50,000 Landranger Series. and 1:25,000 Pathfinder Series. In the sections that follow, the map number refers to the Landranger series.

Guidebooks: to walk the whole of the South West Way takes about 6 weeks. Few people have time for this and most must content themselves

with walking one or more sections of the path. The South West Way Association publish an annually updated guide, *The South West Way* (Devon Books), available from the Ramblers' Association or the South West Way Association (see below). It provides a comprehensive list of accommodation *en route*, camp sites, public transport, ferries, tide-tables, maps, publications and

sectional notes on the path, with distances and gradings of physical difficulty. As a complement to this essential compendium, take with you the best of the other available guides: *The South-West Peninsula Coastal Path* by Ken Ward and John Mason (Letts Guides, 3 vols), with excellent maps and commentary.

A word of warning: especially in Cornwall, the cliffs can be high and rocky and go up and down all day as much as 1,000ft (305m) at a stretch. If you are a hardened walker this should be within your capacity. If not, check the relief of the route before you set out and see if there is an escape route or refreshment available *en route*.

Occasionally there are other hazards. Sea mists roll in without warning and obscure the path ahead and behind. Tides move in swiftly to cut off coves and beaches. Rain can make rocks wet and slippery. Gale-force winds can make it difficult to keep your balance, especially if you are carrying a large pack.

It is preferable to walk the path anti- or counter-clockwise, so that the prevailing south-westerly wind is at your back: this is the order followed here.

For much of its length the South West Way runs through unspoiled coastal scenery. But inevitably some stretches have to wend their way through towns, ports, caravan and motor home parks and recreation beaches, so not all of the South West Way is of interest to the wild traveller or naturalist. The sections outlined below have been chosen because they are the wildest and finest (and often the toughest) stretches of the sea coast in the west of England. For a rock-by-rock account, refer to the recommended guides. Nature reserves adjoining the South West Way, and other areas of particular interest, such as islands like LUNDY and the SCILLIES, are dealt with alongside the adjacent section of the coast path.

GETTING THERE
For invaluable information on how to get to or near the South West Way by public

One of Britain's most typical inland water birds, the heron still flourishes despite the loss of many wetlands

transport refer to *The South West Way*, available from the South West Way Association (see below).

WHERE TO STAY
For complete up-to-date list of all accommodation available along the 560 miles (896km) of the South West Way see *The South West Way*. For further details contact YHA, Ramblers' Association, Holiday Fellowship, Countrywide Holidays Association, and West Country Tourist Board.

ACCESS AND CLOSURES
There is free access to all parts of the coastal path at all times of year. Certain short sections, however, are inaccessible from time to time because of the

tides, or closed for army practice. For walkers who wish to take short cuts across tidal beaches and estuaries, annual tide-tables are published in *The South West Way*, and daily tide-tables are printed in the relevant local papers. Ferry timetables are also included in *The South West Way* for crossings at high tide. Closures by the army mainly affect the Lulworth stretch of the coastal walk in Dorset. For details see the DORSET COAST PATH (p.40).

FURTHER INFORMATION
Contact the South West Way Association at the following addresses: Secretary (Fred White), 'Delamein', Bracken Rise, Paignton, Devon TQ4 6JU, T:0803 842844; Membership Secretary (Mary Macleod), 1 Orchard Drive, Kingskerswell, Newton Abbot, Devon TQ12 5DG, T:080 47 3061.

THE SOMERSET AND NORTH DEVON COAST PATH

OS Landranger Series Map Nos. 180, 181 and 190

This section of the South West Way is 82 miles (131km) long and runs from Minehead on the Bristol Channel in Somerset to Marsland Mouth, overlooking the Atlantic on the North Devon–Cornwall border. The route passes along the coast of the Exmoor National Park and the North Devon Area of Outstanding Natural Beauty. Before starting the walk in this direction, naturalists may want to visit the nature reserves at Brean Down, Bridgwater Bay and Steepholm Island. The finest section of the walk on the Bristol Channel coast runs from Lynmouth to Combe Martin, and is outlined briefly below.

Walkers who follow the coast round to Bideford Bay will find themselves in the vicinity of the remarkable sand-dune reserve at Braunton Burrows. Bideford itself is the point of departure for any trip to Lundy Island. I have included the best section along the Atlantic coast, from Hartland Point to Marsland Mouth, under the heading of the Cornish Coast Path, of which it is geographically and logistically a part; nature does not always respect county boundaries.

Steepholm

Nature Reserve (Kenneth Allsop Memorial Trust)

Small, steep, 50-acre (20-ha), 300-million-year-old limestone island in the Bristol Channel off Weston-super-Mare, Avon. Geologically an outlier of the Mendip Hills, Steepholm is remarkable for its unusual flora and fauna, and remains of Victorian, World War I and World War II military emplacements. Several rare plants were introduced by Augustinian monks in medieval times, including wild leek, wild peony, henbane, alexander and the caper spurge. A few plants (for example the stagshorn plantain) are found nowhere else.

Nesting herring gulls dominate the cliff scene in summer, along with lesser black-backed and great black-backed gulls, cormorants and shelduck. Other notable birds include peregrine falcons, merlins, buzzards and ravens, while the small range of animals include muntjacs, pipistrelle bats, grey seals, and enormous slow worms – a specimen caught in 1984 was 20in (50.8cm) long, a British record.

Getting there: by boat from Weston-super-Mare – for reservations phone 0963 32583. Day trips for public on Saturdays from April to October, and for organized groups on other days; 2-mile nature trail round island – time required, 2 to 3 hours. **Recommendations:** take waterproof clothing, stout shoes, binoculars. No dogs allowed. No swimming (lethal currents). No rock scrambling (dangerous, unstable cliffs and scree). **Where to stay:** in dormitories of Victorian Barracks by special arrangement only. **Further information:** from Resident Warden (Rodney Legg) in main hall of Victorian Barracks, Kenneth Allsop Memorial Trust, Mellborne Port, Sherborne, Dorset, T:0963 32583. **Further reading:** Legg, Rodney: *The Steepholm Guide* (Dorset Publishing Co., Wincanton, Somerset).

Brean Down Sanctuary

NT Reserve
RSPB Sanctuary

160-acre (64.5-ha) limestone headland jutting into the Berrow mud flats of the Severn estuary near Weston-super-Mare, Avon. An outlier of the Mendip Hills, with the island of Steepholm in front and the Somerset Levels behind. Important landmark for migrating birds and insects.
Access: via coast road from Brean; open all year. **Where to stay:** various in Weston-super-Mare. **Further information:** booklet from NT.

Bridgwater Bay

NCC NNR

The reserve consists of 6,000 acres (2,400ha) of mud flats, salt marshes and lagoons in the tidal estuary of River Parrett, 5 miles north-west of Bridgwater on Somerset coast. Main interest is the large number of wildfowl and waders that can be seen there. Thousands of ducks congregate in winter: mallard, shelduck, widgeon, pintail, shoveler and teal, together with white-fronted geese occasionally, and large flocks of waders, including many thousands of dunlin, lapwing and curlew. At migration times dunlin, lapwing, redshank, oystercatcher, black-tailed godwit, knot turnstone and grey plover stop here to feed and rest on passage – a fabulous sight when they take to the air *en masse*. Bridgwater Bay is the only known place in Britain where shelduck gather in such large numbers for their mid-summer moult.

Access: to shoreline from car park at Steart village but limited to public rights of way and bird hides. Permit required to visit Steat Island and Fenning, and no visitors allowed 1 Nov–31 Mar. **Where to stay:** accommodation on site, various in Bridgwater. **Recommendations:** take care on mud flats – they are treacherous. Report unexploded bombs to warden or police immediately. **Further information:** from Warden, Dowells Farm, Steart, nr Bridgwater, Somerset, T:0278 652426; leaflet from NCC Taunton, Roughmor, Bishop's Hole, Taunton, T:0823 283211.

Lynmouth to Combe Martin

13-mile (21-km) walk along Exmoor coastline

A pleasant introduction to the South West Way, through some lovely Devon greenery and scenery. A gentler stretch than some, and less remote

The jagged pinnacles of the Valley of the Rocks loom above the Bristol Channel on the North Devon coast

from the haunts of man, though not without its rigours and cliff-top palpitations. You could begin this stretch further back at Porlock or Minehead,

or better still at Wingate, on the eastern side of Lynmouth, with a spectacular track to Foreland Point and a view over Lynmouth from a thousand feet above the sea. But the walk back from Lynmouth, along what amounts to the north-west seaboard bounds of the

31

Exmoor National Park, is probably the finest continuous stretch: marvellous cliff-top views, craggy valleys, tangled woods, green combes, grassy old coach roads, exquisite bays, 600-ft (180-m) cliffs, cliff-top moorlands and, from the highest eminence along the route – the 1,044-ft (318-m) Great Hangman Hill – tremendous panoramas up and down this lovely coast and across the Bristol Channel to Wales. **Distance:** 13 miles (20km). **Grading:** strenuous. **Warning:** no pit stops on long stretch from Heddon's Mouth to Combe Martin.

Braunton Burrows

2,400 acres (971ha) of sand dunes and mud flats to the north of the rivers Taw and Torridge near Braunton in north-west Devon
NCC NNR
UNESCO Biosphere Reserve

One of the largest sand dune systems in Britain, Braunton Burrows is internationally famous for its plant and animal life. The reserve offers a wide range of habitats, from the open sands of the beach, through the richly vegetated wet slacks and damp hollows, to the thick scrub of the inland dunes, some of them 100ft (31m) high. An immense variety of flowering plants – more than 400 different species – flourishes here.

At the front line of the dunes, on the upper beach above all but the highest equinoctial tides, specialist plants like prickly saltwort, sea rocket, sea holly, sea bindweed and the rare and lovely sea stock cling to their precarious beachhead. Marram grass binds the sand of the foredunes in large tussocks which shelter the rich plant colonies behind them. The wealth of plants attracts many insects; among the butterflies are the dark green fritillary, marbled white, common blue, meadow brown and gatekeeper, while snails thrive on the lime-rich sand which helps build their shells.

Mammals include rabbits (from whose warrens the Burrows derive their name), fox, hedgehog, weasel, mink, wood mouse, common and pigmy shrews, short-tailed and bank voles.

In spring and autumn migrating birds rest and feed here, and flocks of waders congregate on the estuary. In summer shelducks and wheatears nest in disused rabbit burrows and in winter merlins, harriers and short-eared owls join the kestrels and buzzards to hunt for voles and shrews and other prey.

Braunton Burrows were used in the war for training American troops; this resulted in severe damage to the dunes, but since 1964 the NCC has leased the area from the Ministry of Defence and has largely restored it to its original pristine state. **Getting there:** turn left down Sand Lane off B323 Braunton–Saunton road, or turn down toll road (Ferry Road) off A361 at Wratton. 2 free car parks at boundary of reserve: the north-east one at end of Sandy Lane, the south-east one at Broadsands end of Ferry Road. No transport inside reserve. **Access:** reserve open to public all year, but no access to military training areas in northern and extreme southern sections of reserve when training exercises are in progress; at such times red flags are flown and sentries posted. Most unexploded missiles have been removed but some may come to the surface in the shifting sands. If you find one, don't pick it up or kick it; mark the spot, run and report it to the army (see red notice boards), police or Warden (T:0271 812552). **Where to stay:** various types available in Barnstaple, Braunton and the surrounding villages. **Further information:** leaflet from NCC Taunton, Roughmor, Bishop's Hole, T:0823 283211 or Warden, Broadeford Farm, Heddon Mill, nr Braunton, North Devon, T:0271 812552, will arrange guided tours for groups or educational parties.

Lundy Island

Small granite island 12 miles (19km) off North Devon coast in Bristol Channel Reserve owned by NT and leased to Landmark Trust

Lundy is a super lump of rock with fine sea cliffs and tremendous views of England, Wales and the Atlantic. Three miles long, half a mile wide and up to 400ft (122m) high, the island covers just over 1,000 acres (405ha) of largely uncultivated land and is inhabited by a permanent population of 25, one of Britain's smallest communities.

With more than a whiff of the far horizon about it, Lundy is not always easy to land on, or to leave, on account of wind and weather. I recall having to free-fall from the galley hatch of a heaving

Butterflies found at Braunton Burrows include (from left to right) pearl-bordered fritillary, silver-studded blue and small copper

steamer into an open boat which rose and fell 20ft (6m) with each wave of a huge Atlantic swell off the landing beach on Lundy. No one would be expected to do that in the normal course of events, but you might be delayed until the weather improves.

The island is a haven to wildlife, both above and below sea level, and the waters around it were declared a marine nature reserve in February 1987, the first such reserve in Britain. Four hundred species of birds have been recorded on Lundy and 40 species nest there, including razorbill, guillemot, fulmar, lesser and great black-backed gull, herring gull, and kittiwake, a few Manx shearwater and puffins (now much reduced in numbers). Mammals include grey seals, wild goats, island ponies, Sika deer, Soay sheep and black rats (on one of their last British outposts on nearby Rat Island). The Lundy cabbage is found nowhere else in the world, nor are the two species of beetle that live on it.

The underwater rocks and seabed around the island are like a garden in full bloom, with colourful and showy marine invertebrates such as corals, sea anemones, sea fans, sea fingers and sponges, mainly of an Atlantic-Mediterranean distribution. Coastal fish include wrasse and the red-band fish (*cepola rubescens*), which burrows in the sand.

Getting there: the 300-ton MS *Oldenburg* (an experience in itself) leaves every Saturday of the year from Bideford, North Devon, and also on certain other days; Lundy's 32-ft (10-m) launch operates on days when the *Oldenburg* is not sailing. Landing on open beach on Lundy, so arrival and departure can be delayed in bad weather. Timetable and reservations via Landmark Trust (head office), Shottebrooke, Maidenhead, Berkshire SL6 3SW, T:062 882 5925. Helicopter trips from Hartland Point in summer only. **Where to stay:** day or overnight visits are possible: small hotel (Millcombe House), tavern, restaurant, campsite, self-catering accommodation and vacation homes in a number of old, romantic and often remote renovated buildings, including the Castle Keep, the Old Light (lighthouse keepers' quarters in the highest light in Great Britain), The Old School (known as the Blue Bung), and Tibbetts (a granite-built Admiralty look-out from whose remote eminence 14 lighthouses can be seen on a clear night), along with more modest quarters in the Cable Station, the Fridge Room and the Radio Room, and communal accommodation for groups. Campers welcome – camp-site large, grassy, and sheltered from west by granite wall. Full details and bookings from Landmark Trust. **Access:** visitors have unrestricted run of whole island, but rock climbing may be restricted during nesting season (Apr–Jul). No dogs or cats allowed on ship or island; babies only by prior arrangement. Visitors under 16 must be accompanied by someone older. **Facilities:** don't take supplies to the island as this causes problems when embarking and landing. There is a fully stocked shop on the island. **Further information:** can be found in the *Landmark Handbook* and. *Lundy Guide* (both from Landmark Trust, Maidenhead main office or 21 Dean's Yard, London SW1). For information on rock climbing, underwater diving, transport of bulky equipment and special supplies from shop, contact the Agent (John Puddy), Lundy Island, Bristol Channel, Devon EX39 2LY, T:0271 870870.

THE CORNWALL COAST PATH

OS Landranger Series Map Nos. 190, 200, 201, 203, 204

The Cornwall Coast Path, the longest continuous section of the South West Way, runs for 268 miles (429km) from Marsland Mouth on the North Devon border overlooking the Atlantic to Cremyll Ferry near Fowey on the English Channel seaboard. Much of the route passes through the Cornwall Area of Outstanding Natural Beauty. Certain stretches of this route traverse some of the most authentically wild places in the West Country, a world of thrusting headlands, plummeting ravines, wheeling seabirds, windswept moors, vertiginous cliff walls of stark granite, vast views over coastline, ocean, sky and weather, and the exhilaration of standing at one of the great land frontiers on the edge of 3,000 miles (4,800km) of empty ocean. The sections of the path outlined below contain some of the wildest stretches.

Hartland Point to Pentire Point

From Hartland Point to Marsland Mouth the path lies in Devon, but it is such an integral point of a long coastal walk around Cornwall that I have included it here. Hartland Point, 325ft (99m) above the sea, is the real start of the wild west coast. Beyond the point the path follows the sheer cliffs, up and down steep-sided combes and in and out of primordial views. Few parts of the British coastline provide such perfect examples of folded and contorted rocks as this. Approaching Marsland Point the going gets tougher and is not recommended for the unfit. But the last few miles to Bude are straightforward enough, some of them along the beach.

South of Bude, between Boscastle and Port Isaac, lies some of the best cliff walking

in the whole peninsula, with a particularly wild and unspoiled stretch between Tintagel and Port Gaverne. The towering cliffs provide good nesting sites for fulmars, guillemots, razorbills, shags and, on Lye Rock, puffins; and the uncommon rock samphire clings to its foothold on the west-facing rocks.

Beyond Port Isaac, the cliffs are lower, the scenery gentler; and approaching Padstow Bay the sedimentary slates and shales give way to igneous rocks, like the splendid lava of Pentire Point, the fossilized flow from an ancient submarine volcano. At Pentire you have the best all-round views on the whole South West Way and here you can actually feel the shock of the Atlantic rollers as they burst against the headland. The South West Way Association breaks this section down as follows (beginning and ending each stretch with nearest towns):

Hartland Quay to Bude.
Distance: 13 miles (21km).
Grading: severe.
Bude to Crackington Haven.

Distance: 9 miles (14km).
Grading: strenuous.
Boscastle to Tintagel.
Distance: 5 miles (8km) .
Grading: moderate.
Recommended as short stretch of good cliff walking with transport available at each end.
Tintagel to Port Isaac.
Distance: 8 miles (13km).
Grading: severe. Warning: 'The stretch from Trebarwith Strand to Port Isaac is surprisingly wild and rough. This is not a section to be lightly undertaken and probably includes one of the steepest gradients on the whole of the official South West Way. Do not leave Trebarwith Strand unless you have plenty of time in hand, it will take longer than you think to reach Port Isaac.' (South West Way Association).
Port Isaac to Polzeath.
Distance 8 miles (13km).
Grading: strenuous.

St Ives to Mousehole

AONB

Along this stretch of the South West Way, all of it cliff and most of it Cornwall Area of Outstanding Natural Beauty, you round the toe of England on a trail that crosses a land of solid granite. The first 16 miles (26km) of Cape Cornwall are the West Country coast at its wildest: rugged, savage, unpeopled, with soaring cliffs to one side and high moorland to the other.

Beyond Cape Cornwall, as desolate a place as any on the English coast, the landscape seems almost foreign, more like Brittany perhaps, but devastated by old abandoned tin and copper mines. Land's

End, the westernmost point in Britain, is a rock wilderness ruined in the high season (though not in the low) by mass tourism. Half a mile further on, turning the corner of western England and starting east, the cliffs are empty again, the orbit of walker and seabird and the ceaseless murmuration of the swell.

The path from Land's End to Porthgwarra is generally regarded as the finest stretch of cliff in the West Country, and the going is relatively easy. After Gwennap Head the cliffs grow gentler, the climate warmer, the vegetation lusher. Another superb stretch of secluded coast walking ends at the little Cornish fishing village of Mousehole (pronounced 'Mowzel'). You can, of course, carry on past it, but our next recommended stretch cuts out Penzance and its environs and picks up the Cornish Coastal Path again at Mullion Cove.

The South West Way Association breaks this section down as follows (beginning and ending each stretch with nearest towns):

St Ives to Pendeen Watch. **Distance:** 13 miles (21km). **Grading:** severe. **Warning:** 'You are now starting on the longest and most deserted stretch of coast road on the whole of the South West Way. There is only one seasonal place of refreshment on the path and that is after 18 miles (29km) at Cape Cornwall. It is magnificent walking but do not undertake it unprepared.' **Pendeen Watch to Cape Cornwall. Distance:** 13 miles (21km). **Grading:** moderate. **Cape Cornwall to Sennen Cove. Distance:** 5 miles (8km). **Grading:** moderate. **Sennen Cove to Porthcurno.**

Distance: 6 miles (10km). **Grading:** moderate. **Porthcurno to Lamorna.** **Distance:** 5 miles (8km). **Grading:** strenuous. **Lamorna to Mousehole.** **Distance:** 3 miles (5km). **Grading:** strenuous.

Mullion Cove to Black Rock

AONB

Some 20 miles (32km) of scenic grandeur through the Cornwall Area of Oustanding Natural Beauty. By now the granite has given way to new kinds of rocks: schists, slates and shales, serpentine and gabbro. Rock climbers.haul themselves up this tortured geology, walkers pick their way across it. The rewards are considerable: vast views from points and headlands like Predannack Head (St Michael's Mount one way, the coast to Tol-Pedn-Penwith the other, the bare moor of

Brilliant yellow gorse flowers on wasteland below the ruins of the Cornish tin mine of Carn Galver

the Lizard peninsula behind), extraordinary natural formations like the dramatic sea-filled amphitheatre of Pigeon Ogo, and the marvellous cove at Kynance, with its caves, blowholes and pinnacles of multi-coloured serpentine rock.

Rounding the Lizard the landscape changes, the cliffs grow gentler, the soil richer and the valleys lusher – and you pass the half-way point along the South West Way.

The South West Way Association breaks this section down as follows:

Mullion Cove to Lizard. **Distance:** 6 miles (10km). **Grading:** strenuous. Very spectacular and enjoyable walking, no superhuman effort required – a good stretch for people who want to sample the best without fearing the worst.

Lizard to Coverack. **Distance:** 9 miles (14km). **Grading:** strenuous in parts.

The Isles of Scilly

Also known as Scillonia, but never the Scilly Isles

An archipelago of small, low islands, a few inhabited, 28 miles (45km) out in the Atlantic west of Land's End. Strict conservation protection under Duchy of Cornwall and NCC nature reserve (bird sanctuary) on Annet

The Isles of Scilly are the southernmost points of land in the British Isles. Little granite outliers of the Cornish landmass, these 200 or more islands, islets and named rocks lay untidily strewn across the teeth of the wind and grain of the sea. Their isolation is also their salvation, at least from a natural history and conservation point of view. Only five of the islands are inhabited – St Mary's (the largest, most developed, with most of the islands' inhabitants in the 'capital', Hugh Town), Tresco (the most urbane, and privately owned), St Martin's (the finest beaches, longest cliffs), St Agnes (the most oceanic and least developed) and

Bryher (the roughest terrain and smallest population) – and only 2,000 people live on them, 1,700 on St Mary's.

Because of the southerly position of the island the climate is extraordinarily equable. The winter is frost-free, the spring very early, daffodils bloom in December, and sub-tropical plants flourish all the year round. But don't be misled. When the Atlantic winds itself up for one of its wilder blows, the sea almost engulfs the islands, and howling gales raise waves nearly a hundred feet high, almost as high as the islands' highest land, and shift whole beaches with the awesome power of the wind and water.

The Scillies are far enough removed from the British mainland to remain free from wind-borne and water-borne pollution. The air has a startling clarity and the sunlight a brilliance never found on the mainland. The off-shore waters are so pure and clear that even moonlight can illuminate the bottom. Down there the underwater swimmer and marine naturalist can dive on wrecks galore and view a host of remarkable marine creatures such as bristling sea urchins and feather stars on the tidal rocks and sandy bottoms.

Above the surface of this crystal sea, the blinding white granite beaches and the windblown dunes, rocky cliffs and inland heaths support a characteristic range of native plant life and a large number of alien species that have colonized the islands or been planted there.

May and June are the best times to see breeding birds, especially on the uninhabited island of Annet, a bird sanctuary with such a dense cover of thrift that hay fever victims are almost asphyxiated in a cloud of pollen dust. The Scillies are world famous for their birds, especially the incredible number of rare and exotic migrants and vagrants from as far away as Brazil and the USA, which birdwatchers flock to the islands to see every October. Among the 374 species recorded here are large colonies of native seabirds and land birds, many of which are remarkably tame due to absence of predators: there are no snakes, foxes, badgers, stoats or weasels.

The sea holly (a member of the carrot family) uses its exceptionally long roots to reach down to water lying deep beneath the surface of the sand dunes

Of the islands' animal population, only the small shrew is unique to the Scillies, a pretty insectivore that has been evolved by island isolation into something slightly different from its mainland counterpart, and can be commonly seen rummaging about the heaths and among the rocks on the shore. Giant basking sharks, porpoises and dolphins can be seen in the sea around Scilly, and colonies of grey seals on the outlying rocks.

The Scillies were first settled by Bronze Age people from southern Portugal, rediscovered by the Phoenicians from Asia Minor looking for tin in Cornwall, later used by the Romans as a kind of Devils' Island for Celtic dissidents and deserters from the legions, and by the Vikings as a plunder and pillage base. Today these beautiful little islands are invaded by gentler souls, refugees from post-industrial civilization – ex-Prime Minister Lord Wilson among them – who come to refresh their spirits amid the space and silence of oceanic island life, and stare out at one of the clearest horizons in the world.

BEFORE YOU GO
Map: OS Outdoor Leisure Series Map No. 25.
Guidebook: *The Isles of Scilly Standard Guidebook* (Bowley Publications, PO Box 1, St Mary's, Isles of Scilly).

GETTING THERE
By air: British Airways Helicopters Ltd operate 20-minute service from Penzance to St Mary's throughout the year, and additional service to Tresco, Apr-Sept. Advance reservations essential. Information and telephone reservations from Penzance Heliport (T:0736 63871) or St Mary's Airport (T:0720 22646). Brymon Airways operate direct services to Scilly from Bristol, Exeter, Plymouth, Newquay and Heathrow; phone City Airport, Plymouth for reservations (T:0752 707023). Skybus Air Taxi run charter and air taxi services by Islander aircraft between Land's End and St Mary's, and also spectacular scenic joy flights round the islands – enquiries and reservations Isles of Scilly Skybus, Land's End Aerodrome, St Just, Penzance, Cornwall TR19 7RL, T:0736 787017.
By sea: ferry service between Penzance and Scilly (daily late Mar-Oct, less frequently during winter) takes just over 2½ hours. Advance reservations necessary Jul-Aug. Enquiries and bookings to Isles of Scilly Steamship Co. at Quay Street, Penzance (T:0736 62009) or Hugh Street, St Mary's, (T:0720 22357).
Inter-island travel: inter-island launch service between St Mary's and off-islands leaves shortly after arrival of ship. Further information from Isles of Scilly Steamship Co. St Mary's Boatmen's Association and independent operators on other islands run daily between St Mary's and the islands, including uninhabited ones, Mar-Oct.
Motor vehicles: caravans, motor homes, trailers and similar vehicles are not permitted on the islands. Private cars are not encouraged – there are only 8 miles (15km) of road on St Mary's and taxis and buses serve visitors' needs. Cars are best left either at Penzance Harbour car park or Heliport.
Bicycles: can be hired in Hugh Town and High Lanes, St Mary's.

WHERE TO STAY
There is a wide variety of accommodation on the 5 inhabited islands, most of it on St Mary's. For a complete list of hotels, guest houses, bed and breakfast, self-catering vacation homes and camping accommodation, get the annual accommodation list and monthly updated vacancy list from the Tourist Information Centre, Town Hall, St Mary's, Isles of Scilly TR21 0LW, T:0720 22536. Advance reservations in high season strongly recommended.
Outdoor living: camping is restricted, and prohibited on open spaces. Advance reservations are essential. Strict control is kept on the landing of animals. Very few hotels and guest houses accept dogs, and on Tresco dogs must be kept on leads at all times.

ACCESS AND CLOSURES
Most islands are open to the public all year, but some uninhabited islands, including Annet, a seabird sanctuary, are closed to all visitors 15 Apr-20 Aug to protect the nesting birds. Genuine naturalists can apply to NCC Taunton for visitors' permits. Keep to the public rights of way and do not uproot the plants or take cuttings from shrubs and trees.

ACTIVITIES
Boating and fishing: pleasure launches leave St Mary's Quay every day for all the inhabited

St. Agnes in the Scillies is the farthest inhabited land in England; beyond it lie scattered islets, the Bishop Rock lighthouse and the open Atlantic

islands and for Bishop Rock Lighthouse and sometimes Samson and other uninhabited islands, including Annet during non-nesting season. The same boats run evening fishing trips — good fishing for mackerel, pollock, wrasse, plaice. Boats are not usually hired without a boatman, due to many concealed hazards in Scilly waters.

Sailing: good sailing in St Mary's Road for capable helmsmen and in inner harbour for less experienced ones. Visitors are encouraged to bring their own boats and will be made welcome by the local Sailing Club, St Mary's.

Swimming and diving: the only dangerous places are the sandbars connecting St Agnes and Gugh island and St Mary's and Toll's island at high tide. Diving by organized groups under expert supervision is preferred. A code of conduct for divers is displayed at the town hall and the museum. Details from the **Underwater Centre**, Warleggan, Church Street, St Mary's (T:0720 22563) and Marine Study Centre, Pelistry, St Mary's (T:0720 22415).

Walking: the islands are ideal for walkers, and lanes, tracks and cliff and moorland paths abound. There are 2 nature trails on St Mary's – the Lower Moors nature trail starting at Hugh Town, and the Higher Moors nature trail via Old Town. Recommended viewpoints for sunset-watchers on St Mary's: Star Castle, Streval Point, Porthloo, Carn Morval, Buzza Tower and Peninnis Head.

THE SOUTH DEVON COAST PATH

OS Landranger Series Map Nos. 192, 193, 201, 212

This path runs for 93 miles (150km) from Plymouth to the Dorset boundary, just west of Lyme Regis, through the East Devon and South Devon Areas of Outstanding Natural Beauty. The section below is most likely to appeal to the wild traveller, but anyone wanting to stretch their legs over a longer distance could try the 53-mile (85-km) hike from Turnchapel to Torcross, of which the Bolt Tail to Start Point section is a part.

Bolt Tail to Start Point

Heritage Coast

About 15 miles (22km) of the best coastal walking in South Devon round the peninsula that juts into the English Channel between Plymouth and Torquay. The path climbs steeply from Inner Hope to the headland of Bolt Tail and follows the coastline high above the sea to Bolt Head through the longest stretch of National Trust land in England. As far as Start Point this stretch is spectacular walking and you will need to be fit to get up the steep sides of Sloan Mill Cove.

The rocks of the cliff face in these parts are metamorphosed mica schists, wrung out by gigantic pressures and populated by shags and fulmars, ravens and buzzards, and wild flowers like wild thyme, pink thrift and blue vernal quill. From the high cliff top the path winds down through pleasantly wooded slopes into Salcombe, the most southerly resort in Devon.

A ferry takes you across the estuary to East Portsmouth, where the South West Way winds back up to the cliff tops for the stretch to Prawle Point – the loneliest and wildest part of the South Devon Path, with dramatic cliff formations and lung-bursting gradients. This is a good place for the naturalist. In late summer butterflies abound in the more sheltered places – silver-studded blues, small coppers, pearl-bordered fritillaries. And there are all kinds of birds to be seen – seabirds like kittiwakes, terns, gannets and shearwaters, waders like turnstones, oystercatchers, whimbrels and dunlins, migrating birds like warblers, wagtails, pipits and wheatears.

After Prawle Point the landscape changes once again, giving way to a flat table of farming land with a raised beach – the original line of cliffs, 300ft (91.5m) high and complete with caves – half a mile inland. Start Point is a nature reserve and a marvellous spot for watching migrating birds in spring and autumn.

The South West Way Association breaks this section down as follows (beginning and ending each stretch with nearest towns):
Hope Cove to Salcombe.
Distance: 7 miles (11km).
Grading: strenuous, Some of

the finest coastal walking in South Devon.
Salcombe to Torcross.
Distance: 11 miles (18km).
Grading: strenuous. First-class walking as far as Start Point.

Exe Estuary

12 square miles (31sq km) of open water, mud flats, salt marsh and sandy spit on the estuary of the River Exe

The most important wetland area in the whole of the West Country, but as yet no formal conservation status. Enormous numbers of wildfowl and waders of many species in winter, including less frequent visitors such as avocet, greenshank, spotted redstart, ruff, curlew sandpiper, purple sandpiper, whimbrel and others.
Access: there are views of the estuary from footpaths along the shoreline – north from Powderham on west bank, and south from Lympstone on east bank.

Aylesbeare Common

450 acres (182ha) of lowland heath with valley bog and woods RSPB Reserve and SSSI

Wildlife includes nightjar, stonechat, linnet, yellowhammer and curlew on heath; tree pipit, marsh tit and great spotted woodpecker in woods; and hobbies visit the reserve to hunt dragonflies. Raven and buzzard can also be seen, but the Dartford warbler is now a rarity following two disastrous winters in the 1960s and 70s. Thirty-two species of butterflies, several dragonflies, roe deer, badger, harvest mouse, adder and wood cricket. Dwarf gorse, pink butterwort, bog pimpernel, royal fern.

Access: via car park 2 miles (3km) west of Newton Poppleford on A3052 Lyme Regis–Exeter road. Open all year but keep to waymarked trail. **Recommendations:** best time – spring, early summer. No smoking because of danger of fire. **Where to stay:** bed and breakfast in Newton

Poppleford and surrounding villages. Hotels in coastal resorts (Sidmouth, Budleigh Salterton, Exmouth) and larger towns (Honiton, Exeter). **Further information:** contact summer Warden (Apr–Aug), c/o Newton Poppleford Post Office, Sidmouth, Devon.

THE DORSET COAST PATH

OS Landranger Series Map Nos. 193, 194 and 195

The Dorset section is the shortest section of the South West Way. It runs for 72 miles (115km), or up to a week of steady walking from Lyme Regis in the west to Shell Bay near Studland in the east. Though never as wild and lonely as the Cornish coast, the Dorset path passes through some of the loveliest and most varied coastal scenery in England – most of it Heritage Coast and Areas of Outstanding Natural Beauty.

Axmouth to Lyme Regis Undercliffs

NCC Reserve

Heavy rainfall and an inherently unstable geological structure cause small landslips every year along this stretch of the chalk and sandstone sea cliffs. Bigger landslides occur at much greater intervals, and the famous landslide of Christmas 1839 was the biggest of all. A ravine (known locally as the Chasm) was opened up and 15 acres (6ha) of land (known locally as Goat Island) was isolated from the mainland.

In due course a wild wood grew up in the Chasm and today this is one of the wildest and most unspoilt tracts of country in southern England. On the windward side of the woods grows a low, wind-pruned scrub; in the shady places the woods are thick with all kinds of ferns.

As many as 120 species of birds have been recorded here. Roe deer and badgers lurk in the thickets, adders and common lizards bask on the open slopes, and a host of insects throng the flower banks and woodland glades. The Jurassic limestone is famous for fossils, including huge ammonites and nautiloids. The most celebrated of all was a 25-ft (7.5-m) ichthyosaur, a fish-like reptile found in 1809 by Mary Anning of Lyme Regis. **Access:** by footpath, either at east end from Underhill Farm approach near Lyme Regis, or at west end from stile at top of Bindon Cliff. Permit required to leave right of way or collect specimens – apply in writing to NCC Taunton. **Further information:** leaflet from NCC.

Chesil Bank and the Isle of Portland

The 5-mile (8-km) storm beach of Chesil Bank is one of the five largest pebble ridges in Europe. Behind it lies a shallow tidal lagoon, the Fleet, where mute swans

---

DO'S AND DON'TS FOR FOSSIL HUNTERS

Do keep your collecting to the minimum
Do check the local tide conditions
Do take care on unstable cliffs
Do beware of falling rocks
Don't let rocks fall on other people
Don't collect from walls or buildings
Don't leave dangerous or untidy holes or debris behind you
Don't disturb the wildlife
Don't collect on SSSIs or other protected areas without a permit.

---

breed at the Abbotsbury swannery and large numbers of wildfowl feed on the rich supply of brackish-water plants in winter. Chesil Bank is an important nesting site for common and little tern, so there is no access to the beach during the nesting season.

The Isle of Portland itself is a massive limestone outcrop jutting 6 miles (10km) into the English Channel and connected with mainland by pebble ridge of Chesil Bank. Bird observatory and ringing station in converted lighthouse. Staging post for migrant birds and marvellous place to watch birds at sea, such as sooty, Manx and little shearwater. Odd birds of passage have included Egyptian nightjar and pallid swift. **Getting there:** via A354 from Weymouth, following signposts to Portland. **Access:** all year. **Where to stay:** in small dormitories at observatory lighthouse, including evening meals, 1 Mar–31 Oct, at other times by arrangement with Warden, Portland Bird Observatory and Field Centre, Old Lower Light, Portland, Dorset.

Ringstead Bay to Durlston Head

Includes Heritage Coast and ANOB

More than 20 miles (32km) of superb walking over the open cliff tops of the chalk and limestone Dorset coast, with some stiff climbs that bring you up to 550ft (168m) above the sea. There is plenty of interest along the way – the great natural archway at

Durdle Door; the huge roofless sea cave at Stair Hole; the circular bay at Lulworth Cove, hemmed in by cliffs pierced by a narrow entrance; the magnificent high-level cliff walk along the Purbeck coast around St Alban's Head; the flora and fauna of the cliffs and downs, including rarities like the spider-orchid, the Lulworth skipper butterfly, and a vagrant bird more common in the Balkans, the wallcreeper.

Durlston Head itself, which forms the south-east corner of the Isle of Purbeck, is a 261-acre (105-ha) country park run as wildlife sanctuary by DCC, an SSSI (geology, wildlife), and part of Heritage Coast and Dorset Area of Outstanding Natural Beauty. Points of interest include great clifftop views across sea to the Isle of Wight, the Tilly Whim Caves, a 40-ton Portland Stone Globe and seabird colonies on the cliffs.

The South West Way Association breaks down this section as follows (beginning and ending each stretch with nearest towns):

Weymouth to West Lulworth. Distance: 11 miles (18km). **Grading:** moderate to strenuous.

Lulworth Cove to Kimmeridge. Distance: 7 miles (11km). **Grading:** severe. Fine walk, but tough. Warning: route runs through RAC Gunnery School, Lulworth Ranges. Information is obtainable from the Range Officer (T:0929 462721 ext. 819, working hours only) or from the Guardroom (T:0929 462721 ext. 824, at any time).

Kimmeridge to Swansea. Distance: 12 miles (20km). Grading: strenuous, then moderate.

Isle of Purbeck

The South West Way ends at Shell Bay where Poole Harbour meets the Isle of Purbeck in Dorset. Purbeck is not actually an island, but one of the most important areas of dry lowland heath in Britain. The RSPB Reserve of Arne, in the south-west corner of Poole Harbour, boasts 190 species of birds and is one of the best places to see the threatened Dartford warbler, along with 800 species of moths and butterflies, 450 species of plants and all 6 British reptiles.

The Studland NNR, on a promontory between Poole Harbour and Studland Bay, remains an important heathland oasis, a good place for birds, rare reptiles, and all 3 British insectivorous plants. Hartland Moor NNR near Wareham harbours Dartford warblers, a number of rare insects and every species of British reptile. Around Kimmeridge Bay, 4 miles (7km) of coast has been designated a DTNC Marine Reserve, while Poole Harbour attracts a good number of wildfowl and waders, which may be viewed from a hide on Brownsea Island NT/DTNC Reserve. **Getting there:** Arne can be approached from Studland village, Brownsea Island by ferry from Poole Quay or Sandbanks Ferry. **Access:** all year at Arne and Studland, end Mar – end Sep for Brownsea, permit only to Hartland Moor. **Where to stay:** hotel in Studland, various in Swanage, Wareham and Corfe Castle. **Precautions:** extreme fire risk at Studland; also unexploded bombs. No dogs on Brownsea, **Further information:** apply RSPB, NCC or DTNC.

CHAPTER 2

South and Central England

There was a time when the whole of Britain from Land's End to John o'Groats, from Orford Ness to St David's Head, was a primordial wilderness of mountain, forest, bog, fen and moor; the haunt of wolves, bears, boars and beavers, where the streams ran pure, butterflies of innumerable species darkened the sun, serried masses of wildflowers dazzled the eyes and the May-time songs of the great choirs of birds in the oakwoods deafened the ear. A land as yet untouched by axe, scythe, plough, shotgun, pesticide or acid rain.

The first colonist farmers to cross the land bridge that then joined Britain to mainland Europe did not like what they saw, and proceeded to knock it flat to the best of their ability. As did all the people who came after them. Over the centuries these land-hungry pioneers laid waste the woods and wildlife of lowland England, creating the pretty patchwork of yellow wheatfields and green pastures we know as the English countryside.

Any of the great broad-leaved woods that had been preserved as royal hunting forests by the Norman and Plantagenet kings were whittled down when the national need for timber became greater than the royal love of the chase, and today only the New Forest in Hampshire retains a substantial part of its former grandeur. The systematic draining of the East Anglian fens, once one of the major wetland areas of Europe, began in the seven-

Dew-covered nettles glisten in the morning sunlight on the banks of the Stour in East Anglia, a lushly green corner of Lowland England where wildness and wet still hold out

teenth century and was virtually complete by the nineteenth; only a few pockets of Fenland, like that at Wicken in Cambridgeshire, now survive.

Until the turn of this century the last relatively undeveloped wild habitats in lowland England were the heathlands – originally a man-made environment brought about by Bronze Age deforestation and grazing – that covered much of Dorset and East Anglia, and for that matter Surrey too. But twentieth-century urban and industrial development have wiped out great stretches of dry heathland. Today only the Isle of Purbeck and the New Forest contain areas extensive enough to support the wildlife which is dependent on this type of habitat.

The wild places are few in southern and central England, and most of them cling on at the extreme perimeters: the North Sea coastal reserves between the Thames and the Humber, wildfowl country *par excellence*, especially along the North Norfolk Coast; the modest outcrop of the Shropshire Hills; and, haphazardly ranged between the two, the woods, heaths and wetlands of the New Forest.

These are not wildly wild places by the standards of the North Country. But they are the best that lowland England offers after the depredations of our forebears. And the New Forest is still big enough and wild enough to get lost in; in an exceptional season the North Sea marshes can offer winter birds and winter blasts on a Siberian scale; and from the top of the Shropshire Hills you peer over a void so vast it encompasses two countries and 12 counties. So let's count our blessings while we may.

BEFORE YOU GO

For the scattered parts of England covered in this chapter, no one organization can give comprehensive advice. For travel information, however, the British Tourist Authority, Victoria Station, London SW1, T:01-730 3488, will put you in touch with the appropriate regional tourist centres.

For details of the county wildlife trusts that manage many nature reserves, contact the Royal Society for Nature Conservation, The Green, Nettleham, Lincoln LN2 2NR, T:0522 752326.

ACTIVITIES

Serious walkers may wish to join the Ramblers' Association, who can provide details of challenging walks in the area and local walking clubs and societies. But good gentle walking can be found all over southern and eastern England, and an OS 1:50,000

Landranger map of any area will be your most valuable guide.

Those who prefer to get their exercise on two wheels will find that the Cyclists' Touring Club, 69 Meadrow, Godalming, Surrey GU7 3HS, T:048 68 7217 provides advice on routes and equipment as well as organizing cycling holidays and vacation packages.

The east coast has much to offer naturalists, and those who wish to undertake some serious study might find the following field study centres of interest:

Activity Holidays, Snape Maltings, nr Saxmundham, Suffolk IP17 1SR, T:0728 88305. Weekend courses on Suffolk bird life and natural history.

Birding, Lattenden's Farm, Ashburnham, nr Battle, East Sussex TN33 9PB, T:0323 833245. East Anglian coastal trips for birdwatchers.

Bradwell Field Studies and Sailing Centre, Bradwell Waterside, nr Southminster, Essex CM0 7QY, T:0621 76256. Environmental study courses on the Essex coast.

Lincolnshire and South Humberside Trust for Nature Conservation, Gibraltar Point Field Station, Skegness, Lincolnshire PE24 4SU, T:0754 2677. 2- to 5-night courses in bird-watching, botany, geology, etc. in old coastguard station.

Pennington Lodge Hotel, South Street, Pennington, Lymington, Hants SO4 18DX, T:0590 75831. Year-round natural history courses in the New Forest.

Preston Montford Field Centre, Montford Bridge, Shrewsbury SY4 1DX, T:0743 850380. Wildlife courses in Shropshire and the Welsh borders.

The New Forest

100 square miles (260sq km) of woodland, heathland and wetland in southern Hampshire
NNR administered by the Forestry Commission and other bodies

I was talking to a head keeper of the New Forest during the course of an abortive project for the Countryside Commission. At the end of our meeting the head keeper remarked: 'And I'll tell you another thing. Some of the people who come here go into the woods and can't find their way out.'

'They get *lost*?' I exclaimed. 'In the New Forest?'

'Town people,' the head keeper explained. 'They can't tell one tree from another and end up spending the night under one. My keepers find them in the morning trudging around in circles dying for a cup of tea.'

Nothing like that, I am sure, could ever happen to my ex-Countryside Commission colleague and myself. After all, between us we had quartered half the earth's unexplored frontiers. We had a map. We even had a compass. We congratulated ourselves that we were old hands at this sort of thing.

It was a hot summer day. A few puffs of cloud floated lazily across the blue sky before a light north-easterly wind. Young foals lay collapsed in the heat on the grass by their mothers. There were no people around and a great silence, an all-pervading, lethargic hush hung over the heath, broken only by the occasional cries of the birds.

The track took us into a subtle, elusive landscape of horizontal planes – the belts of gorse scrub, the low lines of ridges undulating gently away one behind the other, the dark wall of conifers (sequoias, good heavens) on the skyline, wobbling in the heat haze – strata of landscape piled one on top of the other and topped by a broad band of sky. Such a profoundly recumbent terrain induced a sense of space and repose, and an impression of lifelessness.

But when I turned the binoculars on this vast and empty plain, life suddenly jumped out at me from the middle distance: a small group of ponies grazing stilly as if frozen in a kind of Victorian pastoral woodcut, two fallow deer blundering about in a thick gorse copse, a tall pillar of gyrating mayflies suspended above a swampy patch in a valley bottom, a girl with long flaxen hair on a horse ambling down a shallow gulch until the landscape swallowed her up at the valley bend.

We ventured into the woods in a state of heightened curiosity like early Amazon explorers. We came to a glade where the ground underfoot was soft and soggy and covered in green bog moss, and here our ears were beguiled by a very curious and most unnerving sound: an immense, unending hum like a turbine whirring above our heads. It was not until I had sploshed across the mire and turned to face the way I had come that I saw what the cause was. I was now looking into the sun, and high among the branches of the trees a huge swarm of insects, mainly bees, wasps and perhaps a few hornets, invisible before, were now illuminated, each tiny darting form clearly delineated by a golden outline, each contributing its individual insect voice to this raised growl of massed insecthood.

The sundew traps and digests small insects in its leaves

Every forest glade was like a brilliantly lit proscenium where the scenery, like the pastoral backcloth of some eighteenth-century *folie bergère*, was always changing. We looked out from the darkened auditorium of the woods, now at a tiny sunlit meadow, now a gently swelling flowerclad mound, sometimes a small stream where the most exquisite electric-blue dragonflies rested on the mossy stones, sometimes a brilliant emerald-green spread of marshy ground. In one of the glades my attention was arrested by a sudden agitated bird cry,

and I caught a rare glimpse of an exotic yellow bird, a golden oriole scurrying for cover in the tops of the trees – a sight that was for me the fulfilment of a boyhood ambition.

In our absorption, we forgot the time and neglected to check our bearings. The shadows were much longer and the air distinctly cooler when I asked: 'Where are we?'

And so it was that we found we too were lost in the New Forest. Nothing on the ground tallied with anything on the map

In a classical beech wood near Holm Hill in the New Forest, shafts of sunlight pierce the cathedral gloom and dapple the bare ground of a forest floor devoid of undergrowth

and the compass only told us where north was. There were no sounds of civilization to give us a bearing on the outside world, no distinguishable landmark, just trees, and more trees, and clearings, thickets, groves, gullies leading nowhere in particular, and trees again.

For an hour or more we stumbled this way and that, with an increasing sense of urgency and a decreasing sense of humour, and the first star had popped out of a crepuscular violet sky, and we were tired, thirsty, hot and incredulous, when we chanced on a track bearing the marks of horses' hooves leading in one direction. So we were saved from the ignominy of a comfortless night on the forest floor. And we had learned for ourselves what we had long ago read in books, that the New Forest was big, and it could also be wild.

The reasons lie in the accidents of history.

William the Conqueror transformed the whole area into a royal hunting preserve in 1079. Local farmers were forbidden to fence off their land, as this would interfere with the free run of the King's deer. By way of compensation, the farmers were allowed to graze their domestic animals throughout the Forest. Today their successors, known as commoners, still exercise this right, and their cattle, pigs, donkeys and famous New Forest ponies can still be seen browsing among the unenclosed woods and lawns.

These animals are the true architects of the landscape. Their browsing has kept the woodland in check, preserving the balance between it and the open heath. The ancient pastoral economy is an integral part of the eco-system. Elsewhere in the lowlands of Europe it has virtually disappeared. The New Forest survives as it does largely because of this anachronism.

The last king to hunt in the New Forest was James II. Timber became more important than deer and large areas were fenced

47

off by Forest Inclosures to allow new woodlands to grow. Many of these oak and beech woods, now known as Ancient and Ornamental Woodlands, contain some of the most magnificent old trees in the whole of the New Forest.

The New Forest is the largest tract of wild, unsown country in lowland England, six times greater than any other surviving English forest. Parts of it, such as the primary forests of Mark Ash Wood, are the nearest we now have to the ancient Atlantic wildwood that covered two thirds of Britain some 5,000 years ago. A large bird population inhabits the woods. Many of these birds depend on the rich invertebrate fauna to be found there, which in turn depends on the large quantity of dead and decaying wood that is characteristic of natural woodland. At a rough calculation, half of all the insect species of Britain occur in the New Forest, including spectacular beasts like the stag beetle. For many, such as the New Forest cicada, this is their only home.

The Forest Inclosures today form extensive refuges for the larger mammals of the New Forest – badgers, foxes and the seldom-seen deer. They are also home for many of the large population of birds of prey, including merlin and peregrine falcon, which hunt the heathland in winter.

The heathland is a mixture of grassland, heather and mire known as lowland heath. All over Europe lowland heath has suffered the same catastrophic losses as ancient woodland. The most extensive tracts to survive in Britain are found in the New Forest, and only here is the complete heathland fauna likely to continue to survive. Fauna that has declined elsewhere in Britain still holds out here: birds like the Dartford warbler, woodlark, stonechat and nightjar; reptiles like the sand lizard and smooth snake; butterflies like the grayling and silver-studded blue.

The New Forest, in short, is a national treasure house for British wildlife. Because of its size, intact condition and tremendous diversity of habitat the New Forest is a truly unique enclave – a remarkable triumph of wilderness over the ravages of human development.

BEFORE YOU GO
Maps: OS Outdoor Leisure Series Map No. 22 or OS Landranger Series Map Nos. 195 and 196.
Guidebooks: Forestry Commission: *Explore the New Forest* (HMSO 1978) Ordnance Survey Leisure Guide: *New Forest Official Guide* (AA/OS). Both publications contain much useful instruction including detailed maps with roads and paths for walkers and riders.

GETTING THERE
By train: main station and motor-rail terminal is Brockenhurst; most Waterloo–Bournemouth trains stop there. Nearest major British Rail stations are Southampton and Bournemouth. For British Rail enquiries phone 0703 229393 (Southampton).
48

By bus: National Express Service from Victoria Coach Station, London SW1. Local service operated by Hants & Dorset Motor Services, Arndale Centre, Poole, T:0202 673555.
By car: via M3 from London, M27 from SE coast, A34 from North and Midlands.

WHERE TO STAY
Hotels and guest houses: there are plenty of hotels, inns, guest houses and bed and breakfasts in the New Forest, most of them in Brockenhurst or Lyndhurst. A list of accommodation can be obtained from New Forest District Council, Appletree Court, Lyndhurst, Hants SO4 7PA, T:042 128 3121.
Youth hostels: for list of youth hostels in area apply YHA, 8 St Stephen's Hill, St Albans, Herts, T:0727 55215. **Outdoor**

living: Forestry Commission campsites are marked on the recommended maps; complete list with full details available from the Forestry Commission, The Queen's House, Lyndhurst, Hants, T:042 128 3771. No camping permitted in the Forest except at authorized sites.

ACCESS AND CLOSURES
Open access all year, except on private land or enclosed Forestry Commission plantations, where unauthorized vehicles are not allowed, though walkers or riders may pass through. If in doubt keep to public footpaths. Most forest bogs (shown on maps as Bog, Flash or Bottom) are impassable.

WHERE TO GO
The Forest can be divided into three main areas representing

three main terrains: the high flatland in the north; the central forest; and marshes. Anyone exploring on foot would need to divide the area into smaller units. I found the following break-down into 10 areas, evolved with the help of my friend Bud Young, formerly of the Countryside Commission, particularly helpful:

In the *north-west* the area of the Avon tributaries, with its strong, sloping relief and heath-dominated views south-west to the Avon;

In the *north* the area of the Stoney Cross plateau, aerodrome country pervaded by a sense of height and bordered by major forest edges.

In the *north-east* the area of the King's Garn Gutter – steep land with northern aspects. Scandinavian forestry, and alder carr stream bottoms.

In the *east* two adjacent areas of flatland that probably should be dealt with separately: Ashley Rolling Down – heathland with tree-clumps and long-distance landscapes, but close to the Ashburn-Southampton road; and the area of Matley Bog – mixed wet and dry heath, with an overtly boggy centre and enclosed by higher land.

In the *south-east* the area of Beaulieu Heath – flat, dark and featureless, with sinuous green seepage lines that are almost brooks.

In the *south* the area of Hinchelsea Moor, a medium profile landscape with just enough height to set off the horizontals and the soft edges of the deciduous woodland, and just enough relief to emphasize the beautiful curves and shapes.

In the *south-west* the area of Holmsley Red Shoot Bluffs, a Scottish style landscape, with rounded bluffs, Scots pine and

heath, neat narrow gullies and valleys and medium views.

In the *centre* the area of the great central woodlands, which occupy 30% of the forest area. They can be sub-divided into two adjacent units: the woodland that includes Mark Ash, Gritnam Wood and Boldrewood *to the west* of the Highland Water; and that which includes Denny Wood and Frame Wood to the east of the Highland Water.

ACTIVITIES

Walking: serious walkers who want to blaze their own trail ought to have the highly detailed OS Pathfinder series of maps, showing field boundaries and rights of way, four of which cover the New Forest area: SU 20/30, SU 21/31, SU 40/50, SZ 29/39. Take a compass. Even in summer the going can be very wet underfoot; wear stout walking shoes or boots. In winter or wet weather, some parts of the forest, particularly the valleys and wet heaths, can be very difficult to get through.

Riding: for a full list of riding

schools and stables, contact Association of New Forest Riding Establishments, Decoy Pond Farm, Beaulieu Road, Brockenhurst, Hants.

Natural history: all wildlife, plant or animal, is protected by law. Permission to study or collect specimens for scientific purposes must be obtained in writing from the Deputy Surveyor.

FURTHER INFORMATION
Tourist Information Centre, Lyndhurst (T:042 128 2269), Nature Conservancy Council, Lyndhurst (T:042 128 3944), Forestry Commission Information Office, Lyndhurst, (T:042 128 3771).

'A poorer spot than this New Forest there is not in all England, nor I believe in the whole world. It is more barren and miserable than Bagshott Heath.'
William Cobbett:
Rural Rides

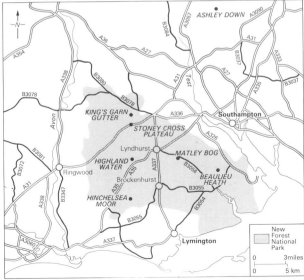

THE SHROPSHIRE HILLS

AONB

Between the Wyre Forest and the Welsh border lie the Shropshire Hills. These parallel ridges of weathered, spectacularly ancient rock – in places as much as 1,000 million years old – grow wilder the nearer they are to the border, where they lift range upon range into Wales.

They offer the best wild walking in the West Midlands, and excellent pony trekking. For the naturalist, and especially the geologist, they are of compelling interest. The Shropshire Hills have one other advantage: the holiday masses tend to pass them by, leaving this sweeping upland landscape to the solitude and tranquillity that is sometimes hard to find in the Cotswolds or the Peak District.

Each of the component parts of the Shropshire Hills has its own distinct geology, landscape and wildlife; but perhaps the most satisfying, from the wild traveller's perspective, are Long Mynd and the Stiperstones.

Long Mynd

Although this broad moorland plateau is only 6 miles (10km) from end to end, its great vistas and its remoteness and desolation make it seem an altogether vaster place. The Long Mynd is divided into rounded blocks by deep, glacial valleys known locally as hollows or batches. Cardingmill Valley, with the Light Spout waterfall at its head, is the best known, though Ashes Hollow and Minton Batch are just as lovely.

From the trigonometric point crowning Pole Bank, the highest point on Long Mynd at 1,695ft (517m), you have an unobstructed view to the Malverns and Cotswolds in one direction and to Snowdonia and the Brecon Beacons in the other.

All but the southern end belongs to the National Trust, which leases parts as grouse moor. Buzzards and ravens

soar above the heights, skylarks sign and dippers bob about in the lower reaches of the streams, where brown trout lurk in the pools, foraging for the larvae of stonefly, mayfly, dragonfly and caddis fly.

Getting there: the Long Mynd is 3 miles (5km) west of Church Stretton off the A49. Minor roads lead west from the B4370, connecting with ancient cattle drovers' tracks (trails) on to the ridge.
Facilities: excellent sail- and hang-gliding; contact Midlands Gliding Club at top of Mintop Batch. **Further information:** leaflets from Information Centre, Church Road, Church Stretton, Salop.

The Stiperstones

NCC NNR

This desolate, rock-strewn heather and bilberry moorland

Range upon range of ridges crest many of the Shropshire Hills on the borders of Wales

is dotted with bogs, cut by deep valleys and crowned with hard white sandstone crags. The best known is the Devil's Chair; when cloud is draped over the Stiperstones (as it often is) it is said that the Devil has taken his seat, and you could well believe it.

Lead was once mined in these hills, but the industry closed down early in this century and only the eerie white landscape of the waste heaps and abandoned

50

smallholdings remain, where redstart and tree pipits inhabit the old walls and hedges. Several tracks lead over the hills, and there are superb, 80-mile (130-km) views from the Devils Chair.

Getting there: follow tortuous minor road from A489 through Shelve and Pennerley and fork left at Bridges and take track (trail) up to Devil's Chair. **Where to stay:** youth hostels at Bridges and Wilderhope. Inn at Stiperstones village. **Facilities:** Field Study Centre at The Bog. Further information: NCC, Shrewsbury.

Cannock Chase

AONB, managed by SCC and FC

A Royal Forest in Norman times, Cannock Chase's location between Birmingham and the Vale of Trent has made it popular with the inhabitants of nearby Midland cities, reducing its wildness but not its wildlife. This ranges from deer (fallow, red, roe, Sika and muntjac) to rare bog plants, a rich crop of fungi (with expressive names like blusher, sickener, razor strop and earthball), butterflies and moths, and birds such as the crossbill, goldcrest, woodcock, grasshopper warbler and nightjar (two-thirds of the whole Midland breeding population).

Getting there: via minor roads off A34, A513 and A460. **Access:** unrestricted. Nature trails, some guided. **Further information:** excellent information pack from SCC. Further details from visitor centre or Head Ranger, T:05438 71773.

51

THE EAST COAST

North Kent Marshes

Between the Channel and the Humber, the east coast of England contains a number of areas that are remarkable either for the wild quality of their landscape on the edge of the ever restless sea or the range of their wildlife. The east coast follows one of the major bird migration routes of Britain; the North Kent Marshes, parts of the Essex and Suffolk coast, the North Norfolk Marshes and the Wash, and parts of the Lincolnshire coast to the south of the Humber Estuary contain vast sand flats, mud flats and marshes with huge views, immense skies and extraordinary congregations of birds.

The North Kent Marshes, which stretch along the south shore of the Thames Estuary from Gravesend to Whitstable, are the best place to watch birds within 50 miles (80km) of London. This bleak Dickensian wilderness is a mere electric train ride from London, but a century away in time; wide, desolate, windswept, and bitter in winter. It is not a pristine horizon: projecting above it here and there rise the ganglions of encroaching industry; and cargo ships slide eerily along the squelching soft grey edge of the land.

Yet this is, I think, an authentic English wild place, and your spirit will be uplifted by the vast congregations of wildfowl and waders, many of them seasonal refugees from the remotest corners of Eurasia. The following are the major areas for wildfowl: the RSPB reserve at Halstow and St Mary's Marshes, with the biggest heronry in Britain at Northwood Hill; the Medway Estuary, especially around Chetney Marshes; and best of all the Isle of Sheppey, which has two reserves along its southern shore, Elmley Marshes (RSPB) and the Swale (NCC, NNR).

Pick of the bunch is Elmley, a vast, flat landscape, featureless except for the domes and towers of distant industry, like the lost city of some vanished civilization. Some 216 species of birds inhabit the area, including the highest nesting concentration of redshanks and lapwings in the country. Many birds stop here to feed on their autumn migration; exotic errant birds like the African crowned crane and Chilean flamingo have been sighted here.

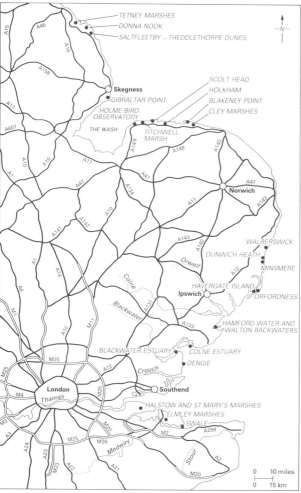

The marsh frog, an outsize defector from Eastern Europe, three times bigger than our native British runt, has successfully found asylum in this reserve and its loud, jubilant croak can be heard over great distances in the early summer. The 140 species of moth recorded here include the rare ground lackey moth, whose eggs can withstand being dried in the sun or drowned in salt water and still hatch normal offspring.

Getting there: for Halstow and St Mary's, turn off A228 to High Halstow. For Medway Estuary turn north off A2 at Rainham. For Elmley Marshes take A249, then farm track 1 mile after Kingsferry Bridge; park at Kingshill Farm and walk to hides at Spitend Marsh. The Swale can be reached from Shellness Hamlet at end of B2231. **Access:** at all times on rights of way. Permit only to Northwood Hill heronry. **Further information:** RSPB or NCC as appropriate.

Essex Coast and Marshes

Essex does not immediately spring to mind as a wild place; and with good reason, as far as the interior of the county is concerned. But the coast is another matter. 'The Essex coast,' the Nature Conservancy Council rightly claims, 'is one of the most important remaining areas of relatively undeveloped coastal estuarine mud and sand flats.'

Hundreds of thousands of geese, duck, waders and songbirds pass up and down this coast during the spring

Clockwise from the left are the crane fly (commonly known in Britain as daddy long-legs), golden-ringed dragonfly and the short-lived adult mayfly

and autumn migrations. Many thousands more arrive each winter from northern Russia and Siberia. To protect the most important of their roosts and feeding grounds, and the plants and insects that live there, the Nature Conservancy Council has established a series of reserves from the Thames to the Stour.

The most important reserves are: the large stretch of almost uninhabited open coast between the mouths of the Rivers Crouch and Blackwater at Dengie; the marshes and mud flats on both sides of the River Colne, among the best in East Anglia; the drowned and lonesome landscape of Hamford Water and the Walton Backwaters, a wetland archipelago of outstanding wildlife interest, inaccessible except by boat.

Getting there: Dengie off B1021. For Blackwater

Estuary, aim for Old Hall Marshes from Maldon. For Colne Estuary, turn off B1027 to Point Clear for east shore, off B1025 to beyond East Mersea for west shore. Hamford Water can be reached by minor roads from B1414 and B1034. **Access:** all year on rights of way, but permit only for St Osyth on east shore of Colne. **Further information:** NCC.

The Suffolk Coast

AONB

The dynamics of the East Anglian coast are confusing, not to say dramatic. At one time you could walk all the way to Denmark without getting your feet wet. Now some parts, such as the Wash coastline, are advancing, while others are being eroded. Dunwich used to send an MP to Westminster; now most of it lies under the sea. Suffolk lies on the major east coast

53

bird migration route and attracts very many common species and a few rare ones as well. Its six river estuaries are wonderful places to watch birds. So are the reserves, especially the RSPB reserve at Minsmere, possibly the most renowned bird spot in Britain; over 280 wetland species have been recorded here.

Wide, shallow lagoons have been bulldozed in an area of derelict marsh which now bears the name of the Scrape. Many migrant waders can be seen here: osprey, black tern, spotted redshank, black-tailed godwit, little stint and a number of rarities like the exotic spoonbill and purple heron, along with the second biggest avocet colony in Britain.

Other important reserves are Havergate Island (RSPB) in the River Ore, which has Britain's largest breeding colony of avocet; an area of coastal heathland known as the Sandlings at Dunwich Heath (NT); and the National Nature Reserve at Walberswick, an extensive area of reed beds, mud flats, woods and coastal heathland overlooking the Blyth Estuary and Westwood Marshes, the largest uninterrupted area of freshwater reed beds in Britain and nesting site to one of Britain's rarest breeding birds, the marsh harrier.

Getting there: for Havergate Island, by RSPB boat from Orford Quay. To Minsmere via B1125 or B1122. To Dunwich Heath off Dunwich–Westleton road. To Walberswick via public footpaths between Walberswick and Blytheburgh.
Access: all year on public rights of way, except Havergate (permit only).
Further information: RSPB, NT or NCC as appropriate.

The North Norfolk Coast

AONB

The North Norfolk Coast between Sheringham and the Wash has been described as 'the finest complex of sand flats, marshes, shingle ridges and dunes in the country'. And every year it gets finer still. Day in, day out, the North Sea fills the Wash with detritus; equally steadily the eastern shore is added to as tide after tide dumps more mud and sand.

The Wash itself is a place where land and water often lose their separate identity – and all too suddenly regain it. The immense foreshore dips imperceptibly towards the sea, so that when the tide comes in it does so at tremendous speed. Trying to record this phenomenon for posterity and the BBC, I was once marooned half a mile out to sea before I had shot half a roll of film.

The sand banks of the Wash are the haunt of the common seal and of enormous flocks of geese, duck and waders. Under these steely, squall-rinsed skies, a multitude of terns and other seabirds go about their cacophonous business. And not a few bird-watchers, rather more discreetly, go about theirs – even in dead of winter, when the east wind seems keen enough to cut your head off.

A number of nature reserves are strung along the

During a harsh winter even welcoming bird sanctuaries like Minsmere in Suffolk can be reduced to icy, inhospitable wild places

North Norfolk Coast to form an almost continuous single reserve of major importance for both birds and bird-watchers. Some are vast, like the National Nature Reserve at Holkham, which covers more than 7,500 acres (3035ha) of marshes, dunes and mud flats between Burnham Overy and Blakeney.

Others are smaller but hugely important for migrant birds, such as the NNT reserve and wild bird sanctuary at Cley Marshes. No fewer than 325 different species have been recorded here, including rare migrants such as bluethroats and spoonbills, as well as a multitude of wildfowl, waders and seabirds.

Also notable are the NNT reserve at Holme Dunes and the NOA bird reserve and observatory at Holme; the RSPB reserve on Titchwell Marsh, where you can see an avocet colony, 12 species of duck, 20 species of wader, 40,000 knot and godwits on a single roost when the Wash is flooded, and the remains of an ancient submerged forest (low tide only); the NT/NNT reserve on Scolt Head Island; the NT reserve at Blakeney Point, one of the most important nesting sites in Britain for terns and other shore nesting birds; and the National Nature Reserve at Winterton Dunes, the largest mainland dune system on the East Anglian coast and a refuge for many rare species, including the natterjack toad, adder, hen harrier and rough-legged buzzard.

Getting there: all these reserves can be approached from the Norfolk coastal road, the A149, though access to the coastal strip is on foot only. Scolt Head and Blakeney Point are best visited by small boat, the former from Brancaster Staithe, the latter

56

from Morston or Blakeney Quays by arrangement with local boatmen. **Access:** at all times, but permit required for the Holme reserves, and no access to Scolt Head ternery during nesting season (May–Jul). **Where to stay:** hotels and bed and breakfasts in villages along the coast, notably in Thornham and Wells-Next-the-Sea; some self-catering and vacation homes; campsites near Titchwell Marsh at Thornham and Choseley Marsh. **Further information:** enquire NCC Norwich, NT, NNT, NOA and RSPB as appropriate.

The Lincolnshire Coast

Northwards from the Wash to the Humber stretches the Lincolnshire coast, the most even stretch of shoreline anywhere round Britain, and one which is constantly growing. North of the Humber the whole Yorkshire coast is being eaten away at the rate of 7ft (2m) a year. Yorkshire's loss is Lincolnshire's gain. The old coastguard station at Gibraltar Point, once on the edge of the sea, is now over a mile inland. At Donna Nook, miles of sand push the sea further and further away from the shore.

From Skegness to Mablethorpe is caravan and motor-home country and the wild traveller will probably want to avoid it. But there are several extensive enclaves of open sand, marsh, sea and birds well worth a visit by

anyone who, like the hordes of migrating birds of this coast, happens to be heading north or south at the time. These include the sand dunes and salt marshes of Tetney Marshes (RSPB) near the mouth of the Humber; the 6 miles (10km) of flats and dunes at Donna Nook between Grainthorp Haven and Saltfleet, a reserve of the Lincolnshire and South Humberside NCT which also runs the 5-mile (8-km) stretch of dunes, flats and marsh comprising the Saltfleetby-Theddlethorpe reserve.

Most outstanding of all, perhaps, is Gibraltar Point. A National Nature Reserve and one of the finest coastal reserves in the country, it stretches for 3 miles (5km) from the Wash to south of Skegness, with a rich variety of marsh and dune flora, wildfowl and waders, and common seals on the sandbars.

Getting there: Tetney Marshes, Donna Nook and Saltfleetby-Theddlethorpe can all be reached off the A1031; for Gibraltar Point, take Gibraltar road south of Skegness. **Access:** all year, except when bombing ranges at Donna Nook and Saltfleetby are in use; watch for red warning flags. **Where to stay:** hostel accommodation for up to 34 people at Gibraltar Point field station and bird observatory. Enquire Resident Warden, T:0745 2677. **Further information:** RSPB, NCC or Lincs and South Humberside Trust for Nature Conservation.

THE NORFOLK BROADS

The Norfolk Broads consist of some 52 lakes (or 'broads') in the valleys of the Rivers Ant, Bure, Thurne, Waveney and Yare. About a dozen of the broads are linked by these rivers, so that it is possible to travel from one to the other by small boat along 125 miles (200 km) of navigable waterways. The broads are the remains of large-scale peat diggings which flooded as the land sank during the fourteenth century. In time they became one of the great wetland wilderness regions of Europe, and a wildlife paradise.

Today, however, the Norfolk Broads are a ravaged Eden; not so much for the quarter of a million holidaymakers and vacationers who come here each summer, as for the lovers of wild places who know all too well of the wildlife, the peace and the solitude that have gone. Motor boats have washed away the banks, destroying reed beds and driving away the birds and mammals that inhabited them. Chemical fertilizers have stimulated the growth of algae, turning the water into a pea-green soup incapable of sustaining life.

The picture is not entirely gloomy. Conservation measures are in hand, pollution is being limited, and several broads are now protected as nature reserves. The broads are still rich in wetland bird life and are the only place in Britain where you can find the swallowtail butterfly. Some 25 species of freshwater fish live in the broads, including some very big pike and the large, predatory zander, introduced from Central Europe.

Only tiny Upton Fen is just like the broads of the past, but access is severely restricted. In the broadland reserves that follow, however, it is still possible to savour something of the mysterious, secretive beauty and wonder of the great Broad wetlands of yesteryear, especially if you go out of season.

entomological interest, and outstanding for its population of marsh birds.

The reserve is renowned for bittern and bearded tit; marsh harrier and Montagu's harrier nest there on occasion; black tern, spoonbills and osprey number among the passage migrants; and predators like the great grey shrike and hen harrier hunt across the marshes in winter. The butterflies and moths which throng this broad include beauties like the swallowtail butterfly, fen dwellers like the bulrush wainscot moth, and winter migrants like the great brocade.

Getting there: by car to Hickling, east of A149. Thence on foot or by boat. **Access:** open 1 Apr–31 Oct; closed on Tuesdays. Entry by permit only; apply to Warden's House, Stubb Road, Hickling, Norwich NR12 OBW, T:069 261 276. Phone 069 261 503 to reserve boat trip to bird hides and observation tower. **Recommendations:** take warm clothing, rubber boots and binoculars. No dogs or other animals. **Further information:** leaflets, permits, reservations and prices from Warden, Hickling.

Hickling Broad

NCC NNR managed by NTT

Hickling Broad is a large shallow lake fringed by reed swamp, sedge beds, marshes and woodland. This superlative, 1,361-acre (550-ha) broadland reserve is of great floristic and

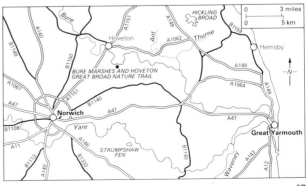

Bure Marshes and Hoveton Great Broad Nature Trail

NCC NNR

These 1,030 acres (417 ha) of wet woodland, fen and broads along the middle reaches of the River Bure east of Hoveton form a wide, green, marvellously peaceful area. Ducks and great crested grebes dot the water and swallows and common terns sweep through the air above the rich banks of sedge, reed, bulrush, milk parsley, yellow iris, bog myrtle, woody nightshade and royal fern. **Getting there:** the nature trail can only be reached by boat from Wroxham, just west of A1151. **Access:** weekdays only, May–mid-Sep. Dogs must be left on boat. Permit required to visit other parts of Bure Marshes reserve. **Further information:** leaflet from site or NCC.

Strumpshaw Fen

RSPB Reserve

This 447-acre (180-ha) fen lies on the east bank of the lower, tidal reaches of the River Yare. The reserve, which also includes Rockland Marshes on the west bank, offers a wide variety of habitats, from the open brackish waters of the river and broad and the reed and sedge beds of the surrounding fen, to the sallow and alder carrs, the damp woodland, the wet grazing marshes and miles of ditches of the outlying pasture.

Over 80 species of wetland and woodland birds regularly breed here, and recently established breeding species include Savi's warbler, Cetti's warbler (except after severe winters), bearded tit and marsh harrier. In summer the reed fens are alive with reed buntings and reed, sedge and grasshopper warblers.

On one of the few surviving broadland meadow sites yellow wagtails, lapwings, redshank and snipe all breed. Rarities like osprey and purple heron pass through here on passage and in winter huge flocks of widgeon and bean geese can be seen down river on the adjacent Buckingham Marshes. With luck you may also glimpse Chinese water deer, muntjac, roe and fallow deer, otter, mink, grass snakes and swallowtail butterflies. **Getting there:** by car through Brundall off A47, taking Low Road to reserve car park; then on foot to reception hide. For Rockland Marsh, take footpath starting opposite New Inn at Rockland St Mary. **Access:** open all year. Nature trail and 4 bird hides. **Further information:** leaflet from RSPB or Warden (Mike Blackburn), Staithe Cottage, Low Road, Strumpshaw, Norwich NR13 4HS.

Broadland Conservation Centre

NNT half-mile wetland nature trail through Ranworth Marshes on River Bure to floating conservation centre overlooking Ranworth Broad in one direction and Malthouse Broad in the other. **Access:** open daily Apr–Oct, except Mondays and Saturday mornings. No dogs.

A channel cuts through Cley Marshes, one of the many fine nature reserves on the North Norfolk Coast, where the bird marshes are among the most extensive in England

Extract from the
BROADLAND CODE

Natural Surroundings
Take great care that you avoid damaging banks, shoreline vegetation and marshland. Do not disturb nesting birds. Avoid shallow water where fish might spawn.

Your Litter
Make sure that you use the litter baskets provided at recognized mooring and parking places and yacht stations. Never leave any litter on land or water, take it home with you. Be particularly careful how you dispose of plastic, cellophane and other indestructible materials; they must never be left about as they can kill or maim wildlife.

Pollution
Do your best not to pollute the water or banks in any way.

Private Property
Remember all the land adjoining the water belongs to someone. Please respect this right. Do not trespass.

THE FENS

In the days of Hereward the Wake, the Fens were a vast, malarial swamp covering most of East Anglia from Peterborough to the Wash; a strange, flat land of enormous skies, empty horizons and endless acres of reed and sedge upon a thick rich silt and a blanket of sedge peat. Ignoring the bitter protests of the peasantry who relied on the reeds, fish and wildfowl for their livelihood, the great landowners drained the Fens to make way for farmland. By the end of the nineteenth century next to nothing was left.

In 1899 a relict area of fen at Wicken came to the attention of naturalists and was purchased by the National Trust, becoming Britain's first nature reserve. A small segment was salvaged at Woodwalton, and an important expanse survives in the Ouse Washes. These vital oases provide a marvellous evocation of the lonely, trackless wilderness the fenland once was.

Wicken Fen

NT Reserve

This square mile of marshland in Cambridgeshire is one of the few undrained areas of the fenland that once covered East Anglia. A windmill, once used to drain the surrounding farmland, now pumps water into the fen, and the vegetation is carefully managed to maintain the widest range of fenland habitats.

One of the classic sites in early ecological management, Wicken Fen is now a lush green haven of rich scrub and stands of tall herbs: meadowsweet, hemp agrimony, yellow loosestrife, wild angelica, milk parsley and many others. Pools and ditches are fringed with great water dock, bulrushes and sedge, spearwort and lesser plantain. The profusion of fenland flora attracts a great variety of butterflies and birds

to this temperate English jungle, and the hush of the wilderness prevails.
Getting there: signposted from Wicken village on A1123. Leave car at NT centre near Wicken Lode and continue on foot along trails across fen.
Access: open all year, best in spring and summer. **Further information:** booklet from site or NT, or contact Warden, T:0353 720274.

Woodwalton Fen

NCC NNR

These 520 Cambridgeshire acres (210ha) encompass a progression of fenland habitats: open water, mixed fen, damp meadows, wet heath and woodland. They shelter unusual plants such as the fen violet, fen wood rush and greater spearwort, and uncommon insects such as the hornet clearwing moth, ruddy sympetrum, large red damselfly and a colony of large copper butterflies,

which were reintroduced here from Holland in 1927.
Getting there: turn off B1040 at Ramsey, drive to Ramsey Heights and continue on foot.
Access: permit holders only. Apply in writing to NCC, Peterborough. **Further information:** contact Warden, Warden's House, Ramsey Heights, Huntingdon, T:0487 812363. Leaflet from NCC.

The Ouse Washes

Various reserves run by Cambient-RSPB-WT SSSI

The Ouse Washes, which occupy about 6,250 acres (2530ha) in a strip half a mile (1km) wide and 20 miles (32km) long, are the result of an ambitious drainage scheme undertaken by the 17th-century Dutch engineer, Cornelius Vermuyden. Two parallel channels, the Old and New Bedford Rivers, were cut across Cambridgeshire into Norfolk; when the River Ouse overflowed, it flooded the meadows in between and not the surrounding farmland.

This strip of land is still grazed in summer and usually flooded in winter, and so remains one of few areas in the Fens which is managed in much the same way as it was in the Middle Ages. A profusion of wetland vegetation grows here, including 280 species of flowering plants; bream, perch and roach teem in these waters, and pike and rudd grow to immense size.

But it is the birds that people come here to see, and with good reason; prodigious numbers of widgeon, teal, mallard, pochard and pintail, as well as whooper swans, hen harriers and short-eared owls. Pride of place goes to Bewick's swan; as many as 4,550 (30% of the European population) have wintered here, and the numbers are increasing each year. Conservation bodies own 60% of the Washes, but this unique treasure will not be safe until it is entirely under conservation control. **Getting there:** the Cambient and RSPB reserves at the south-western end can be reached via the B1093 or B1098. The Wildfowl Trust reserve is in the north-east corner near the village of Welney on the A1101. **Access:** open every day all year, 10am–5pm. Avoid Saturdays Sept–Jan when wildfowling takes place near reserves. Do not disturb the birds; walk below the bank on the side away from the Washes and be as quiet as possible when entering or leaving bird hides. **Where to stay:** accommodation for 6 at Pintail House. No dogs. **Further information:** contact RSPB Warden (Cliff Carson), Limosa, Welches Dam, Manea, March PE15 0ND, or Wildfowl Trust at Pintail House, Hundred Foot Bank, Welney, nr Wisbech, Cambs, T:0353 860711.

Redgrave and Lopham Fen

STNC Reserve

Largest survivor of the once-extensive fens of the Waveny – Little Ouse Valley in Suffolk; an oasis for many rare wetland species, including Britain's biggest spider, the great raft spider. **Further information:** from STNC.

BRECKLAND

The Breckland, some 300 square miles (777sq km) of open heathy countryside between Bury St Edmunds in Suffolk and Swaffham in Norfolk, was once heavily forested. In ancient times the land was cleared, and, with the tree cover gone, the wind blew away the topsoil. Sandstorms buried the medieval farmland, destroying the local economy and creating a treeless desert of sand dunes, which soon become a grassy steppe.

Today, the Breckland is a mosaic of developed and undeveloped countryside. There are military airfields, golf courses, sand and gravel quarries, agriculture and forestry. But large areas remain undisturbed and provide an unusual habitat for snakes, woodlark, nightjar and stone curlew, and many rare plants and insects. Something of the old Breckland can be savoured at the Cavenham Heath and East Wretham Heath.

East Wretham Heath

NNT Reserve

Wretham Heath Nature Reserve, Thetford, Norfolk IP24 1RU, T:095 382 339.

This unusual sandy wild place covers 362 acres (146ha) of Breckland heath, containing grassland with heather and harebell, open scrub of broom and hawthorn, natural birch woodland and a planted hornbeam wood where hawfinch and winter siskin can be found.

Two typical Breckland meres, fringed with aquatic plants, attract a variety of waders and wildfowl, and also a rare leech. Adders, grass snake and common lizards live on the heath, roe deer, red squirrels and badger inhabit the woods and birds of prey such as the hobby, merlin and hen harrier hunt here. **Getting there:** 4 miles (6km) north of Thetford on A1075. **Access:** open all year except Tuesdays. 2 nature trails. Bring warm clothing, rubber boots and binoculars. **Further information:** contact Warden (Peter Steele), East

Cavenham Heath

NCC NNR

One of the finest examples of acid Breckland heath, 502 acres (203ha) in extent, with lovely sweeps of heather and gorse, sandy areas, woodland and fen. A wide range of plants, insects, birds and mammals includes rarer species such as whinchats and nightjars, and a resident population of roe deer. **Getting there:** along track (trail) between Icklingham and Tuddenham, west of Icklingham on A1101. **Access:** main part of reserve open all year; northern part Apr–Jul only, or by permit. Beware of adders; fire is a risk. No dogs in northern part of reserve; keep them leashed elsewhere. **Further information:** contact Warden (Malcolm Wright), Fen Road, Pakenham, Bury St Edmunds, T:0359 30579.

CHAPTER 3

North-West England

This is a cautionary tale of how a latterday Moley immured deep inside his heavily mortgaged bunker and bowed down by the cares of the world, took off for the green woods and the high hills. Like Mole of *The Wind In The Willows*, I had had enough, and one day, when I could stand it no more, I broke out of my London penitentiary and fled north, coming to rest that evening beside the tranquil, sunlit waters of Buttermere, in the very different world of the Lake District's Western Fells. Here, in the green stillness and loveliness of the lakes and hills, my transformation from zombie to human being began.

During the night the sweet, ancient smell of straw and cowpat wafted through the window of my room from the stone cattle byre outside. I awoke to a morning of clear skies and dazzling sun like a man reborn. The simplest, most commonplace image or sound in that pastoral landscape now filled me with intense astonishment and delight, unlocking memories of my Yorkshire childhood: lambs bleating in the buttercup fields; the hum of the wind over the swooping swallows' wings; a fern, like bird chicks in a nest of moss, in the crook of a pollarded oak; and – paradise – a meadow stream flowing swiftly, icily and pure through tangles of reeds and herbs and flowers of almost tropical luxuriance.

Above the wooded meadows that separated Buttermere from Crummock Water the green hills rose like

From the summit of Tarn Crags on Blencathra, the wintry view encompasses the peak of Skiddaw which, at 3,054ft (931m), dominates the mountains in the northern Lake District

gigantic mossy stones with sheep embedded in them. To the south-west towered the three linked peaks of the Buttermere Fells – Red Pike, High Stile (the highest at 2,644 feet or 806 metres) and High Crag. By the standards of the world's great mountains these summits were mere hiccups of geology. To me, finding my hill legs after half a year at a desk, they looked huge, almost monstrous. A rough red track, like a ladder of stones, scrambled upwards towards Red Pike, which was out of sight from Buttermere; the path looked like an instrument of torture and I cast about for an easier route, via the highest waterfall in the Lakes, called Scale Force.

The fall lay deep in a cleft on the open hillside high above Crummock Water. You reached it through a wood of ancient oaks and a walk over hillsides of sprouting ferns where sheeps' wool festooned the gnarled, lichen-

The vivid blue flowers of the spring gentian, an arctic-alpine plant, bring a splash of colour to the most inhospitable rock environments in May and early June

scabbed thorns like beard moss. The cleft was enclosed by high, vertical walls of wet rock, where little stunted oaks, hollies and rowan trees clung tenaciously to minute pockets of soil in the crannies. At the end of the chasm, in a dark and horrid gloom, a 172-foot (52.5-metre) ribbon of white water dropped with fearsome weight and speed into a deep, reed-girt pool – an awesome and killing blow. This was Scale Force.

Lower down, nearer the chasm mouth and the sun, smaller falls busied around rocks and splashed into a brown pool ringed by ferns, foxgloves and green cushions of liverwort. Here lay the body of a sheep that had been swept over the falls to its death. Above the carcass a fluttering bird left a flickering yellow trace in the confined airspace between the rock walls. The bird finally came to rest on the dead sheep's tightly convoluted horns, a wagtail of the most intense canary yellow, the quick on the dead; but when the bird opened its bill to sing the sound was drowned by the thunder of the falls.

I climbed up the rim of the gorge, looking for a place where I could peer down at the waterfall from above. Using a dead silver birch tree for support I leaned over the edge, and as I did so, precariously poised between heaven and earth, the air was suddenly rent by the most terrifying tearing sound, and I was so shocked I almost fell. I looked up in time to see a night-black fighter jet, with wings half folded like a stooping falcon, screech over my head, angle sharply left and skim round the bluff of the hill above. At a dull plod I followed the plane, toiling upstream beside the burbling beck that fed Scale Force.

From where I started it was 2,300 feet (701 metres) of ascent to the highest point of the Buttermere Fells. Most of it now rose before me, a long, unremitting gasper up the convex hump of Red Pike's eastern shoulder. Where the track met the stream I paused to splash my face and drink from the cold, crystal water. I looked at my watch and an inner voice told me: 'Put your watch away, oh busy man! Forget your schedule.'

I sat back. It was a heavenly spot, a soft turfy bank in the sun, blessed with the sweet perfume of rowan blossom, billowing clouds above and a marvellous view down a gap between two fells. And as I paused and looked and dreamed, the cares of the last year fell away. I shouldered my pack and struck up the slope with new-found vigour. Climbing up to the top of Red Pike was like storming Iwo Jima; a steep slope of fine, dark gravel like bloodstained scree, dull red from the syenite in the rock. The view from the summit was majestic. From here I could see five of Lakeland's lakes and many of Lakeland's highest fells, including the four highest peaks: Skiddaw, Helvellyn, Scafell Pike and its twin summit of Scafell. To the south the sun beat down on Ennerdale, Coleridge's favourite lake, and the wildest of them all.

But in this moment of reaffirmation of life, death suddenly appeared before me in the mountains. As I began to climb up the connecting ridge to High Stile, I heard a strange screeching sound and saw two jet fighter planes swiftly receding from each other, groundwards. A very loud explosion reverberated among the fells, and two narrowly separated large balls of very dark, chocolate-brown smoke drifted up behind Robinson.

The cockpits were still intact when I saw them later, but burst open a little, and their innards – the brightly coloured wiring, rods and tubes – lay exposed. From an RAF crane in a field the fuselage of one of the planes hung like the mangled remains of a long-dead shark hauled from the sea. I grieved at the sight of this ill-fated wreckage; but it served only to redouble the *joie de vivre* these Lakeland hills had given back to me.

The route I was following over the Buttermere Fells formed an early stage of the Coast to Coast Walk pioneered by Wainwright between St Bee's Head on the Lancashire coast of the Irish Sea and Robin Hood's Bay on the Humberside coast of the North Sea. I could, if I chose, carry on right through the breadths of the three great national parks that straddle the north Country: the Lake District, the Yorkshire Dales and the North York Moors.

But my ambitions were less heroic; I wished to return to Buttermere before the end of the day or the expiry of my stamina, whichever came first. So I carried on, in my own good time, following the long craggy ridge that connects the rugged, battlemented peaks of High Stile and High Crag. From the summit cairn of High Stile, the highest point of these fells, I could see hazy new land across the blue wash of the Irish Sea and the Solway: the Isle of Man in the west, the Scottish hills of Galloway to the north beyond Crummock Water.

It was mid-evening before I got back to my starting point. I had been out on the fells for ten hours, travelling at a ruminative one mile an hour, every mile a revelation, every hour a joy. I rejoiced at the prospect of tomorrow and a long walk over to Ennerdale. But before that, before anything, there was a pressing priority: my reward, a pint of real ale – Theakston's Best – and then Nirvana.

BEFORE YOU GO

For general information about Lancashire, Greater Manchester, Merseyside, Cheshire and the High Peak area of Derbyshire contact the North West Tourist Board, Last Drop Village, Bromley Cross, Bolton, Lancs BL7 9PZ, T:0204 591511. The rest of the region, up to the Scottish border, is the responsibility of the Cumbria Tourist Board, Ashleigh, Holly Road, Windermere, Cumbria LA23 2AQ, T:096 62 4444.

The Yorkshire Dales National Park falls within the authority of the Yorkshire and Humberside Tourist Board (see Chapter 4).

GETTING THERE

By air: Manchester International Airport has scheduled flights to major cities throughout Europe and the New World. Leeds and Bradford Airport and East Midlands Airport near Derby have flights to major European cities, while Carlisle Airport has a regular London service.

By sea: B&I Car Ferries operate daily between Dublin and Liverpool. Belfast Car Ferries have a daily Belfast–Liverpool service.

By train: Liverpool and Manchester have rapid rail links to most parts of Britain.

By bus: services link all the North-West's principal towns and cities with the rest of Britain. Contact a travel agent or information centre for further details.

WHERE TO STAY

Both the region's tourist boards produce free accommodation brochures. Cumbria's *Holiday Guide* lists a wide range of accommodation, from luxury hotels to farmhouse bed and breakfast, plus a section of campsites. The North West Tourist Board's *Where to Stay* is aimed more at the expense account traveller. Both include addresses of local information centres that provide more comprehensive lists of accommodation.

ACTIVITIES

The three national parks in this area are principal centres for walking holidays. The Pennine Way starts in the Derbyshire Peak District and passes through the Yorkshire Dales on its way to Scotland.

Information about sports and outdoor activities can be obtained from the regional offices of the Sports Council. For Cumbria, write for a copy of the excellent *Northern Sporting and Recreation Handbook*, available from the Sports Council, Northern Region, Aykley Heads, Durham DH1 5UU, T:091-384 9595. For Lancashire, Cheshire, Greater Manchester and Merseyside, send for a copy of the *Sports Directory* from the Sports Council, North West Regional Office, Fifth floor, Astley House, Quay Street, Manchester M3 4AE, T:061 834 0338.

The Peak District

From the Anglo-Saxon *peac*, meaning knoll or hill

National Park occupying 542 square miles (1,403sq km) of the southern Pennines

Hen Cloud is a distinctive mass of rock rising 1,240 feet (378 metres) out of the English lowland plain like a mini Rock of Gibraltar. To the traveller heading north this sudden upward heave of the landscape is both exciting and significant. For Hen Cloud is not only a sentinel guarding the approaches to the open and relatively unspoiled territory known as the Peak, but one of the first bastions of Highland Britain. Here you leave the placid plains and gentle rises of the South and Midlands and enter the starker, more rugged uplands of the North Country. The 150-mile (240-kilometre) Pennine spine of England is a geologically complex world of gritstone plateaux, limestone dales, rocks and crags, great moors and vast peat bogs. The Peak District occupies the first 40 miles (64 kilometres) of this upland chain. Here you can find some of the wildest, least tamed landscape in Britain.

The change in the environment is obvious almost at once. Hedges give way to dry-stone walls, arable fields to rough hill pasture, green slopes to moors and tracts of bog, for as the country climbs the air grows cooler. The cooler climate in turn brings about changes in the flora and fauna. For lowland plants and animals like the nettle-leaved bellflower and nuthatch, the Peak is the northern limit of their range; for highland species like the cloudberry and mountain hare, it is the southernmost limit.

The peak was the first national park in Britain and is still the most popular. Half the population of England are within day-trip distance of it. It is small enough to cross on foot in a day, big enough to get lost in. For the climber it offers hard rock, for the caver an underground wonderland, and for the walker miles of rambling and riding country both on and off the beaten track. For the people of Manchester, Sheffield, West Yorkshire and the Potteries, it is a lung; an escape back to nature, to birdsong and clear skies, the open trail and untrammelled horizon.

There are two kinds of Peak country: the White Peak and the Dark Peak, so called because of the colour of their prevailing rock. The White Peak is limestone country and occupies the southern and central areas of the national park, a dry, porous plateau some 1,000 feet (305 metres) above sea level. It is lighter, brighter, more arcadian countryside than the Dark Peak, and cut through by lovely wooded dales and gorges such as Dovedale, Monsal Dale and Lathkill Dale. These are the famous Derbyshire Dales, renowned for their impressive rock architecture and crystal-clear waters.

For the naturalist, the Derbyshire Dales offer the greatest wealth of interest, above all in Lathkill Dale, one of five dales that form part of the Derbyshire Dales National Nature Reserve. Carved by a torrential river of Ice Age meltwater, Lathkill Dale is a classic White Peak valley which runs through limestone for the whole of its length, a phenomenon which endows it with an exceptional richness and diversity of flora and fauna.

Even today human activity has had little effect on the environment there and many national rarities – most notably, perhaps, the uncommon purple-flowered mezareon – have continued to survive. The ash woods of the Lathkill are among the finest in the country and harbour a tremendous variety of plants. Even on the open, rabbit-cropped grassland of the upper dale, 54 species of plant have been recorded in one square yard alone, while down in the dampish bottom of the dale, between the

rearing limestone walls of the gorge, another rare flower, the deep blue Jacob's ladder, grows in stands as extensive as any in Britain. Further to the north, beautiful Monk's Dale is just as rich and even less affected by man and change than Lathkill Dale. Both comprise the jewels in the crown of the Peak District's natural history heritage.

By contrast the Dark Peak, which surrounds the White Peak like an inverted horseshoe to north, east and west, is gritstone country, altogether harsher, wilder and more sombre, especially along its dramatic rock edges and on the high heather moors and peat deserts at the more northerly end of the park. The high moors are the kingdom of the red grouse and hardy hill sheep. The hill walker who traverses them needs to be well prepared and well equipped for the unpredictable – and often hostile – weather.

The western edge of the Dark Peak rises sharply for more than 1,000 feet (305 metres) out of the Cheshire Plain, and the rock architecture to be found there provides some of the most spectacular gritstone landscape of the national park. Rock outcrops like the Roaches, Hen Cloud and Ramshaw Rocks, with their rearing towers and serrated pinnacles carved by wind, rain and frost, provide some of the best climbing in the country. Some of them are formidably advanced, with encouraging names like Death Knoll and the Crack of Gloom. One of the few genuine peaks in the Peak District – Shutlingsloe, the 'Matterhorn of the Peak', 1,659 feet (505 metres) above sea level – is located in this western part of the National Park.

West of Sheffield lies the eastern arm of the Dark Peak. Extensive peat and heather moors, the domain of the sheep, the hare and the hill walker, give way to a series of odd-shaped tors such as Crow Stones, Cat Clough and Cakes of Bread and spectacular gritstone rock edges, walls of almost continuous rock which run for miles and descend by steps to the plains below.

Through this impressive landscape flows one of the Peak's great rivers, the Derwent, which rises on the Bleaklow plateau to the north. In its upper reaches, the river has been extensively dammed and forested to create a man-made landscape more like Scandinavia than Derbyshire.

For Edale the high Pennine moors stretch northwards all the way to the Scottish border. The Pennine Way starts here, aiming straight at the boggy plateau from which rises the Peak's highest point, Kinder Scout (2,088 feet, 636 metres). This five-square-mile morass of peat bogs and 'groughs', where the water-eroded gullies wind between walls of peat higher than a man, is certainly wild but hardly pretty, and it will appeal more to the dedicated hill walker than to the simple country lover, for it is a desolate and monotonous place, climatically temperamental, squelchy underfoot after rain, fearsome in winter.

The name Kinder Scout probably comes from the Saxon *Kyndwr Scut*, meaning 'water over the edge' and referring, in all likelihood, to the tumbling cascade of nearby Kinder Downfall where the nascent Kinder River drops 100 feet (30 metres) over the rocky escarpment of the moorland edge on its headlong course to the west.

North from Kinder the moorland and bog reach out towards the northern corner of the park. There are two major parts to these northern moors: Bleaklow, to the south of the drowned industrial valley of Longendale, and Black Hill to the north of it. It is a matter of personal experience which of these peat deserts is squidgiest, bleakest, and most vexing for walkers.

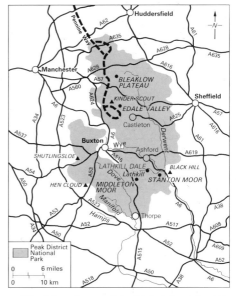

Bleaklow is possibly Britain's only true desert; a semi-tundra of acid peat, once forested, but over the centuries so felled and grazed and burned and drained that not even the humble sphagnum moss can survive here, and the nodding white heads of the bog cotton grass are virtually the only sign of life. For the wild traveller there are compensations in this desolate state of affairs: solitude, a stark kind of beauty, a sense of grappling with primordiality, and the reward of achievement. These are the essential components of all true exploration of the wilderness places.

BEFORE YOU GO

Maps: the Ordnance Survey produce 2 maps covering the entire area in the 1:25,000 Outdoor Leisure Series: the Dark Peak (north) and the White Peak (south).

Guidebooks: visitors will find the Countryside Commission's *The Peak National Park* by Roland Smith (Webb and Bower) a useful introduction.

The Peak District is so close to a densely populated industrial region that visitors tend to forget that conditions can be harsh. Before setting out on a long walk, check the weather forecast and make sure you are adequately equipped.

GETTING THERE

By car: the M1 provides rapid access from the North (exits 28 or 29) and South (exit 36). Main roads through the park include the A515 from Ashbourne to Buxton, the A6 from Matlock to Manchester, the A623 and the A57 from Sheffield to Glossop through Snake Pass.

By train: the Hope Valley Line runs from Sheffield to Manchester with 5 stations inside the park: Edale, Hope, Bamford, Hathersage and Grindleford. Branch lines also run from Manchester to Glossop in the north and Buxton in the south of the park.

By bus: services within the park are listed in the Peak District public transport timetable, available from park information centres. For one

Lathkill Dale, one of the gems of the White Peak in Derbyshire, is lit up in August with bright clumps of rosebay willowherb

day's unlimited travel on bus or train, buy a Peak Wayfarer ticket from British Rail, individual bus operators or the national park office.

WHERE TO STAY
Hotels and bed and breakfast: Bakewell and Castleton are the principal accommodation centres. Ashbourne, Matlock, Buxton and Glossop, on the fringes of the park, absorb many more visitors. The park authority publishes an annual list of accommodation in or near the park. A reservation service is available from Bakewell information centre (T:062 981 3227).
Outdoor living: the park authority publishes a list of approved campsites and operates a site availability telephone service on 062 981

70

4341. It also runs a system of camping barns, stone farm buildings converted into cheap, basic accommodation. Leaflets and further information from the Peak National Park Office, Aldern House, Baslow Road, Bakewell, Derbyshire DE4 1AE.
Youth hostels: at Bakewell (T:062 981 2313), Castleton (T:0433 20235), Edale (T:0433 70302), Elton (T:062 988 394), Eyam (T:0433 30335), Hartington (T:029 884 223), Ilam (T:033 529 212) and Youlgrave (T:062 986 518).

ACCESS AND CLOSURES
Restricted to roads, footpaths and bridle paths in southern park; a special agreement allows visitors to ramble freely over much of the northern moors, except for a few days each year during grouse shoots and when there is a high risk of fire. These periods of closure are posted at park

information centres and advertised in the local press.

ACTIVITIES
Walking: the park authority produces a number of leaflets describing circular walks; it also runs a series of short guided walks, details of which are published in *The Peakland Post*, the annual information sheet available from visitors' centres. The long-distance walker will head for Edale, conveniently located on the Hope Valley Railway, where the PENNINE WAY (see p.88) begins its long route northwards across the park's highest hills – Kinder Scout, Bleaklow and Black Hill in the Dark Park.
Riding and pony trekking: the south offers steep wooded bridle paths, greenways and lanes, exposed and ancient pack horse routes cut across the bare moors of the northern Dark Peak. The park authority's leaflet *Riding and*

Trekking lists a number of centres which organize trekking holidays and vacation packages.

Climbing: both the limestone hills in the south and the gritstone cliffs to the east, west and north are popular training grounds. For names of climbing clubs, contact the British Mountaineering Council, Crawford House, Precinct Centre, Booth Street East, Manchester M13 9RZ, T:061 273 5835.

Caving: the hollow limestone of the White Peak has fascinated cavers since Edwardian times. This is a potentially dangerous activity and even experienced cavers should seek the advice of a local caving club before going underground. A cave rescue service is available by dialling 999. For information on caving in the region, contact the Derbyshire Caving Association, c/o the Sports Council, East Midlands Regional Office, 26 Musters Road, West Bridgford, Nottingham NG2 7PL, T:0602 821887. Several show caves give the visitor a tempting if touristy glimpse of this otherwise closed world. Blue John Cavern and Mine (T:0433 20638), Speedwell Cavern (T:0433 20512) and Treak Cliff Cavern (T:0433 20571) – all near Castleton – are open daily all year round.

Cycling: quiet roads, bridle paths and disused railway tracks offer many suitable routes. Leaflets describing them are available from the park authority's cycle hire shops at: Ashbourne (T:0335 43156), Derwent (T:0433 51261), Parsley Hay (T: 029 884 493), Waterhouses (T:053 86 609), Middleton Top (T:062 982 3204), Hayfield (T:0663 46222) Lyme Park (T:066 32 2023) and Bollington (T:0625 72681).

'A howling wilderness . . . the most desolate, wild and abandoned country in all England.'

Daniel Defoe (1725)

Fishing: the waters once fished by Izaak Walton are still popular with anglers. The Rivers Dove, Wye and Derwent are good grounds for brown and rainbow trout, while several reservoirs are open to the public. Tackle shops issue rod licences and permits and are the best sources of advice on local fishing. The park authority's leaflet *Fishing* gives useful information about trout fishing in the park.

Field studies: courses in all aspects of the natural history and archaeology of the park are offered at the Peak National Park Centre at Losehill Hall, Castleton, Derbyshire S30 2WB; write to the Principal (Peter Townsend) for details.

FURTHER INFORMATION
Peak National Park Office, Aldern House, Baslow Road, Bakewell, Derbyshire DE4 1AE, T:062 981 4321. For all park authority literature.
Nature Conservancy Council, Riversdale House, Dale Road North, Darley Dale, Matlock, Derbyshire DE4 2JB, T:0629 734343. For information on Derbyshire Dales Nature Reserve.
National Trust, East Midlands Regional Office, Clumber Park Stableyard, Worksop, Nottinghamshire S80 3BE, T:0909 486411. For literature on the NT's substantial holdings in the park.
Derbyshire Wildlife Trust,

Elvaston Castle Country Park, Thulston, nr Derby DE7 3EP, T:0332 756610. Holdings include more than 10 small reserves within the park.
The park information centres at Bakewell (T:062 981 3227) and Edale (T:0433 70207) are open year-round. The Castleton centre (T:0433 20679) remains open on winter weekends. Other centres are at Fairholmes, Torside, Hartington and Derbyshire Bridge.

Forest of Bowland

From the Celtic *buland*, a cattle pasture

AONB

A western outlier of the Pennine chain, the Forest of Bowland must be one of the least spoiled and least publicized wild places in England. Once a royal hunting forest and wilderness refuge for Tudor dissidents, it has long since lost its tree cover; today it consists mostly of open heather moor and fell country, 310 square miles (803 sq km) of grandeur and isolation.

This terrain is broken by limestone knolls and gritstone crags, rising to 1,839ft (560m) at Ward's Stone, 1,827ft (557m) at Pendle Hill and 1,786ft (544m) at White Fell, providing tremendous views towards the Irish Sea, Snowdonia, the Pennines and the Lake District.

The area is privately owned and managed primarily for grouse; few people live here and only one minor road crosses the central area. However, there are a few public footpaths for the hill walker to explore the high, bracken-covered fells or the steep, tree-lined river valleys.

Merlin and hen harrier hunt over the fells, curlew and plover call on the moors, dippers bob and flit about by the peaty, swiftly flowing streams and waterfalls, redstarts and pied flycatchers nest in the valley woods and some 20,000 pairs of lesser black-backed gulls breed in a huge gullery on Mallowdale Fell.

Before you go: OS Landranger Series Map Nos. 97 and 102. **Getting there:** via M6 (exits 32, 33 and 34), then by unclassified roads. Buses run from Lancaster to Abbeystead and Wray in the north and from Preston to Chipping and Clitheroe in the south. **Where to stay:** bed and breakfast at Garstang, Chipping, Slaidburn, Dolphinholme, Bolton-by-Bowland and Wray. Youth hostel at Slaidburn. Lancaster and Clitheroe Tourist Information Centres issue accommodation lists. **Access:** few rights of way, but free access in 2 large areas; details in leaflet from Clitheroe information centre. **Further information:** from Head Ranger (T:0524 791075).

The Yorkshire Dales

680 square miles of limestone hills and dales in the central Pennines, one third of which is National Park.

I have a particular fondness for the Yorkshire Dales, for I was brought up in them; and what I am I own in part to them, and to the war. My explorations during those formative years were for the most part limited to how far I could travel in a day by bike or bus; but what they lacked in range they made up for in intimacy, for I experienced the world then in a way that would probably be impossible now, and was part of the natural world to an extent that most people find difficult in adulthood.

A large part of my free time was spent in a fragment of the ancient Forest of Knaresborough, a wood of beech and fir, oak, holly and tangled rhododendron thickets bordering the open rolling dales, where the lapwings cried and the bluebottles huzzahed in the cowpats and the dipper bobbed in the beds of the stream and I could roly poly through fields of cowslips that stretched from one end of the known world to the other.

In that vestigial wood I learned the ways of the forest, learned to stalk, climb trees,

forage for mushrooms, berries, crab apples, hips and haws, beechmast and hazelnuts, wild horseradish and the young fresh leaves of the hawthorn (which we called bread and cheese, and ate). Here I first heard the summer oratorio of the birds' dawn chorus, first set eyes on badgers, weasels and shrews, learned to tell the different birds apart, cut my hand on razor grass, and became aware, with the close proximity that only a child can know, of all the smells and feels and shapes and colours and movements of all the different wild things of the forest. For me that wood was a natural sanctuary.

I went to other places too. At Fountains Abbey I was reduced to silence by the ghosts and echoes of times and people past that crowded round me in this green and haunted place. On the weirdly weathered contortions of Brimham Rocks I learned to clamber around the more awkward eructations of geology, and at Scar Beck I learned to fall off them. But in my mind's eye it is to one small spot in Nidderdale that I return time and again. Call it Becksthwaite: a small grey limestone village and a small grey limestone bridge over a little chunk of paradise. The River Nidd ran clear and cold and fast and shallow here and you could go minnowing and sticklebacking with baited jam jars and feel the fish nibbling your toes and lie back and watch the clouds billowing past and the hot summer sun bursting through the branches of the overhanging trees like a starshell.

A year ago I went back to Becksthwaite.

It had not changed at all in the intervening years, and it was still paradise. But the boys were not boys like the boys when I was a boy.

'Can you still get sticklebacks down in the river?' I asked one local lad by the bridge. He shifted nervously from foot to foot and glanced uneasily at his chum.

'Never heard of anything like *them*,' he replied at last. 'Can't get nowt like that down't river now.'

One boy's paradise, perhaps, is another's purgatory. But for the right person, the Yorkshire Dales are a blessed patch. Part of the Pennine chain, the dales are formed of carboniferous limestone which reflects the light so that, on sunlit days, they positively gleam.

Nowhere in Britain will you find more spectacular examples of limestone scenery. At Gordale Scar and Malham Cove it takes the form of sheer cliff faces of bone-white rock up to 300 feet (91 metres) high. At Southerscales Scars and Scales Moor, as well as Malham Cove, it takes the form of extraordinary limestone pavements, jointed and fissured by millions of years of rain and dirty weather. Or it is dissolved by underground rivers to form an immense network of caves far below the surface. There are 50 major caves in the Yorkshire Dales, including Britain's largest underground cavern, the 350-foot (107-metre) Gaping Gill.

It is the dales, scoured by Ice Age glaciers and cleared, farmed and populated by man, that determine the ground plan of the park. 'Dale' is a Norse word for valley, and there are some 50 of them in the park, the few major ones establishing the layout of the Dales' landscape.

Swaledale, to the north, is narrow, lovely and haunted by the relics of its industrial past. Wensleydale, which runs a parallel course to the south, is the most pastoral of the dales, the gentlest and least wild. It is also the heart of waterfall country; among the many falls (or forces) is the 90-foot (27-metre) drop of Hardraw Force.

Facing south, Bishopsdale leads southward towards Wharfedale, which rises in wild country at the heart of the Dales and flows serenely through the most sylvan of all the valleys. To the south-west of Wharfedale, in the bone-bright Great Scar limestone country, Malhamdale and Ribblesdale wind through a land of gleaming cliffs and scars, while Yorkshire's 'Three Peaks' – Ingleborough, Whernside and Pen-y-ghent, all of them over 2,000 feet (610 metres) in height – peer distantly down over Ribble Head.

There are a score of summits above this height, with high grass and heather moorland fells between the valleys. These Pennine uplands rank among the last wilderness areas of England, where there is only the call of the curlew to keep you company, and the cry of grouse and sheep. It is in the waterlogged peat of the high fells, tumbling and tinkling downhill via the innumerable small tarns and becks, falls and gills, that the rivers in the dales below have their origin.

There is a great range of plant and animal habitats in the park, the products of soil and climate, which are in turn a product of altitude. On the highest ground above 2,000 feet (610 metres) a sub-alpine pasture of moor grasses, heathers, bilberry and crowberry prevails. One zone down, vast areas of the wetter, western Pennine uplands above 1,400 feet (427 metres) are covered in black, sombre, squelchy peat, up to 90 feet (27 metres) deep in places. In this hostile, wilderness environment, the fluffy white cotton grass is almost the only plant that can survive.

Between 1,000 and 1,400 feet (305 and 427 metres), enormous stretches of the

Spring is the best time for spotting adders, when they have just emerged from hibernation and are doing their best to warm up in the fitful April sun

upland Dales are covered by heather moorland. Carefully managed for grouse and sheep, the moors are best seen in August when the heather is in bloom. In bygone times birch woods covered the moors, but now they are confined to the gills, becks and streams which cut ravines on the steep hillsides out of reach of grazing animals. One of the finest gill woods in the park is Ling Gill, a small National Nature Reserve in a limestone ravine in upper Ribblesdale east of Ribble Head, where the dominant trees are ash and hazel and the rich ground flora includes giant bellflower, herb Paris, melancholy thistle, mountain everlasting, marsh hawksbeard, globe flower and ferns of all kinds.

The limestone country has most of the flowers in the Dales. They are everywhere, burning bright or coyly winking, on grassland and rocks, chinks in walls and fissures in limestone pavements. The surface of these pavements is mostly bare rock and there is no soil to support plant life; but in the damp, dark fissures – or 'grykes' – there is not only soil but shade from the heat of the sun and protection from grazing animals, and here a classic English woodland flora flourishes: hart's tongue fern and herb Robert, green spleenwort and dog's mercury, wood anemone and wood sorrel. At Colt Park Wood, a National Nature Reserve near Ribble Head, there is a rare example of a tree-covered limestone pavement, with one of the best native scar ashwoods in Britain and a ground flora totalling more than 150 species.

If the limestone country has more to offer botanists, it is the moors and fells which are likely to be of greater interest to ornithologists, with sandpipers and black-headed gulls round the tarns, ravens, buzzards, merlins, peregrines and kestrels soaring and swooping over the hunting grounds and meadow pipits everywhere between the high fells and the rough grazing. And in the streams that chatter down the gills and dales the dippers dip and the wagtails wag and the kingfishers catch fish in spurts of bright blue and flashing orange flame.

The Yorkshire Dales are a very special and very lovely part of the world. The landscape is remarkable for the harmony between the world of nature and the world of man, his villages, farms and domiciles. You will find peace and beauty wherever you go in the Dales: so go.

BEFORE YOU GO

Maps: OS Outdoor Leisure Series Map Nos 2, 10 and 30.
Guidebooks: a sound background to the park's human and natural history can be found in the Countryside Commission's official guide, *The Yorkshire Dales National Park* by Tony Waltham (Webb and Bower). *Yorkshire Dales* (AA/OS) is informative on a more popular level, and full of excellent maps. The Yorkshire Dales park service's annual information sheet, *The Visitor*, includes useful addresses and details of guided walks and local events. Available free at park information centres or by sending a stamped addressed envelope to Yorkshire Dales National Park, Colvend, Hebden Road, Grassington,

Skipton BD23 5LB, T:0756 752748.

GETTING THERE
By car: from M6, take A65 (exit 36) for southern dales; A684 (exit 37) for Garsdale and Wensleydale; exit 38 for Kirkby Stephen and Swaledale. From A1, take A59 from Harrogate for Skipton and east of park.

By train: the Leeds–Lancaster line serves the south of the park, with stops at Skipton, Gargrave, Hellifield, Long Preston, Giggleswick and Clapham. The spectacular Carlisle–Leeds line, regularly threatened with closure, has recently taken on new life.
By bus: regular services stop at towns on the periphery of the park: Darlington to

---

CAUTION TO WALKERS

Where there are dales there are hills, and potentially treacherous weather. Before setting out on any upland walk, phone the 24-hour weather service on 0898 500417. In emergencies, phone 999 and ask for 'fell rescue'.

Disused lead mines are a hazard in some parts of the park, and open pits still exist near Grassington, Arkengarthdale and Swaledale. Consult a park information centre (see under **Before you go**) for details of any such pitfalls along your projected route.

Many lovers of the Yorkshire Dales consider the undulating limestone scenery of Wharfedale the finest, with its woods, moors and pasture

Richmond, Leeds to Skipton, Lancaster or Kendal to Sedbergh. Within the park, bus services are often infrequent, but certain routes along the principal dales are well served. Schedules available from park centres.

WHERE TO STAY
The park service's accommodation guide, available by post from the central office, gives details of campsites and other accommodation. The 6 park centres, local information points and Yorkshire and Humberside Tourist Board

offices (see below) will provide assistance with reservations.

Youth hostels: in or near the park are situated at: Leyburn (T:096 93 260), Dacre Banks, Harrogate (T:0423 780431), Dent (T:058 75 251), Ripon, (T:0677 60303 – Easter and summer only), Richmond (T:0748 84206), Hawes (T:096 97 368), Ingleton (T:0468 41444), Skipton (T:0756 76232), Kirkby Stephen (T:076 83 71793), Settle (T:072 92 3577). A free leaflet, *Youth Hostels In Yorkshire*, is available from YHA Area Office, 96 Main Street, Bingley, West Yorkshire BD16 2JH, T:0274 567697.

ACCESS AND CLOSURES
Except for Bardon Moor near

Bolton Abbey, where access, has been negotiated, walkers must stay on rights of way specified on OS maps. If in doubt, enquire at a park centre.

ACTIVITIES
Walking: fingerposts and colour coding – yellow for walkers only, blue for riders and cyclists – identify the numerous rights of way. These provide opportunities for walkers of all experience, from endurance tests across high fell country to guided ambles through lowland farms.

The long-distance walker may be tempted by the Pennine Way which winds northwards along high ground through Malham, Hawes and Keld (see under the PENNINE

Britain's smallest falcon, the merlin, hunts over high moorland in summer, but in winter prefers the easier pickings of coastal marshes

WAY, p 88). The Dales Way, which angles up Wharfedale on its way from Ilkley to Bowness, is described in Colin Speakman's *The Dales Way* (Dalesman 1984). The 22-mile (35-km) Three Peaks Walk takes in the summits of Pen-y-ghent, Whernside and Ingleborough. This has become such a cult that in places the peaks themselves are seriously eroded. *The Three Peaks Map and Guide* (Stiles Publications) is one of several descriptions of the route.

Climbing: few long climbs, but challenging cliffs at Malham, Gordale and Kilnsey. *Yorkshire Limestone*, a

76

booklet describing these and other climbs, is available from the Yorkshire Mountaineering Club, P. Scott, (Secretary), 11 Southview Drive, East Brierley, Bradton, West Yorkshire. Climbing holidays (vacation packages) are organized by the park's own centre at Whernside (Yorkshire Dales National Park Outdoor Recreation and Study Centre, Dent, Sedbergh, Cumbria, T:058 75 213) and by the Dales Centre, Grassington, North Yorkshire BD23 5AU, T:0756 752757.

Caving: with more than 125 miles of cave and tunnel already explored, the park is a centre for enthusiasts. For further information, experienced cavers should consult the Whernside centre, or refer to *Northern Caves* (Dalesman, 5 volumes), a publication devoted

exclusively to the caves of the Dales. Three show caves allow casual visitors a brief glimpse of the park underground: Ingleborough Cave, Clapham (T:046 85 242), Stump Cross Caverns, Grassington/Pately Bridge (T:0756 752780), White Star Caves, Ingleton, (T:0468 41244).

Ballooning: for a unique opportunity of gliding over the park in a wicker basket, contact Graham Turnbull (Hot Air Balloons) Flying Club Ltd, Grassington, North Yorkshire BD23 5LR, T:0756 752937. Flights last about an hour and generally leave from Grassington.

Field studies: Malham Tarn Field Centre is ideally situated for the study of plant and animal ecology, geology and birdlife. Open Mar–Nov; 2-, 5- or 7-night courses for students of any level or age. Further information from Malham Tarn Field Centre, Field Studies Council, Settle, North Yorkshire BD24 9PU, T:072 92 331.

FURTHER INFORMATION
For publications and further enquiries, contact the Yorkshire Dales National Park, Colvend, Hebden Road, Grassington, Skipton BD23 5LB, T:0756 752748. There are 6 park information centres, open Apr–Oct, at Aysgarth Falls (T:0693 424), Clapham (T:046 85 419), Grassington (T:0756 752748), Hawes (T:096 97 450), Malham (T: 072 93 363) and Sedbergh (T:0587 20125).

For further regional information, contact the Yorkshire and Humberside Tourist Board, 312 Tadcaster Road, York Y02 2HF, T:0904 707961. They have centres at Bentham, Horton-in-Ribblesdale, Ingleton, Leyburn, Reeth, Richmond, Settle and Skipton.

NORTH PENNINES

The North Pennines are England's last great tract of unprotected moorland – wild, remote country wedged between the Yorkshire Dales, Lake District and Northumberland National Parks at the northern end of the Pennine chain. The region is crossed by the Pennine Way and contains the two largest nature reserves in England, as well as the sensational chasm of High Cup Nick and the Pennines' highest summit, Cross Fell (2,930 feet, 893 metres), where snow can lay into summer.

Important areas include the following:

Upper Teesdale

NCC Reserve

Most visitors to this moorland reserve in Durham come to admire the dramatic waterfalls at Cauldron Snout or High Force, to picnic by the great man-made lake of Cow Green reservoir or to walk one of the barest and grandest stretches of the Pennine Way. But this tundra-like moorland has an extra importance; for more than two centuries it has been recognized as one of Europe's unique wild places, a plant community almost unchanged in 10,000 years.

Several habitats thrive in this living museum of post-Ice Age vegetation: small woodlands, riverside pastures and peat bog uplands. The most unusual and fertile are the grasslands that cover Teesdale's sugar limestone, so-called on account of its granulated surface. Rare Ice Age relict plants include artic-alpines such as spring gentian, alpine bartsia, bird's-eye primrose and Scottish asphodel.

Getting there: via unclassified road off B6277, 7 miles (11km) north-west of Middleton. **Where to stay:** Langdon Beck Youth Hostel (T:0833 22228). **Access:** stay on rights of way, which are unaffected by firing ranges south of reserve at Cronkley Fell. **Facilities:** car park, picnic site and nature trail at Cow Green. **Further information:** leaflet and trail guides on site or from NCC.

Moor House

NCC Reserve

It is said that on a clear day one can see the summit of Cheviot 40 miles (64km) to the north from great Dun Fell in the Moor House reserve. One is more likely to see low clouds and featureless moor, for it rains or snows here on an average of 290 days a year.

Moor House in Cumbria is the largest reserve in England and also one of the poorest in terms of higher plant and animal life. A layer of peat averaging 6ft (1.8m) in depth covers 85% of the area, turning this part of the Pennines into a vast black sponge. Few plants can survive in such an environment; heather, cotton grass, sphagnum moss, moor rush and mat grass are the dominant species. But it is only in the lower plants that the reserve is particularly rich: 260 mosses, 75 liverworts and 120 lichens have been recorded. Few birds and mammals thrive here. Red grouse, curlew, golden plover, snip, mallard, dunlin, teal, widgeon, ring ouzel and dipper are among the nesting birds. Fox, rabbit, field vole, mole and shrew are also residents, though the black-faced Swaledale sheep is the only mammal you are likely to encounter.

Getting there: take footpath from village of Knoch to Great Dun Fell or join the Pennine Way at nearby Dufton – a longer route. Carry a compass. **Further information:** leaflet from NCC.

Asby Scar

NCC Reserve

Situated on the watershed between the Rivers Eden and Lune in Cumbria, the desolate landscape of Asby Scar is a spectacular lesson in the power of water over rock. The limestone pavement of this bare plateau – great slabs known as clints – is deeply notched with fissures, known as grykes, where the rock has literally been dissolved by millennia of rainfall. In this apparently barren world of rock and grass, a few wind-twisted hawthorns are the tallest living things.

But below the surface of the pavement, sheltered from both weather and sheep, an abundant plant life flourishes within the grykes. Of particular interest are the ferns: green spleenwort, brittle bladder fern, limestone

Bird's eye primrose and wood anemone flower below an outcrop in alder and birch woodland on the banks of the Tees

polypody and rigid buckler fern. Other plants to note include mountain melick, lesser meadow rue, hairy

rockcress, herb Paris and hart's tongue. There are even communities of stunted trees in the wider grykes, sunken coppices of sycamore, ash rowan, hazel and elder (see also GAIT BARROWS p. 86).

Getting there: half a mile east

of Orton on B6261, take unclassified road north to Broadfell and Scar Side. A track from Scar Side leads up the fell and through the reserve. **Access:** unrestricted.

Further information: leaflet from NCC.

The Lake District

*The largest National Park in Britain,
covering 880 square miles (2,279sq km)
of Cumbrian lakes, dales, fells and coast*

In few other parts of England are visitors more immediately aware of the geological structure of the land than in the Lake District. The mountains heave up out of the flat plains to greet them. Under their feet lie hard rocks against which they stub their toes, loose scree on which they curse and slide, endless inclines and declines which give them blisters. Beneath their gaze still, deep waters stretch away between the steep slopes of the fells.

Everywhere you look you see geology. The different kinds of rock produce different kinds of scenery, an immense variety of it; and it is old, older than the Alps and the Himalayas, older than almost everything in the world.

Skiddaw is not only the fourth highest mountain in England at 3,053 feet (930 metres), but arguably the oldest mountain in Europe. It is formed of the most northerly of three bands of different rock types that make up the core of the Lakeland fells, a great dome of slates rent by volcanic lavas and covered by later slates and limestones. The name of this rock is Skiddaw Slate, laid down as mud in a shallow sea some 500 million years ago. Most of northern Lakeland, from Blencathra and Skiddaw round via Derwentwater to Buttermere, Crummock and Loweswater, is composed of this dark blue or black slate, which weathers into rounded hills and placid skylines.

The second rock band, in the central Lake District, was formed by a volcanic cataclysm which took place at about the time the Skiddaw slates had been laid down. These Borrowdale volcanics, as they are called, are coloured red, pink and green. Weathered by millions of years of rain, frost and ice, they have produced some of the most fiercely dramatic mountain landscapes of the Lake District: craggy peaks, plunging buttresses, deep chasms, a complex maze of high ridges and crooked valleys across the whole area from Wastwater to the Borrowdale Fells, including the peaks of some of the highest mountains in England, such as Scafell Pike (at 3,210 feet, 978 metres, the very highest point in England), Scafell (3,162 feet, 964 metres), Helvellyn (3,118 feet, 950 metres) and Great Gable (2,949 feet, 899 metres).

The third band of rock, running across southern Lakeland, consists of Silurian slates laid down after the volcanic eruptions had created the central mountains. This rock is blue-grey or black, generally soft and easily eroded, and produces a gentler landscape of rounded hills and lush woods – the lovely, green, seductive Lakeland countryside of Windermere, Esthwaite Water, Coniston Water, Grizedale Forest, the wooded hills and dales to the east of Broughton, the woodlands of the Furness Fells, the Winster Valley and Hawkshead.

Over millions of years, earth movements raised, buckled and crushed the original rock formations. Rivers cut through the surface, forming the pattern of today's fells. The Ice Ages scooped out the mountain tarns, carved out the peaks and razor-edged ridges, shattered the standing rock into long slopes of scree and deepened the valleys. The smaller side valleys were left stranded and hanging, so that today their streams spill spectacularly over the steep walls of the main valley. These waterfalls (or forces), such as Sour Milk Gill at Buttermere, Taylor Milk Gill at the head of Borrowdale or Aira Force near Ullswater, have a wild beauty that has drawn Lakeland travellers since Victorian times.

When the ice at last retreated, life began to return to the stark bare landscape. First came alpine and tundra vegetation, followed by a scattering of birch and pine, and then a luxuriant oak forest into which moved the elk, the bear, the wolf and all the classic fauna and flora of the north European woods – and finally man.

Stone and Bronze Age farmers began to

clear the great forest to pasture livestock and plant crops. Here and there they left mysterious stone henges and circles of unknown significance, like those at Castlerigg, east of Keswick, or at Swinside, near Black Combe, and Long Meg near Penrith. In due course, the native Celt was clobbered by the Romans and then by the Anglo-Saxons, and again by the Viking Norsemen, who came down the west coast from Scotland and Ireland, colonized Lakeland and left their language in many of the place names: dales (from *dalr*), fells (*fjall*), becks (*bekkr*), tarns (*tjorn*), force (*foss*, meaning waterfall), thwaite (meaning clearing or meadow) and how (meaning hill).

And so, as the centuries waxed and waned, the tumultuous landscape of the Lake District was settled according to the pattern of scattered farm and village we see today. The earliest fell walkers, the shepherd and sheep farmer, traversed every inch of the high fells and bestowed their vivid, home-made names upon every nook and cranny: Little Lad Crag and Pots of Ashness, Green Crag Gully and Dollywaggon Pike, Grike, Yoke and Starling Dodd, Beck Head and Windy Gap, White Napes and Green Gable, Base Brown and

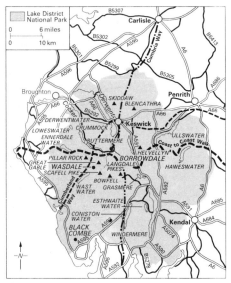

Tom Blue, Hell Gate Pillar and Eagle's Nest Ridge, Raise, Strands and Steeple.

Until the Romantic movement changed the public's perception of wild places, no one in their right senses ever went near the fells unless they had to. During the early years of the nineteenth century William Wordsworth and his circle of Lakeland poets helped to change all that. Besides immortalizing the Lakes in his poetry, Wordsworth also wrote one of the best Lakeland guidebooks, *Guide to the Lakes* (1835), which is still in print today. But it was Coleridge who was the first true recreational fell walker. His many hair-raising ascents pioneered a sport that was to blossom in Victorian times.

The great attraction of the Lakeland fells is that you don't have to be a mountaineer to get up them. The wild traveller will avoid the most popular peaks such as Scafell Pike, Helvellyn and Skiddaw at the height of the summer season, when you may have to wait your turn to get up to the final cairn. They are preferable in winter, especially on a clear day, when the snow is crisp and the sky is blue and with a bit of luck you can have the mountains to yourself. Scafell is a long, slow climb, but not a difficult one. Skiddaw is very easy. Helvellyn is the best of the 3,000-foot (915-metre) peaks, with the finest views and the steepest and most exciting summit; but in poor weather some caution is needed; there are more accidents on Helvellyn than on any other mountain in the Lake District.

The biggest and best known lakes are not ideal places to get away from the madding crowd. Windermere is essentially a summer playground, crowded both on land and water. The same can be said of Coniston Water, Derwentwater and Grasmere, which have busy roads alongside them and heavy tourist traffic in season. This is not to say that they are not immensely beautiful or that one cannot find some measure of peace and seclusion on the quieter sides of these lakes, away from the roads.

But perhaps the wild traveller should turn towards the remoter, less grand lakes such as lonely Haweswater, the most isolated of the lakes; or Wastwater, the gauntest and, at 250 feet (76 metres), the deepest; or Ennerdale, one of the least developed lakes and the only one with no road round it.

I walked to Ennerdale the day after I had slogged over the Buttermere Fells; a gentle, balmy day of complete peace and almost total solitude, as I recorded in my notebook:

'Warm, sunny day, with a wind from the sea. My walk along the edge of Ennerdale is like a stroll by the Med – soft lapping of waves, rich cover of plants, brown fritillaries fluttering, light, sun and sparkling water. On my left, the Buttermere Fells of yesterday. Ahead, Great Gable. On my right, the gaunt wild north face of Pillar, and the 600-foot (188-metre) vertical cliff of Pillar Rock – the Cumbrian Eiger, the tallest vertical crag in England.

'Over a stone bridge and across a wide greensward to the southern side of the lake. See a pied wagtail on a nest deep inside a chink in a dry-stone wall. Almost tread on a male wheatear in the hummocky grass. Why did it wait so long before flying off? A hole in the stones revealed no nest – a cobweb across the entrance precluded that.

'The river is dead – no reeds, no fish, no birds. This is because the water, fed straight from the hard rock of Great Gable, is so pure that it contains insufficient nutrients to sustain animal life. The conifer forest is dead, too – too dark for anything much to grow under the dense cover of the closely compact trees, except where they have cut some of the trees down and suddenly let in the light. Round the stump of one felled conifer I saw an extraordinary explosion of vegetable life – an exquisitely beautiful giant tussock of mosses – emerald, leaf green, black and gold – and foxgloves and rushes and sycamore seedlings and tiny pine saplings all springing in a sudden *feu de joie* out of the very stump itself.

'5pm: sky clouding up and signs of rain.'

In fact, Ennerdale is not entirely lifeless. It boasts a unique freshwater shrimp by the name of *Mysis relicta*, trapped here since the Ice Age but rarely seen since it feeds at night and spends the day deep in the lake. Other glacial relicts in the Cumbrian lakes include whitefish and char, a deepwater trout living in Windermere and other deep lakes. A very rare fish called a schelly, like a freshwater herring, swims in shoals in Ullswater, Haweswater, and Red Tarn on Helvellyn; and another rare fish, the vendace, like a schelly with a pointed head, is found in Bassenthwaite Lake and Derwentwater and nowhere else.

From seashore to mountain top, Lakeland offers an unparalleled wealth and variety of wildlife: sparrowhawk, redstart, red squirrel, and pine marten in the woods; peregrine, raven and golden eagle over the moors and mountains; alpine plants on the mountain tops; meadow and woodland flowers in the gentler, more luxuriant environment of the dales; terns, toads and sea lavender in the dune landscape at the edge of the Irish Sea. Winter is the best time for birds on the lakes: gulls, ducks, various grebes and divers, and – pride and joy of the Lakeland birds – the wonderful wild whooper swan.

BEFORE YOU GO
Maps: OS Landranger Series Map Nos. 85, 86, 89, 90, 91, 96, 97.
Guidebook: the Countryside Commision's official description, *The Lake District National Park* by John Wyatt (Webb & Bower). For books and maps call at Brockhole, the park visitor centre, 2 miles (3km) south of Ambleside on the A591 (T:096 62 2231), and pick up a copy of the *Lake District Guardian* for details of guided walks and park service events.

GETTING THERE
By car: the M6 passes just east of the park, providing easy access from the Midlands and South. For Kendal and the southern lakes take exits 36 or 37; for Keswick and the North, take exit 40. From Scotland, the A74 and A7 – from Glasgow and Edinburgh respectively – join the M6 at Carlisle. Motorists from the East have a slower drive across the Pennines, approaching on the A69 from Newcastle-upon-Tyne or the A66 from Darlington.
By train: mainline trains between London (Euston) and Scotland stop at Oxenholme, Penrith and Carlisle. From Oxenholme a branch line connects to Windermere. From Carlisle change for the

splendid West Cumbrian Line to Barrow-in-Furness, with stops including St Bee's, Whitehaven and Ravenglass. **By bus:** National Express operates daily services from London, Birmingham and Manchester to Whitehaven via Windermere, Ambleside and Keswick. Otherwise, Carlisle, Penrith and Kendal are principal stops for long-distance buses.

WHERE TO STAY
Bowness, Windermere, Keswick and Ambleside are the principal overnight centres, but all grades of accommodation are available throughout the park. All information centres provide details, and most offer a telephone reservation service. **Outdoor living:** dozens of campsites of varying standards are listed in an inexpensive leaflet, *Sites for Touring Caravans and Tents*, available from visitor information centres or by post from the park service. The NT operates 3 tent sites, at Great Langdale and Low Wray Farm near Ambleside and at Wasdale Head near Seascale. It also runs caravan and motor home sites at Sedgwick (T:0448 60186) and Newby Bridge (T:0448 31273). **Youth hostels:** there are youth hostels in all the park's towns and principal villages, as well as several that are very remote. For *Youth Hostels in Lakeland*, a free leaflet, contact YHA Area Office, Elleray, Windermere, Cumbria LA23 1AW, T:096 62 2301/2.

ACTIVITIES
Walking: there are two long walks within the area. The Cumberland Way is an unstrenuous 80-mile (128-km) low-level walk through the Lake District from the Irish

---

Sea to Appleby. OS Landranger Series Map Nos. 89, 90, 91, 96. See *The Cumberland Way* by Paul Hannon (Hillside Publications). The Cumbria Way is a 70-mile (112-km) low-level walk running south to north through splendid scenery in the national park from Ulverston to Caldbeck or Carlisle via Coniston Water, Borrowdale, Derwentwater and High Pike. OS Landranger Series Map Nos. 97, 90 and 85. See *The Cumbria Way* by John Trevelyan (Dalesman 1981). THE COAST TO COAST WALK (see p.89) starts in Lakeland at St Bee's Head.

The park service publishes an excellent and inexpensive series of walking leaflets, available from park information centres or by post from the park office in Windermere. They also run an extensive series of short guided walks; full details are included in the *Lake District Guardian.*

Riding and pony trekking: especially on the lower falls, pony trekking is popular; the solitude and excitement of the high country is also accessible to experienced riders. For enquiries about bridle paths and riding conditions in the Lakes, contact the Secretary, Cumbria Bridleways Society,

2 Compston Villas, Ambleside, T:0966 33188. **Climbing:** many areas provide suitable rock faces, although Wasdale, Langdale and Borrowdale are the most popular. Experienced climbers should contact one of the following climbing shops for advice about routes and local clubs: George Fisher of Lake Road, Keswick (T:0596 72178) or Frank Davies of The Climber's Shop, Compston Road, Ambleside, (T:0966 32297).

FURTHER INFORMATION
In addition to the official park information centres mentioned above, there are Cumbria Tourist Board information centres in Ambleside, Cockermouth, Kendal, Keswick, Penrith, Ravenglass, Whitehaven and Windermere. The CTB's main office is in Ashleigh, Windermere, Cumbria LA23 2AQ, T:096 62 4444. For information about NT land in the Lake District contact the National Trust, Rothay Holme, Rothay Road, Ambleside, Cumbria LA22 0EJ, T:0966 33883.

The three peaks rising above Wasdale Head at the north end of Wastwater in the Lake District are (from left to right) Yew Barrow, Great Gable and Lingmell

THE NORTH-WEST COAST

Between the Solway Firth, which separates the north English coast from the Scottish coast, and the River Dee, which separates it from the Welsh coast, stretches a shoreline of swirling mud and sand. Amid the great tidal flats and shifting dunes lie the popular resorts of Blackpool and Morecambe, old industrial centres such as Workington and Whitehaven, sprawling ports and docklands such as Liverpool, and the nuclear power station at Sellafield.

Not promising stuff for the wild traveller, you might think; an endless string of coloured light bulbs, belching steam, atomic leaks and derelict jetties. Not so, however. Some of the most important wildlife habitats in north-west England lie along this coast, as well as some of the finest wild seascapes. The Lake District coast of Cumbria between St Bee's Head and Haverigg can be as fine as anywhere, and the enormous estuarine mud flats and salt marshes of Morecambe Bay and the Rivers Wyre and Ribble in Lancashire and Dee in Cheshire provide internationally important feeding grounds for huge flocks of wildfowl and waders. The most important sites on this coastline are given here in south to north order.

Gayton Sands

RSPB Reserve

The tide has long since ceased to wash against the red stone sea wall at Gayton Sands on the Cheshire side of the Dee Estuary. A vast expanse of estuarine plants – see club rush, common reed, sea milkwort and sea arrowgrass – seems to stretch unbroken to the Welsh shore.

This ocean of vegetation, together with the mud flats beyond, is one of Britain's richest feeding grounds for wintering waterfowl. Pintail and shelduck, along with oystercatcher, grey plover, knot, bar-tailed godwit, redshank and dunlin are among the many species to be observed here.

The outsider is advised to wait for storms or spring tides

84

when these birds are driven close to shore. The salt marsh is deeply scored with muddy tidal creeks, making the going difficult and at times dangerous.
Getting there: turn off A540 road on to B5135 (Boathouse Lane) to park gate. Turn right at Boathouse Restaurant for reserve car park. **Further information:** the Warden (Colin Wells), Marsh Cottage, Denhall Lane, Burton, Wirral, Merseyside L64 0FC.

Hilbre

Wirral Borough Council Bird Sanctuary

Like most islands once favoured by medieval monks, Hilbre and its two companions

in the Dee Estuary, Little Hilbre and Little Eye, are now a sanctuary for thousands of waders and seabirds such as oystercatcher, ringed plover, grey plover, knot, sanderling, purple sandpiper, dunlin and turnstone.

Autumn and spring bring vast numbers of migrants; the Hilbre Bird Observatory, which rings over 1,000 birds annually, has recorded more than 200 species. Hilbre is frequently visited by grey seals and, at low tide, by foxes.
Getting there: at low tide, the islands are a short walk across rocks and sand from West Kirby. To be safe, set out at least 3½ hours before high tide, when they get cut off, and follow the route in the official leaflet. **Access:** permit only. Apply to Department of Leisure Services and Tourism, Concourse, West Kirby, Wirral, Merseyside. **Further information:** leaflet from Wirral Borough Council.

Ainsdale Sand Dunes

NCC Reserve

The coastal dunes of Ainsdale appeared over three or four centuries, and could easily disappear at the same rate; efforts are continually being made to preserve this volatile environment. Particularly vulnerable to change are the 'slacks', the damp depressions between dunes that harbour an important number of plant and animal species, among them the rare natterjack toad.

The dunes themselves are loosely anchored with marram grass and a variety of other plants, including common stork's bill, lesser hawkbit, biting stonecrop, sand sedge and restharrow; rarities include dune and pendulous helleborine.

The pinewoods were planted in the 1920s to stop sand blowing on to the nearby railway. Natural or not, they are a valuable habitat for the embattled red squirrel.

Getting there: from A565 2 miles (3km) north of Formby, take the coastal road to Ainsdale-on-Sea. Reserve is to the left beyond railway line. **Access:** restricted to official footpaths. **Further information:** leaflet from NCC.

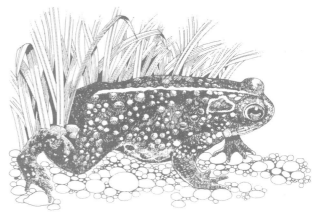

The natterjack toad, Britain's most endangered amphibian, still thrives in the Ravenglass Dunes on the Cumbrian coast

Ribble Marshes

NCC Reserve

Like so many areas beloved of seabirds, the salt marshes and mud flats that flank the mouth of the River Ribble are singularly unfriendly to man. Greenmarsh, a rough plain of salt-marsh grass scored by deep muddy gutters, gives way to featureless mud flats and imperceptibly, to the sea.

This is the wintering ground for 15 to 20,000 widgeon and pink-footed goose, pintail and teal. Waders arrive in even greater numbers during the autumn migration: 50 to 80,000 knot, dunlin, bar-tailed godwit, oystercatcher and redshank, many of which remain for the winter.

Getting there: from coastal road (Marine Drive) off A565 north of Southport, or footpath along sea wall from Crossens pumping station near Banks. **Access:** free to all areas except marked sanctuary zone. Stay off mud and out of gutters unless you are a wader. Beware high tides. **Further information:** leaflet from NCC.

Morecambe Bay

Includes RSPB Reserve

Anyone travelling from Lancaster to the Lake District before the coming of the railway would have set off at low tide, on foot or by stage coach, across the sands at Hest Bank. The turnpike, though safer, added several miles to the trip.

Today this wide and treacherous highway is the undisputed domain of Morecambe Bay's most numerous pedestrian, the wader; indeed, these 120 square miles (310sq km) of tidal mud and sand form the largest and most important area for winter waders in Britain. Huge flocks of bar-tailed godwit, knot, oystercatcher, turnstone, dunlin, redshank and curlew feed on the living sands, roosting at high tide on the coastal salt marshes where greylag geese and widgeon graze.

These marshes, furrowed by muddy channels, are the breeding grounds for meadow pipit, skylark, wheatear, lapwing, oystercatcher and redshank. Even non-bird-watchers, to whom a wader is no more than a long boot, can marvel at the way a few dozen strides from the illuminations and performing dolphins of Morecambe Marineland bring one to a wilderness of sand and water.

Getting there: accessible from many points on Lancashire and Cumbria coast. **Access:** do not venture across the sands unguided. 'Those who do, don't come back,' says the official 'sand pilot' Cedric Robinson. He conducts fortnightly weekend excursions from Hest Bank, May–Sep (T:044 84 2165).

Leighton Moss

RSPB Reserve

A potent combination of shallow meres, reed beds, marsh and woodland brings together a veritable Who's Who of British wildlife in the limited confines of Leighton Moss, near Morecambe Bay. Chief among the celebrities are the dozen or so pairs of

85

breeding bittern, the recently-established bearded tit, the water rail, garganey and gadwall. Pochard, teal, shoveler and a large community of mallard also nest here.

In winter, the reserve is a haven for finches, starlings and huge flocks of wildfowl, while migrants may include osprey, goshawk, merlin and harrier, black tern, whimbrel, bar-tailed godwit and ruff. Both red and roe deer may be found here and otters thrive in eel-rich waters. The wide variety of plant life harbours 24 species of butterfly and more than 300 types of moth. **Getting there:** from A6 via Yealand Redmayne. The reserve is just east of Silverdale. **Access:** Open 9am–9pm (or sunset) every day except Tuesday. Charge for non-members. **Facilities:** car park, visitor centre, 5 bird hides. Public bird hide on causeway off Yealand Redmayne–Silverdale road always open. **Further information:** leaflet from RSPB, or contact the Warden (J. Wilson), Myers Farm, Silverdale, Carnforth LA5 0SW.

Gait Barrows

NCC Reserve

One of the finest areas of limestone pavement in Britain has been preserved within Gait Barrows. The flat, unbroken sheet of stone that covered the ground after the last Ice Age is now fissured, fragmented and grooved. This is the work of water, not man, but the unscientific eye might be excused for seeing here, and in many other parts of the Yorkshire Dales and the North

Pennines, the shattered city pavement of some long-destroyed civilization (see also Asby Scar page 77).

Where there is enough soil between the limestone slabs, or 'clints' as they are known, a wealth of plant life has appeared. Stunted trees, mainly ash, yew and hazel, find just enough root space to survive, but it is the flowers, ferns and small woodland plants that truly flourish in these 'grykes': lily of the valley, herb Robert, biting stonecrop, tutsan, shield fern and the unusual angular Solomon's seal and rigid buckler fern. **Getting there:** via unclassified road between Beetham on A6 and Silverdale. **Access:** permit only off the 2 rights of way. Reserve closed except for rights of way 8 days each winter for shooting. **Further information:** leaflet from NCC or Warden, Orchard Cottage, Waterslack, Silverdale, Carnforth, Lancashire LA5 0UH.

Roundsea Wood and Mosses

NCC Reserve

The reserve consists of two distinct habitats, the wood and the mosses. Roundsea Wood is situated in the main area, surrounded on three sides by a final meander of the River Leven as it carries the waters of Lake Windermere into Morecambe Bay.

The wood encompasses two low ridges, each with its own distinct eco-system. The slate-based west ridge encourages plants that thrive on acidic soil: rowan, hazel and birch among sessile oaks, with hair

grass and bracken on the forest floor. The limestone east ridge supports ash and oak, wild cherry, lime and yew, above a carpet of lime-loving flowering plants: lily of the valley, early purple orchid, bird's-nest orchid, giant bellflower, columbine and false brome.

To the east of the reserve are the mosses, some partly drained by peat cutting and now overgrown with birch, rowan and Scots pine; others still undisturbed beneath primeval carpets of sphagnum moss. The mosses are particularly favourable habitats for moths and butterflies, including the large heath butterfly and clouded ermine moth.

Ellerside Moss, though part of the same reserve, is nearly a mile south-east of the Roundsea Wood area. **Getting there:** take B5278 south from A590 through Haverthwaite village and turn right immediately after bridge over River Leven. **Access:** one right of way; for other paths a permit is required. Apply to NCC, North West Region, Windermere. Reserve is closed to permit holders a few days each year during deer hunting season. **Further information:** leaflet from NCC, or apply to the Warden (Peter Singleton), 39 Allithwaite Road, Flookburgh, Grange-over-Sands, Cumbria, T:044 853 588.

Walney Island

North and South Walney CTNC Reserves

Although Barrow-in-Furness has long since spilled across the Walney Channel to

The Pennine Way and a dry-stone wall follow the contours of the moorland below Pen-y-Ghent, a grand natural belvedere for the Yorkshire Dales

colonize the centre of Walney Island, the extreme ends of this sandy strip 10 miles (16km) long by 1 mile (1.5km) wide have so far been left to nature. The dune slacks of North Walney are home to the natterjack toad, one of Britain's rarest amphibians.

But the noise and excitement is all in the south, where vast numbers of herring gull and lesser black-backed gull wheel and squabble above their nesting sites on the dunes. An estimated 40,000 pairs breed in South Walney. Rich pickings from the corporation dump supplement the food they glean from the sea and beaches.

Other birds managing to breed alongside the overbearing gulls include lapwing, mallard, shelduck, oystercatcher, common tern, little tern and the west coast's southernmost colony of eider. In autumn and winter Walney becomes home to dunlin and oystercatcher, turnstone, knot, teal and widgeon.

In the varied terrain of North Walney, over 300 species of plant have been recorded, ranging from sundew and marsh cinquefoil in the marshy heath to lady's bedstraw, wild pansy and the 'Walney geranium' in the dunes. In the southern reserve henbane, viper's bugloss, mullein and yellow horned poppy are a particular attraction to moths and butterflies.
Getting there: cross bridge from Barrow-in-Furness, turn

left on the Promenade for South Walney, right for North Walney. **Where to stay:** some accommodation for rent on South Walney Reserve. Contact Warden. **Access:** open all year; small admission charge at South Walney. **Facilities:** 2 nature trails and 4 bird hides in South Walney. **Further information:** South Walney guide from CTNC or contact the Warden, Coastguard Cottages, South Walney, Barrow-in-Furness, Cumbria.

Ravenglass Dunes

Cumbria County Council Nature Reserve

The full title of this reserve – Ravenglass Dunes and Gullery – is now a sad irony, for although the dunes are still a distinguishing feature, the gullery is not. In 1985 the birds decided that the level of radioactive pollution from nearby Sellafield had reached unacceptable levels, and the huge colony of black-headed gull and the four species of breeding tern – Sandwich, common, arctic and little – all departed.

This is not to say that Drigg Dunes are dead, only much quieter than before. Plover, oystercatcher, shelduck, red-breasted merganser, wheatear and skylark still nest here. Growing on the dunes themselves are bloody crane's-bill, carline thistle and field gentian, while the ponds and slacks harbour all 6 British amphibians.

Getting there: by lane from village of Drigg, 1½ miles (2km) south-east of Seascale on B5344. Drigg is a station on the West Cumbrian Line. **Access:** by permit only. Apply Director of Property Services, 15 Portland Square, Carlisle CA1 1QQ. **Further information:** from Warden, Middle House, The Square, Holmrook, Cumbria.

The Pennine Way

The north of England is upland England. From Derbyshire to the Scottish border the Pennines run through the middle of the North Country like a 150-mile (240-km) spine. Here can be found some of the highest, wildest and most ruggedly beautiful landscape in England.

A lone, gruelling but rewarding footpath called the Pennine Way traverses almost the entire length of the chain. Although at least one guide has been written describing the route from north to south, for most walkers the Pennine Way begins at Edale on the high moors of the Peak District and ends at Kirk Yetholm, just over the Scottish border. This allows you to walk with the sun and prevailing wind at your back for most of the way; 250 miles (400km) as the boot plods.

It must be assumed that anyone walking the entire Pennine Way will be in reasonably good shape and properly equipped; prepared, that is, for long hauls in cold, uncomfortable weather over steep and rough terrain. Someone in the party must also be a reliable navigator, able to take compass bearing and fold maps in driving rain.

The toughest stretch comes near the start, over the squelchy North Peak moors between Kinder and Standedge; it is not to be taken lightly by beginners. By the time you reach the 750-ft (229-m) BBC transmitting tower at Holme Moss near Black Hill, which sticks out like a whaler's harpoon through a Leviathan's head, the least inspiring parts of the walk are over. Ahead lie the dryer, brighter beauties of the Dales, the rugged eminence of Hadrian's Wall and the long trek over the Cheviots into Scotland.

Before you go: OS Landranger Series Map Nos. 3, 74, 80, 86, 91, 98, 109, 110. These 8 maps are indispensable, and will help you to find a Pennine Way, but not necessarily *the* Pennine Way, as the precise route in some areas is nearly impossible to read, lost in a tangle of footpaths, contour lines and other topographical symbols. The larger scale OS Leisure Series shows the route more clearly, but covers only a fraction of its distance. From south to north the relevant sheets are: No. 1, The Dark Peak Area; No. 21, South Pennines (highly recommended); and Nos. 2, 10 and 30 for the Yorkshire Dales. Even the best maps cannot give the sort of detail you may need along the way, so a guidebook is useful. The perfect guide has not been written; all vary in quality of illustration, information, prose style and size. Go to a good bookshop and choose the one that is best for your needs. None are available in waterproof editions. **Getting there:** Not everyone wishes to walk the entire distance. A number of towns and villages on or near the route allow one to join the Pennine Way or escape from it at convenient points:

Edale, Derbyshire: trains from Manchester and Sheffield.

Marsden, West Yorkshire: A62; buses from Huddersfield and Manchester; trains from Leeds.

Todmorden, West Yorkshire: A646; buses from Burnley and Halifax; trains from Manchester.

Hebden Bridge, West Yorkshire: A646; buses from Burnley and Halifax; trains from Leeds or Bradford.

Cowling, North Yorkshire: A6068; buses from Keighley and Burnley.

Thornton, North Yorkshire: A56; buses from Burnley and Keighley.

Gargrave, West Yorkshire: A65; buses from Skipton and Settle; trains from Leeds.

Malham, North Yorkshire: buses from Skipton and Settle.

Horton-in-Ribblesdale, North Yorkshire: B6479; buses from Settle.

Hawes, North Yorkshire: A684; buses from Kendal and Leyburn.

Middleton in Teesdale, Durham: B6277; buses from Barnard Castle.

Alston, Cumbria: A686/689; buses from Penrith and Carlisle.

Haltwhistle, Northumberland: A69; buses and trains from Carlisle and Newcastle.

Bellingham, Northumberland: B6320; buses from Hexham.

Byrness, Northumberland: A68; buses from Newcastle and Edinburgh.

Kirk Yetholm, Borders: B6401; buses from Kelso.

Where to stay: accommodation is not a problem along the route, but in peak periods it pays to make reservations ahead, especially in the national parks. The *Pennine Way Accommodation and Camping Guide* is published by the Pennine Way Council and available from youth hostels and bookshops along the route or from the Secretary, (C. Sainty), 29 Springfield Park Ave, Chelmsford, Essex CM2 6EL. The Ramblers' Association annual guide also gives details of many useful bed and breakfast establishments. Youth hostels: there are 18 along the way, allowing you to walk the route at low cost and in short stages, except for the last – 27 miles (43km) over the Cheviots from Byrness to Kirk Yetholm. Planning hostelling along the Pennine Way is simplified with the Pennine Way Central Booking Service's free information pack; send a 6×9in (15×23cm) stamped addressed envelope to YHA Area Office, 96 Main Street, Bingley, West Yorkshire BD16 2JH, T:0274 567697.

Camping: carrying a tent allows greater freedom in route planning; the price is extra weight and discomfort. There are many campsites along the way, and a number of youth hostels allow members with tents to use their facilities at half price.

The Coast to Coast Walk

↖↖↖

This long-distance path, running right across the north of England from St Bee's Head to Robin Hood's Bay, was pioneered by the veteran walker Alfred Wainwright. It is 190 miles (304km) long and crosses three national parks: the Lake District, Yorkshire Dales and North York Moors. The walk has a truly satisfying beginning and end, in whichever direction you choose to walk.

This is not an 'official' Countryside Commission route, marked by expensive signposts. In places the way will be difficult and even obstructed; it is, in fact, more an idea for a route than a path to be followed step-by-step. **Before you go:** Wainwright gives a blow-by-blow description of the route in his genially-written and beautifully-designed book *A Coast-to-Coast Walk* (Westmorland Gazette 1972). The relevant maps are the OS Landranger Series Map Nos. 89, 90, 91, 92, 93, 94, 98 and 99. **Where to stay:** beds are scarce along some parts of the route, so get information in advance from the YHA or relevant National Park information services (see separate entries).

CAUTION TO WALKERS

The Pennines are among the wettest and windiest parts of Britain. High and treeless, they can subject a walker to what seem like winter conditions in mid-July. The problem is compounded by tussock grass and peat bog underfoot, a tiring terrain when you are battling with the elements.

For this reason, make yourself familiar with escape routes to towns or sheltered valleys before setting out along a difficult stage. You gain nothing by sticking to the high path in bad conditions and can often find a pleasant alternative at a lower level. The path has a number of official alternative routes, which are well worth considering if the weather is uncertain.

Parts of the way that may need particular attention in bad weather are, from south to north:

Kinder Scout, Derbyshire: high, boggy land criss-crossed with confusing gullies or 'groughs'. Consider official alternative.

Bleaklow, Derbyshire: easy to stray off course.

Black Hill, Derbyshire: avoid high route with its boggy terrain.

Birkdale to High Cup Nick, Durham: route finding can be confusing for these 4 miles (7 km).

Cross Fell, Cumbria: flat, featureless summit. Prepare to use compass.

Cheviots, Northumberland: long rugged stage. Plan escape routes in advance.

CHAPTER 4

North-East England

I first came to the north-east by sea, putting out of Grimsby through the fierce tide race of the Humber Estuary for the long haul to the Pentland Firth and the waters of the North Atlantic. The first patch of terra firma I set foot on was the wild and windblown sand and pebble spit of Spurn Head. It was not a tremendously satisfactory landfall. The Spurn peninsula is a nature reserve run by the Yorkshire Naturalists' Trust, an organization as resolute and worthy as its county cricket counterpart. Then, as now, you needed a permit to visit the seaward tip of the reserve. I had barely moved the length of a fast bowler's run-up over the low and stony ground when a kind of binoculared nature policeman sprang up from behind a buckthorn thicket.

What was I doing here? he asked. Had I made prior arrangements? Where were my credentials? Sadly, reprehensibly, I had none. In vain I protested my bona fide interest in the wildlife and good works of the reserve. Did I realize, the official enquired, that a clumsy size 11 Wellington boot like mine could crush a whole clutch of eggs in a shallow tern scrape in the pebbles? The terns that screamed about my head joined in the remonstrations. Like an illegal immigrant I was escorted back to the sea. Next time make prior arrangements, I was told. Permit only means permit only.

From the huge chalk arrowhead promontory of Flamborough Head to Redcar the boat butted the sea beneath

The vast stretches of sand at Bamburgh are typical of a shoreline that varies little along many miles of Northumbrian coast, one of the longest dune systems in England

some of the highest cliffs in England. For most of their length these soaring battlements form the eastern boundary of the North York Moors National Park, whose rolling hills and heather-covered plateaux stretch mile after mile westward into the northern English interior. Here and there, in a chink in these coastal ramparts, a fishing village has gained a footing, sometimes a precarious one. At the old smuggling haunt of Robin Hood's Bay the cliffs were being eaten away so fast you could almost see them eroding. At some of the cliff-top dwellings you could absent-mindedly put the cat out by the kitchen door and it would free fall to a four point landing on the rocks several hundred feet below. At one house I saw the morning milk bottle on the doorstep, but the step itself hung over an airy void, with nothing beneath it but the beach far below. A great sea wall now protects Robin Hood's Bay from further disintegration, but it is still a spectacularly atmospheric place.

Far to the north, beyond the sprawling industrial seascape of Tees-mouth and Tyneside, the coast under-goes a complete change. Between Amble and Berwick in Northumber-land stretches one of the longest dune systems in Britain. On a great knoll of volcanic rock lies the soaring edifice of the great restored medieval castle of Bamburgh.

It was here that I most recently set foot on Northumberland. It was midsummer night. Above the crescent of the sea horizon a false sunset glowed a dull red in the north-east. As black clouds gathered across the darkening sky I collected driftwood from the tide wrack and with two friends made a great campfire in a sheltered hollow in the dunes.

In every lover of wild places there

beats the restless and anarchic heart of a nomad. In every wild traveller, as in every prisoner, there lies the urge to break out of the confining bonds, actual or metaphorical, of four walls. In those flickering, firelit dunes there were no walls, no roof, no burden of possessions, no agents of bureaucracy yelping like a guard dog at one's heel: only the roar of the distant surf, the occasional splinter of raindrops in the flames, the fitful wind stirring the shadows on the sand, and a deeply satisfying, if briefly won, sense of fellowship and freedom.

'Happy summer solstice!' we mumbled as we raised a toast (in Bulgarian red) at midnight.

There is a village at Bamburgh, a golf course, and a fishing port and small resort called Seahouses just down the road. It is therefore not wild in the sense of being far from the haunts of man. But on the brink of that wildest of wild places, the sea, this coast can at certain times of mood or weather assume the wilder aspect of some far-flung *terra incognita*. Like Lindisfarne bay in midwinter, with a knifing wind and lowering sky, when wildfowl and waders in their thousands settle over the vast mud flats to feed at low tide, and there is not a soul in his senses to be seen. Or like the great desert beach of Goswick Sands under an unclouded late June sun. Look north from the dunes of the Snook and the world seems reduced, like some ultimate expression of abstract art, to its simplest residual parts: cobalt blue sky, ochre yellow sand, and nothing else at all.

Or like the Farne Islands on a morning of mist and rain. Only two miles or so separate these bird rocks from the fish and chips and naughty plastic souvenirs of Seahouses, but those two miles are like a time warp in deep space; after a quarter of an hour at sea you reach an outpost of the primordial era. On the rocky skyline of these cracked dolerite crags, cormorants stand motionless, with wings outstretched like pterodactyls. Creatures with rudimentary animal shapes – inflated bags fitted with eyes and fins – bask on the jagged rocks or float vertically with only their soft humanoid eyes peering above the waves.

In higgledy-piggledy chaos, living embodiments of Darwinism crowd together in messy, intimate and unembarrassed squalor in the fantastic bird tenements of Scale Island. A row of sulking guillemots sit wing to wing on a narrow rock ledge with their backs to the world: from the throat of one of them protrudes the rear end of a wriggling sprat. A green shag rising from its mountainous nest of seaweed and ordure defecates spectacularly over a black-headed gull standing four feet behind it. Puffins, fulmars, kittiwakes, shags and gulls alight and take off, swoop and dive, preen and poke about, sleep, stand and stalk about in a dizzying confusion of random movement. Over the yellow-lichened, white guano-caked rocks a handful of human visitors, reduced by the elemental environment to basic primate status, shuffle gingerly over the slippery, fissured rocks.

Until recently I had never ventured away from the coast into the Northumbrian interior, one of the least populated areas in England. The Cheviot Hills form the northern mass of the Northumberland National Park, and Hadrian's Wall its southern perimeter. A footpath undulates along the top of the wall, emerging to westward from a wood of oaks.

From this wood I saw a lone figure,

Ralph's Cross, emblem of the North York Moors National Park is also know as Young Ralph to distinguish it from an even more ancient neighbour (see p.96)

bowed under a heavy backpack, striding towards me amid the screeching of hundreds of roosting starlings. He was a Yorkshireman with a bushy Edwardian moustache and legs knotted from miles of thumping turf and rocky tracks.

'Where the bloody hell's this?' he asked me in his Yorkshire voice as he drew near.

I told him: 'Vercovicium Fort on the Roman Wall.'

'Bloody hell, is it?' he replied, 'I'm supposed to be on't Pennine Way. I don't suppose there's anywhere round here I can get a cup of tea, is there?' There wasn't, and he wearily turned the way he had come and with a sad 'ta ra' thumped back the way he had come and vanished like some lost legionary amongst the trees and the screeching birds, his knotty legs bearing him over the Cheviots towards the heather and haggis at journey's end beyond the Scottish border.

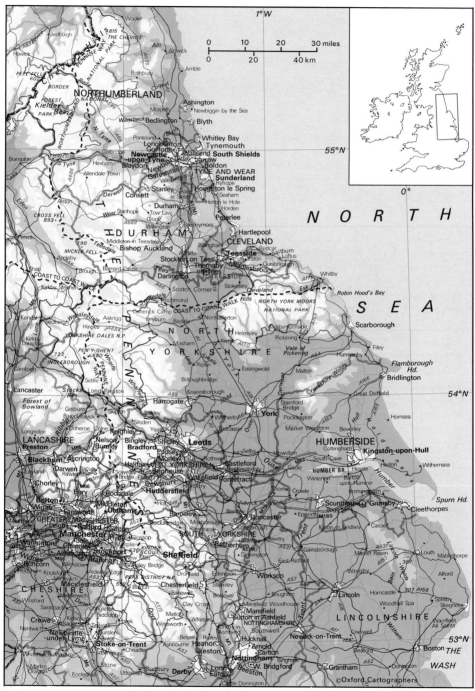

©Oxford Cartographers

BEFORE YOU GO

BEFORE YOU GO

For Cleveland, Durham, Northumberland and Tyne and Wear, contact the Northumbria Tourist Board, Aykley Heads, Durham DH1 5UD, T:091 384 6905. The remainder of the area is covered by the Yorkshire and Humberside Tourist Board, 312 Tadcaster Road, York YO2 2HF, T:0904 707961.

GETTING THERE

By air: Newcastle airport provides the nearest access to Northumberland National Park; Teesside Airport, near Darlington, serves Durham and North Yorkshire. There are regular flights from Amsterdam and Scandinavia, as well as from many points within the British Isles.
By sea: there are daily crossings from Rotterdam and Zeebrugge to Hull by North Sea Ferries. Norway Lines from Stavanger and Bergen and DFDS from Göteborg and Esbjerg sail to Newcastle.
By train: high-speed trains operate between London and Edinburgh, with stops at York, Darlington and Newcastle-upon-Tyne. From York connect via Birmingham for the South-West. The trans-Pennine Tyne Valley line links Newcastle-upon-Tyne with Carlisle and the North-West.
By bus: Newcastle-upon-Tyne, Darlington, York and Hull are principal stops on the National Express network.

WHERE TO STAY

Visitors will have little problem finding accommodation in and around the national parks. For other areas, the Northumbrian Tourist Board's *Official Guide* and the Yorkshire and Humberside Tourist Board's *Holiday Guide* provide useful lists of places to stay, from hotels to campsites. These publications also include full lists of Tourist Information Centres, all of which have details of local accommodation; many offer a telephone book-a-bed-ahead service, enabling you to reserve your next night's accommodation.

For information about youth hostels, contact YHA Area Office, Bowey House, William Street, South Gosforth, Newcastle-upon-Tyne NE3 1SA or YHA Area Office, 96 Main Street, Bingley, West Yorkshire BO16 2JH.

ACTIVITIES

The North-East offers superb and often remote expanses of moorland and hills. See the separate national park entries for further information, or contact the Ramblers' Association for the addresses of area offices, which can provide detailed regional information.
Other facilities: both regional tourist boards prepare fact sheets giving addresses of centres which organize activity holidays and vacation packages. For the addresses of organizations specializing in outdoor activities – pony trekking, cycling, climbing etc. – contact the Sports Council, Northern Region, Aykley Heads, Durham DH1 5UU, T:091 384 9595, or the Sports Council, Yorkshire and Humberside Region, Coronet House, Queen Street, Leeds, LS1 4PW, T:0532 436443.

North York Moors National Park

Note: North *York*, never North Yorkshire, Moors

Upland moors, hills, dales, woodland and coast covering 553 square miles (1,432sq km) of north-east Yorkshire

The North York Moors are one of the classic paradoxes of the wild countryside in Britain today. Their heather-clad plateaux and smoothly contoured hills and dales are loved by many, and fiercely defended by conservationists; yet this landscape is essentially a man-made one.

Bronze Age settlers hacked down the prehistoric forest of oak, elm, lime and yew that once covered the North York Moors, just as the Brazilian pioneers are laying waste the Amazonian rain forest today. With the tree cover gone, the heather that now covers 40 per cent of the park took over. This is the largest and finest stretch of heather moor in England and much loved as such by the 10 million visitors who come here each year.

Few national parks are more easily defined by their physical boundaries than this one, a compact upland which stands on its own above the surrounding lowlands and the sea. Its eastern and north-eastern boundary is marked by 25 miles (40 kilometres) of magnificent North Sea coastline between

Saltburn-by-the-Sea and Scalby Ness, Scarborough. The wild and rolling heather-clad Cleveland Hills, reaching 1,489 feet (454 metres) above sea level at Botton Head, form the natural ramparts of the northern boundary, looking across to the distant Cheviots. The steep scarp of the Hambleton Hills, rising up to 1,000 feet (305 metres), presents a distinctive physical frontier in the west. Along the southern boundary, the narrow limestone belt of the flat-topped Tabular Hills rises gently from the Vale of York, then drops away abruptly in a steep north-facing escarpment that yields impressive 'sudden views' over the moors and dales of the park interior.

It is from the high ground of this grand interior, along the main east–west watershed of the moors, that the main rivers drain. To the north a few short streams plunge down small, deep dales to the River Esk; to the south a series of longer tributaries drain off the central moors along the larger valleys of Bilsdale, Bransdale, Farndale, Rosedale and Newtondale, cutting deep narrow valleys through the limestone scarp of the Tabular Hills before flowing into the river system of the Derwent. It is a country of great scenic variety: wild moors and moorland bogs, pastoral dales, native woods, conifer forests, clear-flowing rivers and a coastline of soaring cliffs fronting the broad and restless waters of the North Sea.

The main attraction of the North York Moors is the sheer quantity of open space they provide. You can walk some 40 miles (64 kilometres) from one side to the other without obstruction from natural barriers or concentrations of humanity. There are over 1,000 miles (1,600 kilometres) of footpaths and bridle paths in the park, and although 80 per cent of the land is privately owned, access is virtually unlimited provided you follow the public rights of way. You don't have to be a Himalayan expeditionary; the ground is level or at worst gently undulating and the springy turf helps put an extra bounce into every stride. In August and September the heather bursts into bloom, so that the moor walker strides through a purple froth of 3,000 million tiny

purple blossoms to each square mile, 120,000 million tiny blossoms for the whole 40-mile (64-kilometre) crossing.

A wide variety of walks have been evolved, long, short and middling, with wonderful vistas and a lot of sky and space. The official long-distance walk for the North York Moors is the Cleveland Way, which follows a U-shaped route from Helmsley, at the south-west corner of the park, north across the Hambleton Hills, then along the Cleveland Hills to Guisborough and the North Sea coast, where it turns south along the cliffs to Whitby, Scarborough and Filey.

The most popular long-distance walk is the Lyke Wake Walk, a 40-mile (64-kilometre) route across the spine of the Moors between Osmotherley and the western border of the park to Ravenscar on the coast. This walk, which takes its name from the old dialect verse Lyke Wake [corpse watch] Dirge, follows the trail of early settlers who buried their dead on the central moor.

There are a number of other ancient tracks over the moor, humbler affairs known as trods or causeways or panniermen's tracks, which were built in the Middle Ages by the local monasteries to enable pack ponies to carry goods across the moorland. The monasteries were also responsible for setting up stone crosses to guide travellers across the featureless moors. More than 30 still stand; the seventh-century Lilla Cross, near Ellerbeck Bridge on Fylingdales Moors, is probably the oldest Christian monument in northern England, while Ralph Cross, in the heart of the moor, has been adopted as the emblem of the park.

Wildlife is probably not what draws most visitors to the park, although the wild variety of habitats provides a home for a corresponding variety of flora and fauna. The heather and grass moor is varied with bracken, bell heather, crowberry, bilberry and cloudberry, bog myrtle, bog rosemary and other bog plants in the wet parts. This is the haunt of the red grouse – grouse shooting is a major source of livelihood on the moor – golden plover, curlew and meadow pipit, and predatory birds such as the merlin, a tiny falcon the size of a blackbird: the moor is its British stronghold.

The broad-leaved woods contain the greatest range of animal, bird and plant life: fox, badger, rabbit, red deer, roe and fallow, a few red squirrel, otter and stoat: carpets of bluebells (*Endymion nonscriptus*) and wood anemones, the archetypal species of the classic English woods. By contrast the limestone country in the south of the park is a botanist's hunting ground, where uncommon plants such as bird's eye primrose, globeflower, white bogbean and a variety of orchids make notable finds.

Of the ten nature reserves in the North York Moors, one is a National Nature Reserve (Forge Valley Woods in the extreme south-east corner of the park), eight are managed by the Yorkshire Naturalists' Trust and can be visited by permit only, while the ninth, in Farndale, is a local nature reserve which protects one of the most spectacular natural phenomena in the park, an immense colony of wild daffodils. Every spring they spread like a brilliant yellow prairie along the banks of the River Dove and its tributaries.

For many people the sea coast is the North York Moors' greatest glory. The eastern flank of the park is part of a spectacular seaboard of hard jurassic limestone rocks stretching from Flamborough Head to the Tees. In places these cliffs tower 600 feet (183 metres) above the sea; and Boulby Cliff, the second highest sea cliff in England, is 700 feet (213 metres) high. The North Sea continues to chew this coast away at an average rate of three inches a year, even up to three feet a year in some places, and the tidal drift bears the detritus south to the Wash and North Norfolk coast. Fossils abound in these sedimentary rock cliffs, especially ammonites. Living plants and birds are relatively few, though there are always petrels to be seen, swooping and soaring above the fearful void, as well as kittiwakes and gulls.

Access to the edge of the sea is difficult. The roads down to the scattering of picturesque old fishing villages like Staithes and Robin Hood's Bay are steep, and yet congested in summer. For the wild traveller a better bet is to get down to the water's edge via one of the wykes, or wooded cloughs, running down to the sea – like Hayburn Wyke, a narrow, almost impenetrably wooded valley (and nature reserve) where a fast-flowing beck tumbles down to the sea via a series of pretty waterfalls.

BEFORE YOU GO
Maps: OS Leisure Series, Map Nos. 26, Western Area, and 27, Eastern Area.

Guidebooks: much essential information is included in *The North York Moors Visitor*, available for a small charge from any information centre or from North York Moors National Park, The Old Vicarage, Bondgate, Helmsley, York YO6 5BP, T:0439 70657. *North Yorkshire Moors* (AA/OS0) provides good maps and popular information. *The North York Moors National Park* by Ian Carstairs (Webb and Bower), is a sound introduction to the park's history, archaeology and wildlife.

GETTING THERE
By car: the A1 provides easy access to the park via York on the A64, Sowerby on the A168 or Northallerton on the A684. The A171 Scarborough to Guisborough road skirts the northern and eastern borders

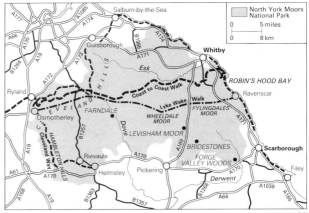

The sparkling water of Eller Beck will soon be turned a muddy brown when the stream plunges down to join Murk Esk

of the park, giving access to the coast. The A170 from Scarborough to Thirsk follows the park's southern border through Pickering and Helmsley.

By train: Scarborough has rail links with York and Hull. Whitby is the terminus of the scenic Esk Valley railway from Middlesbrough, where a rail link connects with the main line at Darlington. Within the park the remarkable North York Moors railway covers 18 miles (29km) between Grosmont and Pickering.

By bus: regular services run to Middlesbrough, Scarborough and York from many major cities. Local bus schedules are available from Tourist Information Centres. United Bus Company, the park's

98

biggest operator, has offices in Scarborough, T:0723 375463, and Whitby, T:0947 602146.

WHERE TO STAY
Accommodation is available in villages and on farms, mainly near Pickering, Kirkbymoorside and Helmsley in the south and near Whitby in the north-east. *The North York Moors Visitor* includes a list of accommodation and camping sites. The park also produces a free leaflet listing campsites and bed and breakfasts near the Cleveland Way. Youth hostels in or near the park: Fyling Thorpe (T:0947 880352), Helmsley, (T:0439 70433), Pickering (T:0751 60376), Northallerton (T:0609 83575), Saltburn-by-the-Sea (T:0287 24389), Scarborough (T:0723 361176).

WHERE TO GO
Nature reserves within the park include:

Bridestones: heather moorland with remarkable weathered outcrops of rock; YWT/NT. Take minor road north from Thornton Dale, 2 miles (1km) east of Pickering. Access on foot to Bridestones from Staindale car park on Dalby Forest Road, an FC toll road.
Farndale: famous for wild daffodils; SSSI managed by national park. 8 miles (13km) north of Kirkbymoorside. Access from an unclassified road running between Kirkbymoorside and Castleton.
Forge Valley Woods: semi-natural woodland; NCC. Access by road or footpath from West Ayton, 4 miles (6km) south-west of Scarborough on A170.
Levisham Moor: moorland and wooded valleys managed by national park. Access by footpath from Levisham Station on NYM railway or

from A169, 7 miles (11km) north of Pickering.

ACCESS AND CLOSURES
As in other national parks, most of the North York Moors is privately owned. Visitors may not roam off designated rights of way, but the many existing foot- and bridle paths provide sufficient opportunity for exploration.

ACTIVITIES
Walking: the park has more than 1,200 miles (1,900km) of public footpath. The OS Outdoor Leisure maps provide the necessary information for experienced walkers; less innovative visitors will appreciate the park service's inexpensive Waymark Walk leaflets, which describe more than 30 circular walks of between 2 and 5 miles (3 and 8km).

The Cleveland Way, a Countryside Commission designated route, follows the park borders for 93 miles (149km) from Helmsley in the south-west to Filey on the coast south of Scarborough. The unofficial Moors Link along the path's southern border from Filey Brigg to Helmsley completes the circuit. The Ebor Way, between Helmsley and Ilkley, links the Cleveland Way with the Dales Way. The park service produces a leaflet on the Cleveland Way.

FURTHER INFORMATION
The park's principal information centre is the Danby Lodge National Park Visitor Centre, Lodge Lane, Danby, Whitby YO21 2HB, T:0287 60654. Other information centres are at Helmsley (T:0439 70173), Hutton-le-Hole (T:075 15 367), Pickering (T:0751 73791), Scarborough (T:0723 373333), Sutton Bank (T:0845

597426), Thirsk (T:0845 22755) and Whitby (T:0947 602674).

Spurn Peninsula

YWT Reserve

This narrow promontory extends 3 miles (5km) into the mouth of the Humber and encompasses 280 acres (113ha) of dunes, pebble beach and mud flats. The first bird observatory on the British mainland was established here in 1946. Today it is one of the best places to see migrants, especially rarities. Large numbers of wildfowl, waders, terns, and smaller birds pass through here, and their 'falls' are sometimes prodigious; 6,000 blackbirds in a single day, for instance.
Getting there: along B1445 to Easington, then minor road to Kilnsea and Spurn. Car parks by bird observatory and information centre at landward end of peninsula or at the tip. **Access:** unrestricted all year. Use of bird hide for observatory residents. **Where to stay:** basic accommodation with kitchen facilities at observatory for up to 17 people. **Further information:** leaflet from YNT or information centre. Bookings through Warden, Spurn Nature Reserve, Kilnsea, Patrington, Hull, Humberside HU12 0UG.

Bempton Cliffs

RSPB Reserve

Three miles (5km) of magnificent chalk cliffs – at 400ft (122m) the highest chalk cliffs in Britain – run north-west from Flamborough Head, Humberside. They are the most southerly of the seabird cliffs on the east coast of Britain, containing the only nesting colony of gannets on the mainland (650 pairs in 1986). In the breeding season the cracks and ledges are packed with nesting birds, including 80,000 pairs of kittiwakes and many thousands of auks.

As many as 160 bird species have been recorded here, many of them, such as terns, skuas, shearwaters, merlins and bluethroats, on migration.
Getting there: along cliff road from Bempton village on B1229 Flamborough–Filey road. **Access:** at all times to clifftop path, where 4 safe observation barriers give excellent views of seabird colonies. Visitors must keep to footpath and observation points, as the cliffs are very high and extremely dangerous.
Further information: leaflet from RSPB or contact Warden, c/o Post Office, Bempton, nr Bridlington, Humberside.

THE LYKE WAKE WALK
The Lyke Wake Walk is one of the most popular long-distance walks on the North York Moors. This is the Lyke Wake Dirge. Repeated *ad infinitum* it grows on you after the first few miles:

'This yah neet, this yah neet,
Ivvery neat an all
Fine an fleet an cannle leet
An' Christ take up thy soul.'

Northumberland National Park

400 square miles (1,000sq km) of hills and moorland between Hadrian's Wall and the Scottish border

The Northumberland National Park is frontier country. For centuries it was a lawless border land where cattle rustlers, border reivers and moss men, whose deeds are vividly recalled in Scottish border ballads and the historical romances of Sir Walter Scott, raided and skirmished.

It is still the most sparsely populated part of the most sparsely populated county in England. There are few settlements here, just isolated stone farmhouses in the valleys; there are hardly any roads, and industrial centres are far away. When one stands by the Roman Wall and peers northward towards the bare, abandoned hills that recede wave upon wave into the interior, one feels one is staring at a fearful void, where the only sound is the wind in the heath, the desolate cry of the curlew and the distant bleat of the white-faced Cheviot sheep.

Most of the park is upland country over 1,000 feet (305 metres) high, formed by volcanoes and shaped by ice. The sombre, smoothly contoured hills and moors rise steadily towards the rounded boss of the Cheviot, a wide, bare, upland heath and grass moor where the wild goats and the blue hares run. At 2,674 feet (815 metres) it is the highest point of the Cheviot Hills. They are the most elevated part of the park, and the core round which the landscape revolves in concentric circles: farmed land on the lower, softer rocks alternating with ridges and crags of harder rocks like the Simonside Hills, with the long volcanic escarpment of the Great Whin Sill, where the Romans built their wall, forming a natural barrier at the southern edge.

The park is made up of five main parts. In the north-west are the Cheviots, which stretch down the west side of the park as far as the Border Forest; in the east lie Coquetdale and the Simonside Hills, only 1,444 feet (440 metres) high but more rugged than the Cheviots; in the centre the softer, more pastoral valley of the Rede; south of the Rede, the farmed valley of the North Tyne; and along the southern border, Hadrian's Wall country.

Locals divide the country more simply into the Black Country, meaning the dark sandstone slopes of the Simonside Hills, and the White Country, referring to the light granite of the Cheviots. Though the Simonside Hills offer outstanding walking, most visitors head for the two most outstanding features of the park, the Cheviots at one end and the wall at the other.

The Roman Wall is not the only man-made feature to be seen in the park – there are older prehistoric hill forts such as Yeavering Bell as well as more recent fortified houses and villages – but it is certainly the most sensational. This long stone battlement sealing off the north-west frontier of the Roman Empire is one of the most impressive remains of antiquity north of the Alps. Constructed between AD122 and 130 on the orders of Emperor Hadrian, it crossed the whole breadth of northern England from the Tyne Estuary on the east coast to the Solway Firth on the west.

One of the best-preserved stretches of the wall runs for 15 miles (24 kilometres) through the Northumberland National Park between Chollerford and Gisland. Here the great grey stone barrier follows the line of the natural, north-facing rampart on which it is built, the basalt scarp of the Great Whin Sill. The well-preserved fort at Vercovicium (now Housesteads), which could garrison some 1,000 infantry, and the milecastle at Cawfields, with accommodation for 30 troops, give a good idea of the solidity of Roman military engineering and the purposefulness of the Roman occupation of Britain.

The Romans pulled out at the beginning of the fourth century AD. Their wall remains. A foray along its foot, up and down the switchback crest of the Whin Sill ridge, offers as intriguing a walk as can be had in any national park in Britain, strong in its sense of remoteness, especially along the section between Sewingshields Crags and Peel Crag, or at Winshields with its vast views towawrds the Cheviots, Pennines, Solway Firth and Lake District, and over the loughs, or glacial lakes, which dot the landscape north of the wall.

After being an outpost of Rome, Northumbria became an outpost of Christianity. Through the centuries that followed the land was fought over by Scots, Vikings and Saxons in endless frontier raids. In the Middle Ages Northumberland remained a virtually independent kingdom, and the havoc years of the border reivers only ended with the Union of England and Scotland in 1603. The legacies of centuries of frontier fighting are everywhere in the form of fortified farms and dwellings known as 'peles' and 'bastles'.

It is the modern works of man which have made the biggest and least welcome impact on the park. The British army has taken over where the Roman army left off and turned one fifth of the park – 90 square miles of the middle portion between Redesdale and the Coquet valley – into the principal military training area in northern England. For 300 days of the year the sounds of battle rise incongruously from the centre of the national park and the birdwatcher and hill walker who innocently approaches the firing ground is welcomed with signs that read: 'DANGER. MILITARY TARGET. DO NOT TOUCH ANYTHING. IT MAY EXPLODE AND KILL YOU.'

Elsewhere the Forestry Commission have installed regiments of a different kind: rank upon rank of conifers that make up the largest man-made forest in Europe. This vast plantation, centred on Kielder and dubbed the Border Forest Park, spreads into the national park, where it is called the Wark Forest. Additionally, a rocket testing site has been established on the western margin of the park, though an atomic waste dump has at the time of writing been successfully resisted.

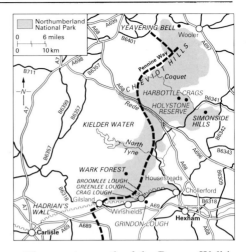

The country north of the Roman Wall is probably the most varied in Northumberland. Moorland, woodland, farmland and the wetland of the glacial lakes, upland streams, bogs and basin mires provide the main habitats, together with the mountain habitat of the rocky ravines high up in the Cheviots. Most of the heather moorland lies in Coquetdale and the Simonside Hills, where it is managed as grouse moor, while the slopes of the Cheviots to the north are predominantly green and grass covered. The hub of the Cheviot Hills is the flat, peat-covered plateau known as the Cheviot, from which bare grass or heather ridges and summits radiate all around, providing superb walking and marvellous views in all directions. Like Dartmoor, the high plateau of the Cheviot Hills is covered in blanket bogs of deep acid peat where granite tors protrude out of the vegetation mantle. Deep valleys run off these hills and swift flowing streams dive over tumbling waterfalls (such as the beautiful waterfall of Harthope Linn) and then broaden out into winding rivers that glide, crystal clear and primordially pure, over pebble and boulder beds.

Ravens and buzzards soar among the hills, and merlins still nest in the deep heather. A regular breeding species on the moors is the short-eared owl, which increases in number during years when the field vole undergoes one of its periodic population explosions. Ring ouzels occupy the higher ground, nightjars the birch- and bracken-sheltered slopes, and red grouse and curlew call loudly from the heather moors and fells. Rabbits and brown hares are the most commonly seen animals on the upland pastures, and wild goats graze in small herds on the Cheviots. Badgers and foxes breed in the valleys and on the high moors; adders, common lizards and slow worms can also be found here.

The high rocky ravines of the Cheviot – Dunsdale, the Bizzle and the Henhole – shelter typical mountain or arctic–alpine plants. These survivors of the arctic tundra world of post-Ice Age Britain include alpine willow herb, alpine club moss, rose root, starry saxifrage, hairy stonecrop and the rare dwarf cornel. In the valleys, rocky outcrops have weathered to deposit a rich brown earth on the cliff ledges, supporting a tall herb community of plants like rose burnet, foxglove, bluebell, golden rod, wild angelica and wood cranesbill.

On the lower slopes of ravines and the steeper valleys, especially in the Coquet-dale and Simonside areas, scattered fragments of the prehistoric forest that once covered much of the region survive. They are mostly sessile oak, with birch, hazel, alder and ash supporting a rich ground layer of primrose, bluebell, meadowsweet, foxglove and enchanter's nightshade, along with an abundance of ferns and fungi like the fly agaric. One of the best of the old woods can be seen in the valley of the Grasslands Burn, separating the Simonside and Harbottle Hills. Two other fine relict woods, Holystone North Wood and Holystone Burn Wood, are managed as nature reserves by the Northumberland Wildlife Trust.

The wetland habitat of the park takes various forms. Bog is one form; the blanket bog of the upland Cheviots, and the raised bogs of the country to the west of the North Tyne, in the middle of the park. Most notable of the raised bogs are the Irthinghead Mires, situated in the prairie landscape of the Wark Forest at the extreme west of the park, far from any roads. Many of these bogs, known locally as mosses or

flothers, are of tremendous ecological importance because of the delicate balance of their plant communities: most of them have been designated as SSSIs, and one of them, Coom Rigg Moss, is also a National Nature Reserve, the only one within the park. These remote, undisturbed and little-visited wild habitats support a wide range of typical bog plants including bog moss, the beautiful bog rosemary, bog asphodel and the round-leaved sundew and rare long-leaved sundew, two unusual plants that supplement the scanty nutrients of their habitat by trapping and digesting small insects in their sticky leaves.

Another kind of wetland in the park is that of the shallow glacial loughs or lakes that occupy the basins gouged by the ice between a series of basalt ridges stretching northwards from the Great Whin Sill to Simonside, Coquetdale and beyond. Some of the most important loughs are visible to anyone walking along Hadrian's Wall; Broomlee, Crag Lough and Greenlee Lough to the north of the wall, and Grindon Lough, the smallest and shallowest (and now a National Nature Reserve), to the south. Some of the loughs, such as Grindon, are still open water; others are slowly filling up with vegetation, evolving from reed swamp and fen to raised bog and willow carr, and growing a profusion of tall marshy herbs such as meadowsweet, skullcap, marsh marigold, water mint and ragged Robin.

The upland streams provide yet another kind of wetland habitat in the park. These are either fed by water from the loughs or by rainwater from the hills, and they can be torrential at times, filling the valleys with the busy tumult of their headlong rush. The most commonly seen creatures of the streams are the dipper and grey wagtail, along with the water rat in the slower streams. The otter, which still clings on here, is seldom seen.

As Hadrian's Wall follows its course eastwards through the Northumberland National Park past Cuddy's Crags and Housesteads, walkers can measure their progress when they reach Milecastle 37

BEFORE YOU GO

Maps: OS Landranger Series Map Nos. 74, 75, 80, 81, 86 and 87. There are no 1:25,000 Outdoor Leisure Series maps for this part of Britain, but the OS/AA Outdoor Leisure Guide called *Northumbria* includes 1in.–1mile maps of the entire region as well as 16 walks illustrated with 1:25,000 maps. The OS also produce a 2in–1mile strip map of the entire 73 miles (117km) of Hadrian's Wall.

Guidebooks: the Countryside Commission's *Northumberland National Park* by Tony Hopkins (Webb and Bower) is an invaluable introduction. The park service's own *Visit Planning Guide*, including information on accommodation, transport, recreation and emergency services, is available from Northumberland National Park, Eastburn, South Park, Hexham NE46 1BS, T:0434 605555.

GETTING THERE

By car: from the East Midlands and south-east England the A1 provides rapid access to Newcastle-upon-Tyne. For Wooler and the Cheviots, continue north from Newcastle-upon-Tyne on the A697; for Redesdale take the A696/68 Jedburgh road; for Hadrian's Wall and the southern region of the park, drive west along the A69. From the west and south-west of England leave the M6 on the A69 (exit 43) for Haltwhistle and Hexham. There is easy access from Edinburgh on both the A68 and A697.

By train: Newcastle-upon-Tyne and Carlisle are linked by the scenic Tyne Valley Line, which stops at Hexham, Haltwhistle and other stations along the park's southern border.

By bus: there are regular daily services from Newcastle to Rothbury and Hexham. For Wooler travel via Alnwick, and for Bellingham change at Hexham. Many villages within the park are on bus routes, but services are often infrequent. Some of the more remote settlements are accessible by post buses on routine runs. *The Northumberland Public Transport Guide*, a comprehensive listing of all bus services, is available from information centres and most post offices. For further information contact the Transport Officer, Northumberland County Council, County Hall, Morpeth, Northumberland NE61 2EF, T:0670 511343.

WHERE TO STAY

Most accommodation is to be found in or near the towns and villages on the western fringes of the park: Wooler for the Cheviot Hills; Rothbury just north of the Simonside Hills; Hexham and Haltwhistle for Hadrian's Wall in the south. The Northumbria Tourist

'Over the heather the wet wind blows,
I've lice in my tunic and a cold in my nose.
The rain comes pattering out of the sky,
I'm a Wall soldier, I don't know why.'
        W.H. Auden:
        Roman Wall Blues

Board's annual *Guide to Northumbria*, available at information centres, includes a list of accommodation.

Outdoor living: the River Breamish Caravan and Camp Site, managed by the Caravan Club for the national park, is 8 miles south of Wooler off the A697 (T:066 578 320). The FC operates campsites at Stonehaugh and Byrness.

Youth hostels: Acomb (T:0434 602864), Bellingham (T:0660 20313), Byrness (T:0830 20222), Greenhead (T:069 72 401), Once Brewed (T:049 84 360), Wooler (T:0668 81365).

MOORLAND SAFETY

The benign face of moorland on a sunny day can change swiftly and treacherously. Before setting out on a long walk, telephone the Newcastle Weather Centre on 0632 326453, telling the forecaster where you are going and for how long. Be prepared to alter your plans if the forecast is very discouraging.

Walkers along the beach below coastal cliffs must anticipate a more predictable natural phenomenon — the tide, which can transform an afternoon's outing into a terrifying race against the clock. Before any such expedition, learn the time and the extent of the next tide; tide-tables are available from newsagents or tackle shops.

Adders, which thrive on the moor, will generally escape long before you see them; if not, keep a respectful distance. You are less likely to encounter an unexploded bomb, but they do still exist; treat any suspicious object with caution and contact the police.

The park service produces *Moorland Safety*, a free leaflet addressing itself to these potential dangers.

WHERE TO GO

Nature reserves in the park include:

Coom Rigg Moss: one of the few areas of peat bog to have survived the reafforestation of Wark Forest, 10 miles (16km) north of Haltwhistle. No rights of way or access except by permission of NCC.

Grindon Lough: important wintering site for waterfowl south of Hadrian's Wall; no access to shore, but entire lake can be observed from nearby roadside. From B6319, ½ mile (1km) west of Fourstones, take unclassified Newbrough road. Grindon Lough is on right after 5 miles (8km).

Harbottle Crags: high moorland with sphagnum bogs and sandstone crags; part of Harbottle Forest (FC). Above village of Harbottle on unclassified road west of Rothbury. No access off nature trail, which starts at Harbottle information centre.

Holystone Reserve: broad-leaved and coniferous woodland, interspersed with bog and heath. 7 miles (11km) west of Rothbury. From Holystone village, take Campville road. Visitors for the North Woods (upland oak, birch, holly, etc.) can use FC car park; for the Holystone Valley, continue past park and leave cars in layby where road leads downhill.

For more information contact the Nature Conservancy Council, Archbold House, Archbold Terrace, Newcastle-upon-Tyne NE2 1EG, T:091 281 6316, or Northumberland Wildlife Trust, The Hancock Museum, Newcastle-upon-Tyne NE2 4PT, T:0632 320038.

ACCESS AND CLOSURES

Much of the land is privately owned, and visitors must stay on public roads or rights of way specified on OS maps.

There are 3 areas where walkers have free access: Breamish Valley in the vicinity of Ingram, Harthope Valley south-west of Wooler and the land immediately surrounding Housesteads Fort on Hadrian's Wall. Access to the College Valley is by permit only, from J. Sale and Partners, Glendale Road, Wooler, T:0668 81611, but limited to 12 vehicles a day and closed for lambing 10 Apr–1 Jun.

One great obstacle can be the Ministry of Defence's Otterburn Training Area between the Rivers Rede and Coquet, north-east of the A68. There is no access to this area when red flags are flying, up to 290 days a year. During lambing (14 Apr–15 May), between Christmas and New Year and on public holidays the range is always open.

ACTIVITIES

Walking: countless tracks and paths meander across the park's interior. Be prepared for some serious map and compass reading; this is easy country in which to get lost. Equip yourself as you would for any demanding hill walking expedition; then add another chocolate bar.

Hadrian's Wall has now been designated an official long-distance footpath. The best section is between Steel Rigg and Housesteads fort – park at the former and return from the latter by national park minibus.

The park service's guided walks (Apr–Sep) start from various points and last from 1 to 6 hours. These are described in the leaflet *Discovering Walks and Trails*. Another leaflet describes a series of Sunday afternoon winter walks. Reservations are unnecessary for guided walks.

Walkers can obtain regional information from the Ramblers' Association, Mr M. Ruddick, 14 Moor Place, Gosforth, Newcastle-upon-Tyne NE8 4AL, T:0632 857279.

Climbing: there is good climbing in the Simonside Hills, the Cheviots and at Crag Lough on the Whin Sill. Access is rarely a problem, but make sure that you have the landowner's permission before beginning a climb. For further information contact.

EMERGENCY SERVICES

Mountain Rescue Posts:
Hawick Police Station, T:0450 75051
Kirk Yetholm Police Office, Kelso, T:05732 3434.

Alpine plants of the English Pennines include: (from left to right) alpine lady's mantle. grass of Parnassus, yellow saxifrage and sweet Cicely

the Northumbrian
Mountaineering Club, N.
Jamieson, 52 Angerton
Avenue, Shiremoor,
Newcastle-upon-Tyne NE27
OTU, T:091253 2703.
Field studies: the park has no
official field study centre of its
own, but many of its guided
walks are led by expert
naturalists.

FURTHER INFORMATION
The park runs information
centres in Ingram (T:066 578
248), Rothbury (T:0669
20887) and Once Brewed
(T:049 84 396). It also
operates centres jointly with
the National Trust at
Housesteads on Hadrian's
Wall (T:049 84 525), the
Northumbrian Water

Authority at Tower Knowe on
Kielder Water (T:0660 40398)
and the Northumberland
Wildlife Trust at Harbottle in
Upper Coquetdale.
   For information about
nature reserves within the
park contact the Nature
Conservancy Council,
Archbold House, Archbold
Terrace, Newcastle-upon-Tyne
NE2 1EG, T:091 281 6316, or
Northumberland Wildlife
Trust, The Hancock Museum,
Newcastle-upon-Tyne NE2
4PT, T:0632 320038.
   The Forestry Commission
has 2 regional offices: Walby
House, Rothbury NE65 7NT,
T:0669 20569 and West View,
Bellingham NE48 2AH,
T:0660 20242.

NORTHUMBERLAND COAST

AONB

Northumberland has one of the finest coastlines in
England, with one of the longest sand dune systems.
Buffeted by the North Sea, it can be an exhilaratingly
wild place, and scattered along it are several remarkable
wildlife reserves and bird islands.

The Farne Islands

NTNR

The Farne Islands, 2 to 4 miles
(3 to 6km) off the coast
between Seahouses and
Bamburgh, are the most
easterly forms of the volcanic
outcrop known as the Great
Whin Sill, along the inland
stretch of which the Romans
built Hadrian's Wall. The 28
small islands are mostly low
lying, and only 15 of them are
visible at high tide. A few,
however, boast high stacks
and cliffs, reaching 70ft (21m)
near the Inner Farne
106

lighthouse, which provide
ideal nesting sites for many
species of seabird.
   The fishing boat trip out to
the islands is always a little
adventure, long enough to
give you the feel of the swell
and saltwater tang, short
enough not to feel seasick.
The islands, none of which are
permanently inhabited, enjoy
sanctuary status as a National
Trust Nature Reserve, one of
the most important in Europe.
The public can land on only
three of them – Inner Farne
(the largest), Staple Island and
Longhope. Even so, they
remain among the most easily
accessible and enjoyable bird
islands off the British coast.

More than 250 species of
bird have been recorded on
the Farne Islands, including
puffins, guillemots, kittiwakes,
lesser black-backed and
herring gulls, arctic and
Sandwich terns, eider,
cormorants, shags, fulmars,
black-headed gulls and

common terns; a good number of oystercatchers, ringed plovers and meadow pipits; some score of razorbills and a few roseate terns. Most of the terns breed on Inner Farne and if you land there you will need to protect the top of your skull or the irate terns will give you a sharp peck on the head.

There have been grey seals on the Farne Islands for more than 800 years. They are not hard to see, particularly on the nursery islands of North and South Wamses and Northern Hares.

The stacks of Staple Island, one of the Farne Islands, form desirable detached columns for guillemots and other sociable seabirds

Hermits and monks lived on Inner Farne for nearly 900 years, the most famous of them being the 7th-century

107

Lindisfarne
(or Holy Island)

NCC NNR

The largest reserve in north-east England, these 8,100 acres (3278ha) of dunes, salt marsh and mud flats extend from Holy Island north to Goswick Sands and south to Budle Bay. They are world famous for their large winter flocks of divers, grebes, wildfowl and waders.

The inter-tidal flats of the broad Lindisfarne inlet are sheltered by the natural breakwater of Holy Island, a low hump which can be reached at low tide by a causeway from the mainland village of Beal. Behind this shelter, enormous flocks of wintering birds congregate to feed when the flats and marshes are exposed by the receding tide.

Lindisfarne is the only regular wintering ground in Britain for the pale-bellied Brent goose, which flies down from Spitzbergen when the polar ice covers its summer nesting grounds. Lindisfarne is also the most important coastal site for widgeon (peaking at 40,000) and the place where the largest wintering flocks of whooper swan in England are to be found. The huge swirling flocks of waders include internationally important numbers of knot, dunlin and bar-tailed godwit, as well as many other wader species, rare passage migrants, and regular birds of prey like the peregrine, merlin and short-eared owl.

All this is in winter, when the sub-polar climate at the edge of this northerly sea may well shiver your timbers, so to

prior, St Cuthbert. Subsequently the only inhabitants have been the lighthouse keepers, including William Darling and his famous lifeboat daughter, Grace, on Longstone. For a bracing foray on the ocean wave and an intimate view of teeming bird life at close quarters on an almost desert island group, the Farne Islands are hard to beat. **Getting there:** all sailings from Seahouses, 3 miles (5km) south of Bamburgh on B1340. Boats leave daily, weather permitting, from Easter to October for trips around the Islands and from April to September for landings on Inner Farne, Staple Island, and sometimes Longhope if conditions allow. No dogs allowed. Contact National Trust Centre, Seahouses, T:0665 72042, or individual boatmen: W. Shiel T:0665 720308, W. McKay T:0665

720155 and H.J. Hanvey T:0665 720388. **Where to go:** around the islands for the best viewing of grey seals. Inner Farne for nesting colonies of puffins, terns, and elders. Staple Island for vast colonies of kittiwakes, also shags, guillemots and puffins. **Access:** only islands open to public. Access restricted during breeding period (15 May–15 Jul). **Facilities:** information centre and public lavatories on Inner Farne. **Further information:** National Trust Information Centre, 16 Main Street, Seahouses, Northumberland NE68 7RQ, T:0665 720424 for annual bird report, colour guide and leaflets.

speak. In summer, bird life is much less evident, still less so when the tide is in and the mud flats are covered by the sea. On the other hand, the summer wild flowers of the dunes can be a reward, especially the marsh orchid, common spotted orchid and marsh helleborine. And if it's pouring and all else fails, there are always the beautiful ruins of the 11th-century priory, or Sir Edward Lutyens' marvellous restoration of the 16th-century castle perched on a high rock above the sea.

Getting there: 8 miles (13km) south of Berwick-upon-Tweed on A1, an unclassified road leads to Lindisfarne via the village of Beal. The causeway to the island is impassable from 2 hours before and 3½ hours after high tide: check tide-tables at causeway. Buses run from Berwick to Beal with connecting services to the island dependant on the tide.

Where to stay: there are 2 hotels on the island: Lindisfarne Hotel, T:0289 89273, and Manor House Hotel, T:0289 89207. No caravans, motor homes or tents are allowed, but there are campsites nearby at Beal and Haggerston. **Access:** free access to reserve, but permits from NCC required for field work. Parking off causeway at low tide only. **Further information:** leaflet from NCC, or contact reserve office, T:06683 386.

Coquet Island

RSPB Reserve

Among the common seabirds of the north-east coast are: on the cliff-top (from left to right) guillemot, fulmar, kittiwake and cormorant, all highly successful breeders on crags, cliffs and stacks; and in the air a common tern, which has a much poorer breeding record, not least because its colonies are in exposed locations on the ground

Officially it is not possible to land on this small island off the Northumberland coast, for fear of disturbing the nesting birds. I would not have included it in this book were it not for the fact that I once spent a jolly afternoon on the island in the company of the lighthouse keeper and a few friends; so obviously it is possible for the serious observer to make visiting arrangements with the relevant authorities. I recall landing through choppy seas in a rubber boat and stepping ashore amid a mass of birds' nests on the flat ground under my feet and an even bigger mass of jittery, abusive terns hovering excitedly immediately above my head.

Unless you are a real enthusiast it is probably easier to hire a boat in Amble and view the bird colonies during a sea trip around the island. They include large colonies of Sandwich, Arctic and common terns, a small but very important population of roseate tern, Britain's most threatened seabird, and large colonies of puffins and eider ducks. Arctic skuas and bonxies come raiding in late summer.

Getting there: island is 1 mile (2km) offshore from Amble, which is on A1068. Nearest railway station is Acklington. **Access:** no landing permitted, but round-the-island trips from Amble can be arranged with Gordon Easton, T:0665 710384 or 712460. **Further information:** Summer Warden, c/o the Post Office, Amble, near Morpeth, Northumberland.

109

CHAPTER 5

Wales

Wales would be guerrilla country, if it ever came to it. It was into this great mountain fastness in the west that the early Celts beat a permanent strategic withdrawal from the invaders of lowland England, there to lick their wounds, and nurse their language, and live their own peculiarly Welsh kind of Celtic life. Few were inclined to pursue them over the windswept upland moors, the black bogs and bristling mountains of the wild Welsh heartland. For centuries the line of English castles along the Welsh Marches marked the beginning of a no-man's land beyond which there was only Merlin, wizardry and red dragons, a dark, stocky tribe of proud, defiant hill people and an upland wilderness, the haunt of red kites and the swooping falcon, where even angels and Angles feared to tread.

Wales has had a rich history. There were cave dwellers like those who lived in the now classic sites at Cae Gwyn in Flintshire and Paviland on Gower. In the upland depths of Wales to this day there are folk who, in their physical appearance and their blood groups, are akin to some of those early peoples – an indication of the wild remoteness of these regions which later invaders like the Normans never quite overcame. For the historian, Wales seems well blessed with ancient ramparts, hill and promontory forts, and castles, not just the great Norman and Edwardian strongholds, but Welsh castles; like Dinefwr, standing proud on its limestone crag where it guards a crossing of the middle Tywi.

Not all that much has changed. The

The tranquility of this sunset over St Bride's Bay on the Pembrokeshire coast is deceptive; the sea here is often tempestuous

red dragons are no more and the red kites are greatly reduced, but much of the wilderness remains, and to anyone approaching Wales from the lowland English plain the country seems to be an impenetrable mountain fastness, as it has always done. In no other part of Britain is the landscape so solidly and uniformly mountainous. True, Scotland's mountains are higher, but they are more widely dispersed, and there are extensive lowlands and vast stretches of level moor. In Wales, by contrast, the uplands extend north and south from coast to coast, and east and west from the Marches to the sea. Wales is literally stuffed with mountains, from the great ramparts of Snowdownia – the highest mountain in all England and Wales – in the north west to the wild sweep of the Brecon Beacons in the south east; and the vast highland plateau of the Cambrian Mountains that occupies the middle of the country, though less dramatic than the spectacular rock piles to the north and south, is as remote and solitary as almost anywhere in Britain, where the only sounds to be heard on a still summer afternoon are the mewing buzzards and the distant bleating of the sheep. Numerous rivers fan out to sea from the highland interior, though a few – notably the Dee, Severn and Wye – drain in the opposite direction, down to the lowland English border. Some of these rivers meander in slow and stately fashion across the floodplains, as if wishing to delay their arrival at the sea. Others dash in a wild, headlong charge through narrow, boulder filled defiles, where the sound of water is never stilled. It is the river routes that still allow access to the very heart of wild Wales.

It is an invariable axiom of wild Britain that where there is high ground

there is also wildnerness, and this is indubitably true of Wales. This is the playground – if dangling from a rock pinnacle or snow-bivouacing in a sub-zero icefield can be described as play – of the hard rock buff, the white-water canoeist and the long-distance backpacker who eats granite for breakfast. Being so near to the main centres of population of Great Britain, there are more wild travellers per square mile of scree, cwm and glacial moraine in high Wales than any other part of the country, except perhaps the Lake District. And more accidents too, so take care.

Not that Wales is exclusively upland. In Anglesey in the north and along the Bristol Channel coast in the south there are large tracts of low-lying land. The long stretches of cliff coast, particularly in Pembrokeshire in the far south west, are among the loveliest and most varied in Britain, and at times the most windswept. There is no grander sight than the view from Wooltack Point during the aftermath of a westerly gale, when the great rollers surge across St Brides Bay, or send plumes of spray high over the aptly named Mad Bay on Skokholm Island. Along the South Wales coast in the west you can find places where at very low tides the remains of sunken forests are still visible, trees that once flourished on dry rolling lands several thousand summers ago. It is also along this coast that you can see many of the most spectacular gatherings of birds in Wales, especially in the estuaries with their vast expanses of mud flats and salt marsh, on the bird islands of the Skomer island group and on the many inland lakes which abound in the interior. Some of these are reservoirs, while others were first filled by the meltwaters of the Ice Age glaciers that once gripped the uplands of Wales, and contain in their depths relict fish that are peculiar to Wales, such as the gwyniad of Lake Bala and the fresh-water char of Llanberis.

For the naturalist Wales provides a mixed bag. The flora is impoverished by comparison with the rest of Great Britain; Wales has only 1,100 native plants compared with 1,600 in Britain as a whole. The high proportion of moisture-loving plants such as ferns reflects the rain-laden climate. In compensation, Wales harbours some animals and birds which are either extinct or extremely rare elsewhere in Britain, such as the polecat, the pine marten, a number of pairs of kites, the embattled chough, a moth called Weaver's wave and a beautiful beetle, found only on a small part of Snowdon, which rejoices in the name of *Chrysolina cerealis* and the unique Snowdon lily, like a small white tulip. Throughout Wales a wide variety of habitats ensures a goodly abundance of species, and off the Gower coast there is the added bonus of a breathtaking cavalcade of marine creatures. Much of the natural heritage and beauty of Wales is contained within the generous boundaries of its three National Parks: Snowdonia, the Brecon Beacons and the Pembrokeshire Coast. Much else can be found in the several Areas of Outstanding Natural Beauty, the many nature reserves and along the long-distance paths. Even outside these areas there are wide tracts of unspoiled landscape, as genuinely wild and remote as anything you could hope to find in Britain.

GETTING THERE

By air: Cardiff-Wales airport has scheduled flights to most major British cities. There is also a regular service to Amsterdam and frequent charter flights from the USA and Canada. North Wales is served by Manchester airport.

By sea: 4 ferry routes link Wales with Ireland. Sealink and B&I both operate from Dun Laoghaire to Holyhead and Sealink alone from Rosslare to Fishguard. B&I sail from Rosslare to Pembroke Dock, and Swansea-Cork Ferries operate between Cork and Swansea.

By train: a fast inter-city service operates out of Paddington to Newport, Cardiff and Swansea. Trains from London, Birmingham and Manchester connect via Chester with stations along the north coast, including Colwyn Bay, Conway and Bangor: for mid-Wales, change at Shrewsbury for trains to Newtown, Machynlleth,

Aberystwyth and the Snowdonia coast. *Wales by Train* and *Wales Timetable* are available from principal railway stations or Wales Tourist Board information centres.

By bus: National Express operates regular services from major centres in England to the principal towns of Wales. To Cardiff there is a service

The polecat thrives in the dunes of the Welsh coast, where prey such as rabbits abound

from London every hour, every other hour from Birmingham and twice daily from Manchester. There is also a daily service to Aberystwyth – via Newtown and Llanidloes – from London and Birmingham, and several daily services to Bangor and stations along the North Wales coast from London, Birmingham and Manchester. Travellers from Scotland will generally have to change at Liverpool or Birmingham for connections to Wales.

WHEN TO GO

The weather in Wales is at its most welcoming in summer, but it is wise to avoid the congested roads and booked-up accommodation of the National Parks in August and on bank holiday weekends. The Cambrian Mountains in Mid Wales, on the other hand, are relatively neglected by tourists and can still offer peace and space even in mid-summer. Bird watchers will often choose spring and autumn to visit coastal Wales in order to observe migrating wildfowl and waders. Mountaineers find Wales an exciting challenge year-round, especially Snowdonia, where several centres organize winter climbing holidays.

WHERE TO STAY

The Wales Tourist Board has two useful publications: *Wales – Where to Stay*, including hotels, guest houses, farm houses, self-catering accommodation and caravan and camping sites; and *Wales – Bed and Breakfast*, a comprehensive list of inexpensive overnight accommodation. There is also a booklet listing 'Dragon Award' caravan parks, which provide first-class facilities. These publications are available from information centres or from the Wales Tourist Board, PO Box 1, Cardiff, CF1 2XN, T:0222 499909.

Individual tourist information centres generally print lists of local accommodation, including camp sites. Most of them will book accommodation free of charge, and many operate a telephone 'Book-a-Bed-Ahead' service. By ringing the Holiday Hotline, a visitor can reserve accommodation – ranging from tent space to 5-star hotel – numbers are 07902 474308 for South Wales, 0654 3101 for Mid Wales and 0492 34626 for North Wales.

ACTIVITIES

Walking: Wales offers some of the best and most accessible walking in Britain. There are few places where you cannot find an attractive, impromptu walk within minutes of stopping your car or getting out of a train. For those who need more structure to their outings, the Wales Tourist Board publishes *Wales Walking*, with brief descriptions of 625 graded walks throughout the country, mostly under 10 miles (16km). The 3 National Parks also produce leaflets of walks within their boundaries. *The Welsh Peaks* by W.A. Poucher (Constable 1962) is still considered the classic guide for the mountain walker.

The Forestry Commission has substantial plantations in Wales, all of them criss-crossed with footpaths. For leaflets with recommended forest walks, contact the FC, Victoria House, Victoria Terrace, Aberystwyth, Dyfed SY23 2DA, T:0970 612367.

Riding and trekking: riding centres abound, particularly in the Brecon Beacons and the Cambrian Mountains. For further information, contact the Pony Trekking and Riding Society of Wales, c/o 32 North Parade, Aberystwyth, Dyfed SY23 2NF, or the British Horse Society, Stoneleigh, Kenilworth, Warwick CV8 2LR.

Climbing: the principal centre for climbing in Wales is Plas y Brenin, the National Centre for Mountain Activities in Betws-y-Coed (see SNOWDONIA). Run by the Sports Council, Plas y Brenin offers modern facilities and expert tuition in a wide range of mountaineering skills. Centres that offer climbing courses outside Snowdonia include:

Butterfields, Pen-y-Nant Cottage, Minera, Wrexham LL11 3DA, T:0978 750547.

Five Seasons Guiding, Coed Derw Isaf, Betws-y-Coed, Gwynedd LL24 0BD, T:06902 366.

Solid Summit, 9 Burlington Drive, Prestatyn, Clwyd LL19 8AN, T:07456 6492.

Fishing: there are good opportunities for game and coarse fishing throughout Wales, as well as excellent sea angling. To be thoroughly prepared for Welsh waters, purchase a copy of the *Welsh Angling Guide* from the Fisheries Officer, Welsh Water Authority, Cambrian Way, Brecon, Powys, T:0874 3181.

Caving: natural cave systems suitable for exploration exist almost exclusively in South Wales, where there are 54 caving clubs; in the north, caving activity is restricted to disused mines. Anyone who has acquired a taste for caving is urged to seek the advice of a local club. For a list of clubs, as well as for leaflets about cave systems throughout South and Mid Wales, contact the Cambrian Caving Council, The White Lion, Ynys Uchaf, Ystradgynlais, Swansea SA9 1RW, T:0639 849519.

FURTHER INFORMATION

Wales Tourist Board, PO Box 1, Cardiff CF1 2XN, T:0222 499909. For general information on where to go and where to stay in Wales.

Mid Wales Development, Ladywell House, Newtown, Powys, T:0686 26965. Central source of information for the large and relatively neglected area between the Brecon Beacons and Snowdonia.

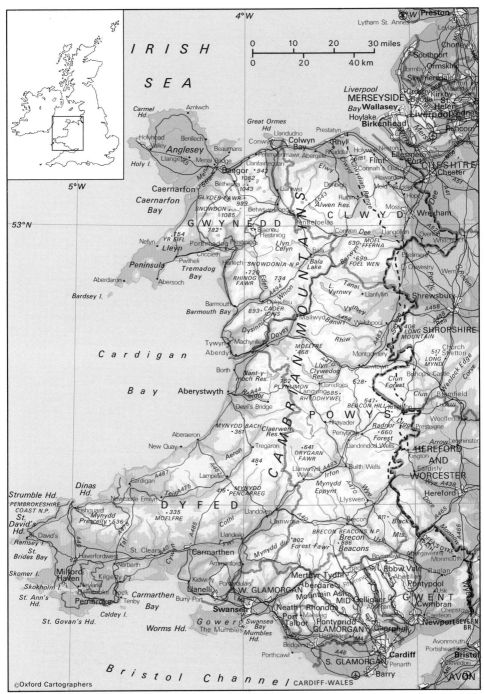

115

Pembrokeshire

Includes the 225-square mile (580sq km) Pembrokeshire Coast National Park

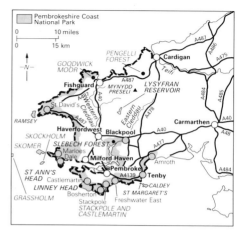

Pembrokeshire, the most south-westerly part of Wales, containing the smallest National Park in Britain, is a maritime county of windswept headlands, of islands large and small, and of superb beaches. Some of these beaches are very public, but many others are secluded, almost secret, so do not reveal their location even to your friends. Nowhere is further than 16 miles (25 kilometres) from salt water, for the great waterway of Milford Haven, a valley drowned when sea levels rose at the end of glacial times, wends its way some 21 miles (33 kilometres) inland. The entrance is guarded by the Old Red Sandstone cliffs of St Ann's Head, where a lighthouse now fulfils the function of the beacon that long marked the dangers to mariners.

The cliff-top flowers here – and indeed all along the Pembrokeshire coast – are superb in early summer; scurvy grass with white flowers and fleshy green leaves, sea campion, thrift, spring quill, kidney vetch and wild carrot, to mention but a few. It was at St Ann's that I first encountered fulmars, on a wild March day when one could barely stand on the cliff top. Despite the weather, these magnificent seabirds swept effortlessly past the cliff face, dropping down with a quick twist of the wings over the Atlantic swell.

Ideally, one should sail here; that is the real way to explore the waterway eastwards to the headwaters of the Western Cleddau at Haverfordwest, where the castle guards the first of the ancient crossings of the river. Alternatively, take the Eastern Cleddau to Blackpool where the old mill has been restored for visitors, and where in most years a pair of dippers nest within a few feet of the wheel shaft. There is a heronry nearby, residents of which can always be seen along the estuary together with shelduck and Canada geese. From September to March large numbers of wildfowl and

waders gather here, and the estuary takes on a special importance during severe weather further east. Sea aster turns some of the saltings mauve during late summer, following on from the carpets of sea lavender. At several points the stately marsh mallow can be found; its roots were once used to make the sweets.

Leave the coast and the waterways, and you will find south-west Wales equally enchanting. In the north Mynydd Preseli rises to 1,535 feet (468 metres); it was from here that early inhabitants are said to have taken the famous 'blue' stones to Stonehenge. This land is an archaeologist's dream; you cannot go far here without seeing earthworks, cromlechs and castles.

The lower slopes of Mynydd Preseli, especially the great sweep above Brynberian, are of special interest to naturalists. In spring, botanists should search here for insectivorous species like the pale and common butterworts, long-leaved and round-leaved sundews. In late summer the tiny bog orchid may be revealed by a hands and knees search, so be prepared for wet legs. In the same location you may well encounter one of Britain's rarest dragonflies, the southern damselfly, a delicate species with azure blue segments; take care, however, not to confuse it with several similar and widespread species.

The fragments of lowland heath

surviving in the agricultural lands between Fishguard and St David's contain more treasures for the naturalist. These windswept areas are a blaze of colour in late summer, with three species of heather contrasting with the saffron of western gorse. On the footpaths you can find special plants such as three-lobed water crowfoot early in the year and yellow centaury towards the end. More conspicuous will be the lesser butterfly orchid, bog asphodel, and devil's bit scabious, a food plant for the often scarce marsh fritillary butterfly. In days gone by Montagu's harriers nested here; now, alas, they are rare visitors. Hen harriers, in contrast, are regular visitors in winter, when you may be lucky enough to see several of these fine raptors going to roost in a patch of willow scrub.

Virtually the whole of the coastline, including the headwaters of Milford Haven and a large block of Mynydd Preseli, lies within the Pembrokeshire Coast National Park. A long-distance footpath runs from Amroth in the south east to the Teifi estuary in the north. There are ancillary routes across several of the headlands and around the upper reaches of the Cleddau.

BEFORE YOU GO
Maps: OS Landranger Series Map Nos. 145, 157, 158.
Guidebooks: Countryside Commission Official Guide: *Pembrokeshire Coast National Park* (Webbs and Bower) and *The Nature of West Wales*, edited by David Saunders (Barracuda) are recommended.

GETTING THERE
By road: the M4 brings the visitor within an hour of south-west Wales, where the main routes are the A40 to Fishguard, A477 to Pembroke and A487 to St David's. Most visitors approaching from the North will do so by the A487 from Aberystwyth through Cardigan and Fishguard to St David's. There are a number of B roads, but most other roads are unclassified and many are narrow. There are good car parking facilities at most points.
By rail: services run from London Paddington; on most, travellers have to change at Swansea for the West Wales line through to Milford Haven, with some services to Tenby and Pembroke in the south and Fishguard in the north.
By bus: buses run from London with links from other centres to Haverfordwest, Milford Haven, Pembroke and Tenby. Public transport within the area, even close to the main towns, is extremely limited.

WHERE TO STAY
Major accommodation centres outside the Pembrokeshire National Park are Fishguard, Haverfordwest, Milford Haven and Pembroke; within the Park, St David's in the west and Tenby in the south. A telephone bed booking service run by the Wales Tourist Board is available at the Information Offices at Kilgetty (T:0834 812175) and Haverfordwest (T:0437 66141); also at the Tourist Board Office in Fishguard (T:0348 873849).
Youth hostels: at Poppit (T:0239 612936); Castell Mawr (T:03485 233); Fford-yr-Afon (T:03483 414); Llaethdy (T:0437 720345); Broad Haven (T:043783 688); Runwayskiln (T:06465 257); The Old School, Pentlepoir (T:0834 812333).
Outdoor living: park information centres will provide information about camping and caravan (motor home) sites, with which the park is well provided. *Coastal Path Accommodation*, published by the park authority, is a comprehensive list of camp sites and bed and breakfast establishments, indispensible for the long-distance backpacker.

ACCESS AND CLOSURES
Much of the Castlemartin Peninsula is an MOD tank gunnery range; access to Range West is only possible on the National Park Authority's escorted Sunday visits.

ACTIVITIES
Walking: the coastal path and its adjacent routes offer several hundred miles of walking. Much of Mynydd Preseli is open common land, while there are some special routes like that around Lysyfran Reservoir, or through the conifers at Slebech Forest. A programme of walks is organised by the National Park Authority. Full details are given in the free annual publication *Coast to Coast*. For the 168-mile (269-km) Pembrokeshire Coast long-distance path from Amroth to the Teifi Estuary, see *A Guide to the Pembrokeshire Coast Path* by C.J. Wright (Constable).
Climbing: some of the sea cliffs, especially in the south,

offer striking and varied climbs. Seasonal restrictions apply in certain areas to safeguard nesting seabirds. The *Climbers Club Guide to Wales – Pembrokeshire* by Pat Littljohn and Mike Harber (Climbers Club 1981) lists many routes.

Fishing: the rocky coastline, sandy beaches, rivers and reservoirs of south-west Wales offer many opportunities for angling. Enquire at information centres or fishing tackle shops. Sea angling is catered for from ports such as Tenby and Dale.

FURTHER INFORMATION

The National Park operates 7 Tourist Information Centres, at Broad Haven (T:043783 412), Haverfordwest (T:0437 66141), Kilgetty (T:0834 812175), Newport (T:0239 820912), Pembroke (T:0646 682148), St David's (T:0437 720392) and Tenby (T: 0834 2402). The headquarters is at County Offices, St Thomas's Green, Haverfordwest, to where postal enquiries should be addressed. Other sources of information are Preseli District Council, Cambria House, Haverfordwest, and South Pembrokeshire District Council, Information Bureau, The Croft, Tenby.

Pembrokeshire Islands

Part of Pembrokeshire Coast National Park Grassholm RSPB Reserve, St Margaret's and Skokholm WWTNC, Skomer NNC NNR and Ramsey

The islands of Grassholm, Skokholm, Skomer and 118

Ramsey are without compare, for they support some of the most spectacular seal and seabird colonies on the coast of Britain. Part of the Pembrokeshire Coast National Park, they are noted for their seabird colonies, maritime flowers, grey seals and, in the case of Skomer, an indigenous sub-species of bank vole found nowhere else. Lonely Grassholm – a bare cone of granite rock in the wild Atlantic – is home for 30,000 pairs of gannets, the third largest colony in the world. It is the most difficult to reach; the boat journey can be well over an hour in duration and one cannot always land. With so many birds, however, there are always spectacular views from the sea.

Skokholm – site of the first bird observatory to be established in Britain – and Skomer are of international importance for their seabirds, especially the nocturnal Manx shearwater of which the two islands support 140,000 pairs, and some 6,000 pairs of storm petrels which come ashore to breed on Stokholm. Razorbills, guillemots and puffins are much more readily seen, while the garrulous kittiwakes endlessly call their name from the cliffs.

Everywhere there are birds, and then the flowers, not just the maritime species one might expect, but two surprises for offshore islands; vast acres of bluebells quickly followed by equally dramatic sweeps of red campion, with a few foxgloves standing nobly along the old walls for good measure.

Choughs apart, Ramsey is disappointing for birds, as brown rats, possibly survivors from some long forgotten shipwreck, mean that there are no burrow-nesting seabirds. This is the place to

observe seals, however, for Ramsey has the most important grey seal breeding colony in Wales; there can be few more dramatic sights than the west coast of Ramsey viewed from a boat, with seals watching from cave entrances or sprawled on offshore rocks as you pass by. The inland waters around Skomer and the Marloes Peninsula are now protected as a marine reserve.

Getting there: the islands can be reached between Easter and late September; don't forget that even in midsummer, high winds may make the crossing impossible. Skomer is open daily by boat from Martin's Haven, a rocky beach west of Marloes (T:06465 349). Skokholm is normally open only to weekly visitors, with full board provided for up to 15. For details, phone 0834 812175. There are only occasional day visits. Grassholm may also be reached from Martin's Haven; landings (Mon only from mid-June) or round-island trips at any time, weather permitting, but no landings before 16 June (T:06765 349); authorised boatman Campbell Reynolds of Dale Sailing Co. For Caldey and St Margaret's, where landings are not permitted, several boats ply out of Tenby. Boats for and round Ramsey leave the lifeboat slip at St Justinian to the west of St David's. **Access:** to all these islands is strictly controlled by WWTNC.

Facilities: guided walks on Skomer and Skokholm; make your reservation in advance from any Pembrokeshire National Park Information Centre or phone 0834 812175. Skomer has limited

This Ramsey Island beach makes a pleasant sun trap for grey seals, all spent bulls and non-breeding cows

accommodation for WWTNC members only. Skokholm offers weekly residential natural history courses; details of accommodation on both islands from WWTNC, Haverfordwest (T:0437 5462). **Further information:** leaflets from WWTNC, 7 Market Street, Haverfordwest, Dyfed SA61 1NF

Stackpole and Castlemartin

Part of the Pembrokeshire Coast National Park
NCC NNR

A limestone coastline all the way from Stackpole Quay to Linney Head, and one of the finest stretches of the Pembrokeshire Coast National Park. In the east there are nearly 2,000 acres (800ha) of dunes, rabbit grazed warrens, cliffs and the freshwater lakes at Bosherton. The lakes were formed nearly two centuries ago when the valleys were flooded after the construction of several dams. Now this is one of the best areas in lowland Britain for its aquatic flora, the most striking of all being the huge rafts of white water lilies. In winter many duck may be seen; rarer visitors include bittern and the North American ring-necked duck. The cliffs at Stackpole, with their caves, stacks and wave-worn arches, are noted for their flowers and nesting seabirds, even a few pairs of puffins, though look hard for these. Choughs and peregrines are two other species which occur. Elegug is the Pembrokeshire name for guillemot, and at four limestone stacks midway along the Castlemartin Peninsula is a large colony, certainly the
120

most easily viewed colony of these birds in Wales, if not the whole of Britain.
Getting there: well signposted south from Pembroke. Stackpole Quay is to the east, Bosherton village and Broad Haven South in the centre and Elegug Stacks in the west. Castlemartin is a tank range, and access is only possible on one of the Sunday escorted visits organized by the national park. The road to the Stacks is frequently closed on weekdays when the tank range is operational, but is always open at weekends and on bank holidays. **Where to stay:** Pembroke and Freshwater East are the main centres. **Where to go:** if time is short then make sure you go to Elegug Stacks and the ponds at Bosherton. For the more energetic there is the 4-mile (6.5-km) cliff walk from Elegug Stacks to St Govan's.

Pengelli Forest

WWTNC Reserve

The largest remaining block of ancient woodland remaining in south-west Wales. Pengelli Forest covers 163 acres (66ha). In Elizabethan times, when a local historian left so

much fascinating information about the forest, it was much larger. The forest consists mainly of sessile oak, with a range of other species, including three specimens of midland hawthorn at its only known location in this part of Wales.

Polecats, and dormice too, may be found here although, like the white-letter hairstreak butterfly which has also been recorded, they are extremely elusive. Woodland birds include sparrowhawk, redstart and pied flycatcher. Many nestboxes have been erected for hole-nesting birds.
Getting there: from the village of Velindre, 12 miles (20km) east of Fishguard on the A487, take a secondary road to Trewilym. Access to the forest is through a gate about 1 mile down this road on the right. **Access:** open all year on marked paths only. **Facilities:** 4 nature trails. **Further information:** Tourist Information Centre, Town Hall, Fishguard; leaflet available from West Wales Trust for Nature Conservation.

The Skomer vole is an evolutionary rarity found only on the Pembrokeshire island from which it takes its name

SOUTH WALES

South Wales is bounded in the west by the wild limestone cliffs of Gower, and in the east by the Severn estuary with its vast brown tidal mud flats and even browner water. Running northwards from the estuary is the Wye valley, the frontier with England; and what a superb frontier it is, this steep, wooded valley with its natural defences underlined by the ancient fortifications of Offa's Dyke.

Between these extremes lies the industrial heart of Wales, though it beats less strongly than in earlier days: the mining valleys, the great works, the docks, marshalling yards and power stations. The casual observer speeding west might think that nature had passed the area by, but there is much to explore and many delights to savour.

There can be few greater contrasts than that which exists between the tiny pools in the heart of Gower, and the vast lowland fen of Crymlyn Bog (paradoxically situated in the industrial heartland of Swansea). But the key to it all is water, whether it be river, lake, reservoir or sea; it is water that makes South Wales so rich in bird life and such a joy to naturalists and ornithologists.

Gower Peninsula

AONB Includes much NT land, several NNRs and GWT Reserves

This delightful peninsula, barely 5 miles (8km) wide, extends 20 miles (32km) westwards from the outskirts of Swansea. Virtually every habitat, save for uplands and mountains, is represented here, though in a coastal area such as this the range of maritime habitats is the dominant feature.

At the extreme south west is Worm's Head, which takes its name from the Saxon word for 'dragon' on account of its shape. It is rich in maritime flora, and has the only seabird colonies of note in South Wales. There are kittiwakes, razorbills and guillemots, possibly even a pair or two of puffins. To the east of the Worm the cliffs are a botanist's paradise, rich in special species such as the yellow whitlow grass which grows nowhere else in Britain, spring cinquefoil, white rock rose, hoary rock rose, spiked speedwell and clary.

Two rather special insects may also be found here. One of these is the marbled white butterfly, the other insect is a great green bush cricket, a very local insect in Wales where it is restricted to a few areas on south and south-west coasts. This massive beast, over 1 ½ in (4cm) in length, is more often heard than seen, though its strident note, which it plays until well after dark, is too high-pitched for some naturalists to hear in the evening of their years.

Oxwich NNR is a mosaic of fen, marsh, open water, sand dune and woodland. The aquatic habitats are exciting, bitterns are regular winter visitors and in some years remain to boom. Another East Anglian species, the bearded tit, has nested here for the past 10 years, while the Cetti's warbler is a more recent colonist. Adder, grass snake and slow worm inhabit the drier slopes.

In the north the Burry Inlet, flanked by nearly 9 miles (15km) of salt marshes and guarded by the large sand dune system of Whiteford Burrows NNR, is one of Britain's major estuaries for wildfowl and waders. Of particular importance is the only regular flock of wintering Brent geese in Wales; the resident eiders are also worth attention, since this species normally breeds no further south than Cumbria.

Getting there: the A4118 leaves Swansea and traverses south Gower to Port Eynon, beyond which the B4247 carries on to Rhossili. In the north, the B4271 and B4295 both terminate at Llanrhidian; then it is unclassified roads all the way to the remote north west. **Where to stay:** there are plenty of hotels and guest houses in Mumbles and west to Caswell Bay, beyond which there are bed and breakfast houses and a number of caravan and camping (motor home) sites. **Access:** permit only off marked paths at Whiteford Burrows; unrestricted access to the dunes and woodland paths at Oxwich; for access to other areas within the Whiteford and Oxwich reserves apply for a permit to the Regional Officer, NCC, South Wales Region, 44 The Parade, Roath, Cardiff CF2 3AB. For conservation reasons, visitors are urged to keep to footpaths or designated nature trails along the coastal reserves.

121

The long spine of Worm's Head emerges in the dawn light of Rhossili Bay

Crymlyn Bog

NCC NNR

The largest lowland fen in Wales, Crymlyn Bog is a remarkable example of a fast-disappearing type of habitat with its wealth of rare plants and birds. Although the great sundew has vanished, both the round- and long-leaved sundews are still found here. In midsummer, the yellow of bog asphodel, great spearwort and yellow sedge make a splendid show. Reed and sedge warblers are numerous in summer, while Cetti's warbler is a recent arrival. This is one of the few places in the extreme south of Wales where snipe can still be heard 'drumming'. Strangely situated in the heart of industrial Swansea, it is continuously threatened but somehow, miraculously, it still survives. **Getting there:** via A42217 in east Swansea. Car park and information centre on Dinam Road, south of Pentre Dwr. **Access:** permission from NCC required to leave footpath. **Further information:** leaflet from NCC.

Kenfig Pool and Dunes

Mid-Glamorgan CC Reserve

These 2,525 acres (1,022ha) of dunes, flanked on the seaward side by the expanse of Kenfig Sands, contain a reed-gist dune-slack lake called Kenfig Pool in the middle. Long recognized for its wealth of flowering plants, the reserve also boasts a variety of birds, including uncommon species such as purple heron and bittern. Several hundred tufted duck and pochard

Worm's Head is only accessible for 2½ hours at low tide; visitors are requested not to visit this important nesting site from March to July. **Facilities:** NCC information kiosk at Whiteford Burrows;
122

information centres and nature trails at Rhossili and Oxwich. Advice available at Rhossili on rock climbing and sea fishing. **Further information:** NCC leaflets from information centres. For Wardens at NCC Oxwich, Whiteford and South Gower contact Oxwich Reserve Centre, Oxwich, Swansea SA3 1LS, T:0792 390320/390626.

gather in winter, while the flock of up to 80 gadwall is the largest concentration in Wales.

Small numbers of seabirds pass offshore in late summer and can be observed by those who watch patiently from Sker Point. Among the dune plants are carline thistle, viper's bugloss and even primrose, while the slacks support several species of orchid.
Getting there: signposted from Pyle and Porthcawl; junctions 37 or 38 from M4. Regular bus services from Porthcawl and Bridgend. **Access:** open all year; several footpaths.
Facilities: lectures and guided walks regularly scheduled by information centre. **Further information:** Warden, Kenfig Nature Reserve Centre, Ton Kenfig, Pyle, Mid Glamorgan CF33 4PT, T:0656 743386.

The Wye Valley

NCC scheduled Grade 1 site

The Wye rises at 2,000ft (600m) on Plynlimon not far from the sea in Cardigan Bay, but like its near neighbour the Severn chooses an easterly course to the Bristol Channel where eventually the waters mingle. For the last 21 miles (35km) of its journey the Wye forms the boundary with England, and here it has carved a meandering course through a magnificent river gorge from just downstream of Monmouth to the sea at Chepstow.

The gorge contains many fine woodlands – among the few ancient woods left in Britain – with oak, beech, ash, wych elm where these have escaped the ravages of Dutch Elm disease, and field maple. A number of scarce species

occur, including small-leaved lime, and the rare whitebeams of which several species are recorded here.

The whole area is renowned for its invertebrates, the butterfly fauna being especially rich; nearly half of all the species in Britain can be found here. The riverside cliffs contain caves, the winter hibernation site of greater horseshoe bats, one of our rarest mammals.

Shelduck breed on the lower reaches of the river, while cormorants and grey herons are always to be seen. Look out for common sandpipers in the summer months. This delightful wader has a nervous disposition, or so it seems as it bobs its way along the water's edge, drawing attention with its shrill 'willy-wicket' song. Were they here when the monks from Tintern Abbey fished these waters 800 summers ago?
Before you go: OS Landranger Series Map No. 162.
Getting there: the A466, which clings to the banks of the river Wye for its last 18 miles (29km) from Monmouth to the Severn, makes the lower Wye Valley one of the most accessible of Britain's beauty spots. Exit 22 on the M4, at the Welsh end of the Severn Bridge, is a logical starting place for southern visitors. From the Midlands and North, turn off the M5 at exit 8 and take the M50 to where it ends near Ross-on-Wye, 12 miles (19km) from Monmouth.

Chepstow is on a direct line between Swansea and the Midlands, and one stop away from the main London-South Wales line. **Where to stay:** there is no shortage of tourist accommodation along the valley, with Chepstow and Monmouth at either end offering a wide range of

overnight facilities. Book your accommodation ahead at the Wales Tourist Information and National Trust Centre, Church Street, Monmouth, T:0600 3899. Four youth hostels are evenly spaced along the valley at Welsh Bicknor (T:0594 60300); Monmouth (T:0600 5116); Lydney (T:054 530272); Chepstow (T:02912 2685).
Where to go: both banks of the river are criss-crossed with footpaths and rights-of-way. The following nature reserves are of especial interest.

The Wyndcliff Nature Trail is operated jointly by the FC and the NCC. About 3 miles (5km) north of Chepstow, turn left off the A466. The trail leads from the FC car park. Spectacular views from the Eagle's Nest on cliff top. From there, a path (including 365 steps) descends to the Wye.

Cleddon Bog and Cleddon Shoot (GTBC), an area of ancient woodland, are both accessible from the village of Trellick. Take the Llandogo road off the B4293, 5 miles (8km) south of Monmouth.
Access: Lady Park Wood open to permit holders only. Apply to NCC. Cars not permitted on FC roads; riding by permit only on FC bridleways.
Facilities: trails for the handicapped and visually handicapped at Whitestone, operated by FC (leaflet available).
Further information: Tourist Information Centres are at Church Street, Monmouth (T:0600 3899); The Gate House, Chepstow (T:02912 3772); Tintern (T:02918 431).

Booklet on reserves from Gwent Trust for Nature Conservation, 16 White Swan Court, Monmouth, Gwent NP5 3NY. For further information about FC holdings contact FC, Wentwood, Llanvaches, Newport, Gwent NP6 3AZ, T:0633 400849.

123

Brecon Beacons

*National Park extending over 519·square
miles (1,350sq km) of mountains and
valleys in southern Wales*

One of the finest views in all of Wales, where there are so many to choose from, can be obtained from the A470 just north-east of Brecon. Look south, and you behold the high peaks of Brecon Beacons encompassing all the beauty and majesty of the region. At times they are covered by winter snow, at others shrouded in mists that leave only the foothills visible. Whatever the conditions, the Brecon Beacons are always a lure.

This huge tract of land straddles three counties and is divided into several segments by valleys. From the corrie cliffs of the Carmarthen Van in the west it is nearly 40 miles (64 kilometres) eastward to where the Black Mountains extend their formidable welcome to the intruders from across the English border. To the south is industrial Glamorgan, to the north more high ground, the Mynydd Eppynt, base of the central spine of Wales.

The westernmost section of the park is known, confusingly, as Black Mountain. From the youth hostel at Llanddeusant at the base of its northern slopes, the two main peaks of this spectacular region, Bannau Sir Gaer, 2,460 feet (750 metres), and Fan Brycheiniog, 2,366 feet (721 metres), are a popular challenge.

To the east of Black Mountain lies Fforest Fawr, once a hunting preserve for the Lords of Brecon. It is now less frequented by hikers than its towering eastern neighbours, the glamorous Beacons; this may, however, make it a more attractive area to lone rangers wishing to escape the company of their fellow beings.

Much of the park is composed of Old Red Sandstone; in the park's eponymous heartland, the Brecon Beacons themselves, it rises to 2,907 feet (886 metres) at Pen-y-Fan, the highest point in South Wales. There are two lesser peaks hard by: Corn

Du, 2,863 feet (873 metres) and the pointed summit of Cribyn, 2,608 feet (795 metres). If you make your way by means of the path from Storey Arms, you may be surprised to come across a memorial obelisk commemorating the death from exposure in August 1900 of young Tommy Jones. It serves as a salutary reminder that the high ground can be dangerous, even in mid-summer, for the ill-prepared.

There are numerous reservoirs which provide water for South Wales, while among the natural sites are the lakes of Llyn-y-Fan Fawr and Llyn-y-Fan Fach below the 650-foot (200-metre) cliffs of Bannau Sir Gaer. The latter is renowned for the folk tale of the Lady of the Lake, a beauty who lived happily with her farmer husband before the spell was broken and she returned to the waters. One of her sons, so further legend has it, became the first of the physicians of Myddi, a village a few miles to the north, where you can still see the graves of the last of these healers.

Just south of Llangorse is Llangorse Lake, the largest area of natural fresh water in the southern half of Wales. Famous as a breeding ground for wetland birds, it has unfortunately lost some of its natural history interest as a result of its extensive use for waterborne sports. The number of breeding birds has dropped and some plants have vanished, though several scarce species remain. It is best to visit the lake in the winter, when there is a good range of wildfowl. Pochard and tufted duck are the most numerous, while small parties of Bewick's and whooper swans are regular visitors. The access route is well signposted from the A40 at Bwlch, the pass over a low shoulder of the Black Mountain.

The park contains several notable reserves such as the one at Craig-y-Ciliau, where the densely wooded limestone cliffs and screes contrast sharply with the open moorland above. Bordering the River Enig near Talgarth is Pwll-y-Wrach, a reserve of the Brecknock Naturalists' Trust, a woodland with dog's mercury, enchanter's nightshade, woodruff and wild strawberry.

Botanically the lakes are important for several plants which reach the southern

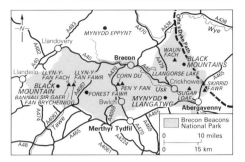

limits of their range. A visit in late July is best, for then the pale lilac flowers of water lobelia dance in the wavelets.

At the southern edge of the park the sandstones give way to millstone grit and carboniferous limestone. This is a dream land for the geologist and the caver. There are more swallow holes per square mile than in any other part of Britain. Like bomb craters they litter the southern boundary. The rivers and streams are in confusion; some vanish below the ground to reappear after a short distance, others pass through gorges and over waterfalls. There can be few more classic falls than the one at Henrytd with its 100-foot (30-metre) drop, or at Sgwd yr Eira on the Hepste where you can drive a herd of sheep behind the cascade.

If you really wish to go behind water, to follow its ancient routes, then visit the Dan-yr-Ogof show caves in the upper reaches of the Tawe. The system was first explored in 1912 by the Morgan brothers and their friends, first on a raft and then by coracle. What better way to explore a Welsh cave than by Welsh coracle? For the experienced caver there are numerous other systems including that at Agen Allwed, where over

nine miles (15 kilometres) of underground passages penetrate into the heart of Mynydd Llangatwg, and the cave system at Ogof Ffynon Ddu NNR, one of the deepest in Britain.

The park comes to a dramatic conclusion in the east in the daunting peaks of the Black Mountains. Waun Fach, at 2,660 feet (811 metres) is the highest, but Sugar Loaf, 1,955 feet (595 metres) and Skirrid Fawr, 1,595 feet (486 metres), set apart to the south of the main range, are equally popular with hill walkers. Offa's Dyke Path (see page 140) passes through the Black Mountains, skirting the eastern boundary of the park.

BEFORE YOU GO
Except for its extreme western and south-eastern corners, the Brecon Beacons National Park fits obligingly into two OS Landranger Series Maps, Nos. 160 and 161. The serious walker, however, is better equipped with Nos. 11, 12 and 13 of the Outdoor Leisure Series, which give the entire park in 1:25,000 scale, or about 2½ inches to the mile. The best introductory guide book is the Countryside Commission Official Guide, *The Brecon Beacons* (Webb and Bower).

A good place to start any visit is at the Brecon Beacons Mountain Centre, 5 miles (8km) south-west of Brecon. The largest of the park's 4 information centres, it is open every day except Christmas.

GETTING THERE
By car: from the south and east, the M4 brings motorists to within 20 miles (32km) of the park's southern boundary. Take exit 26 at Newport for Pontypool and Abergavenny. From exit 32, take the A470 for Brecon. From the Midlands and the North, the M50 (exit 8 of the M5) leads to Ross-on-Wye. Continue on the A40 for Abergavenny at the east of the park. The A40 angles north-west across the park to Brecon and from there due west to Llandovery. Most of the major roads, however, run roughly north-south: the A4069 over Black Mountain, the A4067 through Fforest Fawr, the A470 through the

Brecon Beacons and the A479 to the west of the Black Mountains.
By rail: from Newport and Cardiff – stations on the main London line – change respectively for Abergavenny and Merthyr Tydfil. Abergavenny also connects via Crewe with cities in the Midlands and North. The beautiful Central Wales Line from Swansea to Shrewsbury serves both Llandeilo and Llandovery and connects via its termini to points throughout Britain.
By air: Cardiff, the principal airport in South Wales, has regular flights to London, Birmingham and Glasgow, and a limited international service.
By bus: from major coach

stations in Newport and Cardiff change for local buses to points within the park. A regular coach service from Cardiff to Bangor crosses the park via Merthyr Tydfil and Brecon.

WHERE TO STAY
The park has within or just outside its boundaries a number of towns which offer a wide range of self-catering and serviced accommodation. Brecon, with a population of just over 7,000, is the largest community in the park; Hay-on-Wye, Crickhowell and Talgarth are also centres for accommodation and information. Outside the park, Abergavenny to the south east, and Llandovery and Llandeilo to the west are the principal dormitory towns for tourists. Equally convenient, though less tourist-oriented, are the industrial 'heads of the valleys' to the south, Merthyr Tydfil the largest among them.

Bed-booking services are available during the tourist season from the national park information centres at Abergavenny (T:0873 3254); Brecon (T:0874 4437); and Llandovery (T:0550 20693). The National Park Authority issues a useful list of serviced and self-catering accommodation.

Outdoor living: another leaflet issued by the park authority lists some 30 camping and caravan (motor home) sites within or near the park. Camping elsewhere, even on common land, requires the owners's or tenant's permission. Motorists towing caravans are urged to avoid minor roads which may not be wide enough to accommodate two vehicles.

The FC operates 4 camping sites for walkers only. Further information from the National Park Office, 7 Glamorgan Street, Brecon, Powys LD3 7DP, T:0874 4437.

Youth Hostels: there are 5 youth hostels within the Park, at: Capel-y-ffin (T:0873 890650); Llanddeusant (T:05504 634); Llwyn-y-Celyn, Libanus (T:0874 4261); Ty'n-y-Caeau, Groesffordd (T:087486 270); Ystradfellte, Aberdare (T:0639 720301).

ACCESS AND CLOSURES
While the unfenced uplands of the park seem to invite ramblers to walk where they will, it is well to remember that most of the open country is common land, used for grazing by the local 'commoners'. In practice, there is rarely a conflict between visitors and commoners, but when in doubt concerning your rights, stick to signposted paths or to rights-of-way indicated on the OS maps.

The Forestry Commission, which has a substantial presence in the park, generally welcomes well-behaved walkers along its many trails. Its 4 major forests are Coed Taf, 5 miles (8km) north of Merthyr Tydfil; Talybont, just west of the village of that name; Mynydd Du, in the heart of the Black Mountains; and Coed y Rhaiadr – with its spectacular waterfalls – bordering the park to the south of Fforest Fawr. For complete information about FC forests and facilities, visit the Garwant Visitor Centre, 5 miles (8km) to the north of Merthyr Tydfil.

For access to nature reserves (see above), which are not served by rights-of-way or signposted nature trails, contact the NCC or the local Trust office for the appropriate county. Most of the park lies in Powys, but Dyfed, Gwent and Glamorgan nibble at its corners.

> 'There are, as perhaps the reader knows, no jaguars in Wales – nor pumas – nor anacondas . . . What I feared most was lest, whilst my sleeping face was upturned to the stars, some one of the many Brahminical-looking cows on the Cambrian Hills might poach her foot into the centre of my face.'
>
> *Thomas de Quincey: Confessions of an English Opium Eater*

ACTIVITIES
Walking: despite the relative proximity of all the major peaks to main roads and the comforts of civilization, the walker in the park should remember that the high ground here is as exposed and the weather as unpredictable as anywhere in Britain. Plan your route carefully and equip yourself for rough terrain, then set out to enjoy some highly accessible and beautiful hill walking.

With the aid of the OS maps (see **Before you go**) it is an easy park to improvise an attractive expedition. Some of the standard routes, however, are not to be missed. From Crickhowell, for instance, you can take in all the major hills of the Black Mountains on the way to the youth hostel at Capel-y-ffin. From Brecon there is a circular ridge walk which includes as many of the highest beacons as you have the energy to encounter in a single day. **Riding:** in a land so full of ponies, it is no wonder that pony trekking is a well-established activity. *Pony*

Winter emphasises the remoteness of Brecon at Pen-y-Fan, the highest of the Beacons

Trekking, a leaflet issued by the park authority, lists some 2 dozen centres, mainly in the Black Mountains, from which you can ride – or learn to ride.

For further information write to The Pony Trekking and Riding Society of Wales, c/o 32 North Parade, Aberystwyth, Dyfed.

Caving: in the narrow strip of limestone that extends across the park's southern boundary are some of the longest and deepest caves in the country. From west to east, the principal caving areas are:

The Tawe Valley and Black Mountain.

The Nedd, Mellte, Hepste and Sychryd valleys.

The Nant Glais valley north of Merthyr Tydfil.

The Llangattock escarpment and Clydach gorge south of Crickhowell.

Caving is an enthusiast's sport and not for the adventurous novice. If you are a caver, contact one of the many clubs whose members have experience in the Brecon underground. The National Park Authority issues a leaflet which lists some of the region's caves and caving clubs. For further information contact the Cambrian Caving Council, Hon. Secretary F. S. Baguley, 15 Elm Grove, Aberdare, Mid Glam. CF44 8DN, T:0685 872585.

Non-cavers should content themselves with a visit to the Dan-yr-Ogof and Cathedral caves in the Tawe valley.

Climbing: The crumbling red sandstone that lies beneath so much of the park makes a treacherous playground for the rock climber. Although some climbing is possible on limestone quarry faces in the south of the park, these hardly justify a special visit.

FURTHER INFORMATION
Information centres within the park:

Brecon Beacons Mountain Centre, near Libanus, Brecon, Powys LD3 8ER, T: 0874 3366. Open all year.

Monk Street, Abergavenny, Gwent NP7 5NA, T: 0873 3254.

Broad Street, Llandovery, Dyfed SA20 0AR, T: 0550 20693.

Watton Mount, Brecon, Powys LD3 7DF, T: 0874 4437.

Enquiries by post to National Park Office, 7 Glamorgan Street, Brecon, Powys LD3 7DP.

CENTRAL WALES

The western gateways to Central Wales are the valleys of the Twyi and Teifi in the south, Ystywth and Rheidol in the centre, and Dyfi in the north. Each is a superb route into the very heartland of Wales, the last refuge for some species, of which the red kite is the most notable. Eight centuries ago it was the beaver, building their last lodges in Britain on the Teifi; Hywel Dda the law giver valued their skins at six score pence, five times that of marten skins and ten times any other.

All five westerly flowing rivers, and the Severn and Wye which travel east, rise in the great moorland massif of central Wales, the Cambrian Mountains. Some 500 square miles (1,280 square kilometres) in extent, this is one of the most remote and sparsely populated areas south of Scotland; a land of open windswept hills and deeply incised valleys with thickly wooded slopes where the sound of the axe has hardly been heard this century. The real threat to the wilderness here is forestry. There are some, usually those with vested interests, who claim that ugly blocks of alien conifers support more birds than the open grouse and heather moor. No one who truly loves Wales would wish to exchange the hilltop call of red grouse for those of the conifer woodpigeon, the song of the golden plover with that of the blackbird, or the dashing merlin for the dunnock.

Upper Twyi Valley

Includes RSPB and WWTNC Reserves

Llandovery, described by George Borrow as 'about the pleasantest little town in which I have halted in the course of my wanderings', is an ideal base from which to explore the valley. Hard by the town is Poor Man's Wood, gifted to the town 3 centuries ago by Vicar Pritchard with a stipulation that the poor people could remove such dead wood as they could carry on their backs.

Go right to the head of the valley, to Llyn Brianne Reservoir on the borders of Carmarthen, Ceredigion and Brecon. A huge block of conifers extends north for a further 10 miles (16km), stretching eastwards to the Irfon and westwards to the Camddwr. The open uplands seems to be your own until a low flying aircraft on a training mission sweeps by and you look down on the pilot and, depending on your inclination, marvel at or curse the jet engine.

Some 2 miles (3km) below the great rock and clay dam of Brianne, the RSPB have their Dinas Reserve. Here, a nature trail passes round the base of a conical wooded hill almost surrounded by the rushing Twyi and its tributary the Doethie.

To these same valleys the red kite retreated towards the end of the last century. Even now it is still restricted to central Wales. This tiny fragile population had a record year in 1987, but even then only 39 fledged, a pitifully small number.

Getting there: leave the A40 in Llandovery and make your choice, for the unclassified roads follow the river north to Rhandirmwyn village and beyond. The Central Wales railway from Shrewsbury to Swansea stops at Llandrindod Wells, Builth Wells, Llanwityd Wells and Llandovery. **Where to stay:** the Tourist Information Centre in Llandovery will help with accommodation; there is a youth hostel at Hafod y Pant, Cynghordy, Llandovery, T:05505 235. **Further information:** Wales Tourist Board Information Centre, Broad Street, Llandovery, T:0550 20693.

Dyfi Estuary

Includes NCC NNR and RSPB Reserve

Here is the border between Central and North Wales. To the south the rolling hills of Ceredigion, to the north the ramparts of Cader Idris and Snowdonia. Few estuaries can encompass such a range of habitats, and there can be few better places to start an exploration than at the Ynyslas Dunes. Don't rush through to the shore, but stop to examine the dune slacks; these moist level areas among the dunes are botanical treasure houses particularly noted for their orchids.

To the south-east, trapped by the coastal ridge, is another of the great mires of central Wales, Cors Fochno – part of Ynyslas NNR and one of the largest raised bogs in Britain – with its bog plants such as myrtle, rosemary, cranberry and royal fern. The rosy marsh moth thrives here, a

128

century after it became extinct in East Anglia.

The estuary, wide at first, twists its way inland where on its southern shore is Ynys Hir, a reserve of the RSPB with habitats ranging from the saltings to woodland and bracken-clad hillsides, and of course the birds for each. **Getting there:** easily accessible from the A487 Aberystwyth to Machynlleth road. For Ynyslas, take the B4353 9 miles (14km) north of Aberystwyth. The Ynys Hir reserve is signposted near the village of Eglwysfach on the A487, 7 miles (11km) from Machynlleth. **Access:** the dunes and shore at Ynyslas are open at all times; a road runs direct to the point. Ynys Hir is open daily from 9am to 9pm or sunset when earlier. Charges are made for non-RSPB members. Access to the rest of the estuary reserve, including Cors Fochno, is by permit issued by NCC, Aberystwyth. **Facilities:** nature trails at both Ynyslas and Ynys Hir (wear rubber boots at the latter). 4 bird-watching hides at Ynys Hir. **Further information:** information centres at both Ynyslas (NCC) and Ynys Hir (RSPB) provide leaflets, or contact NCC. Plas Goggerddan, Aberystwyth, Dyfed SY23 3EE. Further details about Ynys Hir from the Warden, RSPB, Cae'r Berllan, Eglwysfach, Machynlleth, Powys SY20 8TA.

Cors Caron

NCC NNR

A huge upturned saucer of peat, in places 30ft (9m) thick, resting on the bed of a lake formed in glacial times and now one of the largest and best preserved raised mires in

The kite is now a rare spectacle away from Central Wales

western Europe. It lies immediately north of Tregaron, surrounded by low hills, the haunt of the raven and buzzard. This is one of the best places to see the nearly extinct red kite, especially in winter. Whooper swans and other wildfowl also feed on the pools in winter, and may be watched from a tower hide reached after a 1-mile (2-km) walk along the disused railway line. **Getting there:** access from B4343, 1½ miles (4km) north of village of Tregaron, south-east of Aberystwyth. **Access:** limited road-side parking on B4343; public access only along nature trail. Permit required for other areas. **Further information:** leaflet from NCC. For further information and permit, contact the Warden, Minawel, Ffair Rhos, Pontrhydfendigaid, Ystrad Meurig, Dyfed SY25 6BN, T: 09745 671.

Lake Vyrnwy

RSPB Reserve

The largest man-made lake in Wales, nearly 5 miles (8km) long and with a perimeter of

11 miles (18km), has supplied water to Liverpool for nearly 100 years. The reserve extends through the superb woodlands right on to the upland catchment at the southern edge of the Berwyns, the most extensive area of heather moor left in Wales. Here birds such as hen harrier, merlin and short-eared owls breed, while other species that are scarce in Wales, such as the golden plover, may also be encountered. In the woods there are woodcock and even the elusive long-eared owl, best located early in the year when its characteristic triple hoot may be heard. The breeding goosanders are probably the highlight among the waterfowl. **Getting there:** 20 miles (322km) north-west of Welshpool. From Welshpool, take the A490 to Llanfyllin, then continue to Llanwddyn on the B4393, which encircles the lake close to the shoreline. **Where to stay:** the Lake Vyrnwy Hotel provides bed and breakfast, as do a number of local farms. **Access:** unrestricted. Some of the best views, however, from B4393. **Facilities:** RSPB interpretation centre; 2 public hides; 2 nature trails. **Further information:** leaflets and guides at RSPB centre, Llanfyllin, Oswestry, Salop.

NORTH WALES

North of the Dyfi, west of the Shropshire and Cheshire plains are the hills and mountain fastnesses of North Wales, where the Welsh princes once held sway. The coastal regions heard the tramp of many an invading army, and after the death of Llywelyn ap Grufydd, Edward I had a series of magnificent fortifications erected at key points such as Flint, Conwy, Caernarfon, Beaumaris and Harlech, proud on its rock high above the sea; a sea now receded almost a mile to the west.

Half of North Wales is within the Snowdonia National Park, but there are many delights beyond its boundaries. Anglesey, separated from the mainland by the lovely shores of the Menai Straits, is a land of broad flat-topped ridges and shallow valleys, of superb beaches, of cliff headlands, of lakes thronged in winter with Siberian waterfowl. One visitor has said that 'all the softness of Anglesey has marched down to the edge of the water', a spot 'not only one of the fairest in Britain but in Europe'.

Further west is the narrow peninsula of Lleyn, its hills descending in height to the west. With its quiet countryside, narrow roads and tiny coves, it is an area much underrated and worthy of your exploration. Beyond it lies Bardsey Island, now a bird sanctuary, but formerly a religious one.

Bardsey Island

Bird Observatory and Nature Reserve

Some 1½ miles (3km) off the tip of the Lleyn Peninsula, Bardsey is the legendary burial place for 20,000 saints, a place where fact and legend are inextricably woven. It has a long ecclesiastical history, for a holy man called Einion Frenchin had a cell here early in the 5th century, followed by St Cadfan about 100 years later.

Quite unlike the Pembrokeshire islands, Bardsey has a long tradition of a farming community rather than as a single homestead. Although only one family now farms the island, many of the houses are in good condition and from one the Bardsey Bird Observatory is operated.

The island is renowned for its bird migration, partly as a result of its infamous lighthouse where in certain conditions following a new moon large numbers of birds are killed by flying into the glass or nearby structures. A breathtaking list of rare vagrants has been recorded on the island and includes honey buzzard, sora rail, bee-eater, tawny pipit, penduline tit, yellow warbler and grey-cheeked thrush. Ten species of native seabirds also breed here, as do a few pairs of the rare and diminishing chough.

Getting there: the Bardsey Island Trust operates a regular Saturday service for visitors staying on the island for a week or more. Depending upon the weather conditions and the number of interested passengers, day trips with local boatmen can also be arranged through the Trust. Journey time, approximately 2 hours. Contact the Trust Officer, Stabal Henn, Tyddyn Ddu, Criccieth, Gwynnedd, T:076671 2239. **Where to stay:** the Bardsey Island Trust rents cottages to groups or to individuals willing to share. Contact the Trust Officer. The Bardsey Bird and Field Observatory runs residential courses. For enquiries and reservations, contact The Booking Secretary, 21A Gestridge Road, Kingsteignton, Newton Abbot, Devon, T:0626 68580. **Further information:** *Bardsey, Its History and Wildlife* is available from the Bardsey Island Trust. Nearest Wales Tourist Board Information Centre is in Pwllheli (T:0758 61300).

Newborough Warren

NCC NNR

Newborough Warren, the site of one of the finest sand-dune systems in Britain, was once threatened by conifer planting; fortunately, it was stopped before it was too late, and nearly 1,605 acres (650ha) were declared an NNR in 1955. In addition to the dunes there is a freshwater lake, an estuary, a beach and the rocky islet of Ynys Llanddwyn, an island only at high tide. In the extreme west at the head of the Cefni estuary is Malltraeth Pool, made famous by the bird artist Charles Tunnicliffe who lived here from 1945 until his death.

Montagu's harriers used to breed here. (How often one has heard this statement.) They are seen often enough

Carnedd Llywelyn looms giddily east-south-east of Bethesda near the North Wales coast

on passage, however, to raise hopes that one day they may return. In winter various waterfowl including red throated and great northern divers, eider, long-tailed duck and goldeneye frequent the bay.

Getting there: signposted access from A4080 in village of Newborough. **Access:** entire area is very well served with rights of way and Forestry Commission trails. Permit required for access to areas off these paths. **Further information:** information centre at Dinas-lwyd and kiosk at FC car park. Leaflet and permits from NCC, Penrhes Rock, Bangor, Gwynedd LL57 2LQ. For further information, contact the Warden, 'Serai', Malltraeth, Bodorgan, Anglesey, Gwynned LL62 5AS.

South Stack

RSPB Reserve

The cliffs extend for 2 miles (3km) at the most westerly extremity of the island of Anglesey, and are easily accessible by road from Holyhead. They are much used by climbers, for whom

they offer excellent opportunities. Sharing parts of the cliffs that are out of bounds to climbers during the breeding season are large numbers of seabirds, including up to 3,000 guillemots and smaller numbers of razorbills, puffins and kittiwakes.

Peregrines nest and there are usually choughs to be seen, often in close proximity to Ellin's Tower, the observation room and information centre. When you make your visit, spend a little time on the heaths where there are superb late summer flowers, including some special species such as the field fleawort and spotted rock rose.

Getting there: secondary road signposted from Holyhead leads out to cliffs; several nearby car parks. **Access:** unrestricted cliffside walks. Rock climbers are asked to avoid the cliffs between Ellin's Tower and the area just north of South Stack from February to the third week of July. **Facilities:** Ellin's Tower information centre (open Easter to September); displays on birdlife and fine views from first floor. **Further information:** leaflet from RSPB. Warden on duty Apr-Sep at Plas Nico, South Stack, Holyhead, Anglesey, Gwynnedd; at other times contact RSPB, Frolic Street, Newtown, Powys.

Anglesey's Offshore Islands

Two small islands on opposite sides of Anglesey have something to offer birdlovers and islandgoers alike. On the west coast the offshore islets at Rhosneigr support the largest roseate tern colony in Britain, as well as summer populations of common, arctic and Sandwich terns and passage waders like whimbrel in winter. On the east coast the small, green, whale-backed cliffs and grassy slopes of uninhabited Puffin Island, where St Seiriol, a Celtic monk, established a sanctuary in the 6th century, provide nesting sites for numerous seabirds, including razorbills, cormorants, shags, guillemots and, of course, puffins. The island also boasts an old telegraph station, part of a chain of signalling stations for shipping news between Holyhead and Liverpool. Neither of these places enjoys any official conservation status and both can be visited at any time, provided you can find a small boat to take you.

Getting there: the small seaside town of Rhosneigr on the A4080 is the jumping-off point for the Rhosneigr islets; Penmon village (on an unclassified road north-east of Beaumaris) for Puffin Island. Though both Puffin and Rhosneigr islands are only separated from the main shore of Anglesey by narrow stretches of water, you will need to hire boats privately to take you to them. **Access:** at all times – but take extreme care not to disturb nesting birds from the end of April to July, especially the ground-nesting terns on Rhosneigr. **Further information:** Tourist Office, Holyhead or Bangor.

The Manx shearwater, which spends most of its life skimming the Irish Sea, nests on Skokholm and Skomer

Great Orme

Nature Trail

This massive headland, jutting into the Irish Sea to the north of Llandudno, is a botanist's paradise, with a profusion of maritime flowers and scarce species like goldilocks aster, spotted cats-ear, Nottingham catchfly and spiked speedwell. Five bushes of a cotoneaster not found elsewhere in Britain cling on here. There is a fine seabird colony with fulmars, kittiwakes, guillemots, razorbills at the Head. **Getting there:** access from Marine Drive (toll road) in Llandudno, or by tramway to the centre summit and then on foot. **Access:** Public nature trails along cliffs. **Further information:** leaflets from Wales Tourist Board, Chapel Street, Llandudno.

Dee Estuary

RSPB Reserve at Point of Ayr

The Dee Estuary, the third most important in Britain for its waders and wildfowl, straddles the border with England and Wales, with opportunities for observation on both shores. In mid-winter up to 94,000 waders and 21,000 wildfowl are resident, making use of the rich feeding areas on the sands and mud flats, retreating to the saltmarshes and coastal fields at high water. Among the wildfowl the winter flock of up to 5,000 pintail is the largest concentration in Europe.

The non-breeding herd of grey seals, with, on occasions, up to 200 animals hauled out on the West Hoyle Bank, is memorable. They are some 150 miles (240km) from their nearest major breeding area,

The puffin, one of Britain's most distinctive seabirds, is easily distinguished from its relatives the auks by its colourful bill

the Pembrokeshire coast.

Like many other estuaries, the Dee is under threat; plans are afoot for either a barrage which will create a huge freshwater lake, or to maintain the tidal system as a source of power generation. Will the vast flocks of dunlin, bar-tailed godwit, ringed plover, sanderling, oystercatcher and grey plover one day be but a memory, or will the Dee continue to provide a winter home for these birds which have come to Britain from Arctic breeding grounds? **Getting there:** from Chester the A458 North Wales coastal road runs along the shoreline from Connah's Quay to Point of Ayr. On the Wirral side, a number of towns and villages, all linked by the A540, give access to the shoreline. **Where to stay:** Chester is one of the major tourist centres in

Britain. The North Wales coastal towns of Rhyl and Prestatyn are popular holiday resorts. **Where to go:** there are two nature reserves on the Welsh side of the Dee Estuary, at Connah's Quay, 4 miles (6km) south-east of Flint on A548, and at Point of Ayr, at the mouth of the Dee on the Talacre turn-off from the A548. **Access:** Connah's Quay: a number of public open days – generally Sundays – each year; otherwise access is by application to the Secretary, Deeside Naturalists' Trust, 38 Kelsterton Road, Connah's Quay, Deeside, Clwyd CH5 4BJ. Point of Ayr: no restrictions, but visitors are asked not to disturb roosting waders. **Further information:** for literature published by DNT, contact the Secretary (see above). Nearby Tourist Information Centres are at the Town Hall, Chester, Cheshire, T:0244 40144 and the Scala Cinema, Prestatyn, Clwyd, T:07456 2484.

Snowdonia

National Park comprising 838 square miles (2,170sq km) of Welsh mountain terrain

'Horrible with the sight of bare stones' John Leland wrote of Snowdonia in the mid-sixteenth century. Other early visitors also made disparaging remarks about the terrain and, not surprisingly, about the weather, for the high Snowdonia peaks may receive as much as 200 inches of rainfall in a year. They are rugged and often wet, but don't be put off, for this is the wildest region in southern Britain, a place to savour and to explore, and it doesn't rain every day. The heights may be mist-shrouded on occasions, but then the blue sky appears, with white clouds passing behind the ridges and peaks. Climb to the high ground, and it seems as though you can see to the ends of Wales.

This is upland Britain at its very best. Snowdon, or Yr Wyddfa as it is known in Welsh, soars to 3,557 feet (1,085 metres), making it the highest mountain in England and Wales. It forms the centre of the North Wales massif, a great sweep of moor and mountain that includes 13 other peaks above 3,000 feet (900 metres), from high above the Conwy Valley south-west to the Rhinogs, Cader Idris and the Dyfi. There are valleys, many deep and narrow through which the main routes pass, together with some 22 miles (35 kilometres) of coast, the sandy shore of Merioneth south from Harlech including the Mawddach Estuary.

For the geologist, for those who study land forms and the shaping of the country-side, Snowdonia is the greatest classroom in Britain. Early geologists came here to describe the classic sites, and their interpretations still enlighten our visits today. One of the most dramatic sites is at Cwm Idwal – the first NNR in Wales – a magnifi-

The picturesque countryside of Crawcwellt is overshadowed by the silhouettes of the Rhinogs, rising grimly away to the west

cent bowl gouged by ice out of the surrounding crags with a glacial lake at its base. Above the lake, in the cliff cleft of Twill Du, the Devil's Kitchen, can be seen the base of the great rock fold of the Snowdon syncline, a feature but rarely revealed elsewhere.

To the south of the main Snowdonia uplands, across the tranquil Vale of Ffestiniog and bounded by the beautiful Mawddach Estuary, are the craggy uplands of the Rhinogs. A rough landscape with massive ledges and block screes makes this one of the most intractable places in Wales. One visitor to the highest peak, Rhinog Fawr, claimed that it extracted more perspiration to the yard than any other in Snowdonia. Only ancient trackways and footpaths cross this region, including at one point the so-called Roman steps in the defile of Bwlch Tyddiad. These great slabs of stone are more likely to have been laid by medieval hands than by those of the Romans, but the name persists.

At the south-western extremity of the park, on the peninsula that lies between Barmouth Bay and the Dyfi Estuary, soars Cader Idris. Although this impressive 2,928-foot (893-metre) peak is not, topographically speaking, part of Snowdonia proper, it falls within the boundaries of the National Park and has a nature reserve on its slopes. The ascent to the summit of Cader Idris is spectacular but often rugged; be prepared for treacherous weather and carry a map.

Snowdonia is not all open hill. There are fragments of ancient woodland clinging to some valley sides, while modern forestry has created some extensive tracts, none more so than the Gwydir Forest which extends for over nine miles (15 kilometres) from above the Conwy valley to the south of Betws-y-Coed. Visitors are well catered for with several forest walks and picnic sites for the short distance walker, and there are plenty of opportunities for those who require more arduous journeys. Don't miss Coedydd Aber, a valley running inland from the coast just west of Llanfairfechan, which provides an access to the uplands by way of a footpath past the spectacular Aber Falls.

Snowdonia has long attracted naturalists, one of the most famous being Edward Lhuyd, described by John Ray as 'very learned not only in the matter of plants, but also of all Natural History.' Lhuyd has given his name to many rare species, including *Lloydia serotina*, the Snowdon Lily. Found only on a few limestone cliffs in Snowdonia and nowhere else in Britain, this arctic-alpine plant flowers briefly in early June.

The upland birds are a little disappointing, however. The golden eagles have long since disappeared, but there are still ravens, peregrines, merlins, ring ouzels and choughs. In South Wales the chough is restricted to the coast, but here it ranges high into the mountains and some 30 pairs nest, mainly in quarries and mine shafts. For me, a party of choughs feeding on the sheep-grazed turf and then taking flight, their screaming calls fading into the distance as they cross a valley to fresh ground, is one the great moments of any visit to Snowdonia.

BEFORE YOU GO
Maps: all of Snowdonia National Park is contained in 4 of the OS Outdoor Leisure Series maps: Snowdon; Conwy Valley; Harlech; Bala and Cader Idris/Dyfi Forest. With a scale of 1:25,000 – or about 2½ins to a mile – these are an essential first purchase for the serious walker.
Guidebook: a good book to start with is the *Landranger*

Guidebook to Snowdonia, Anglesey and the Lleyn Peninsula, published by the OS and generously illustrated with full-colour maps. See also the Countryside Commission Official Guide, *Snowdonia* (Webb and Bower).

The weather in Snowdonia is notorious, even by Welsh standards. Phone 0286 870120 for a regularly updated regional forecast.

GETTING THERE
By car: from the south east, take the M1 and M6, then the M54 (exit 10A) to where it ends near Wellington. From there, follow the A5 to Betws-y-Coed and the north of the park, or take the A458 from Shrewsbury – generally a quieter route – to Dolgellau and the park's southern region. Motorists from the north should leave the M6 at

its junction with the M56 (exit 20), then follow the A55 to Colwyn Bay. From there, take the A470, the main north-south route through the park. Alternatively continue westward on the A55 to its junction with the A5, or drive on to Caernarfon, where the A485 and A486 head south-east into the park's most mountainous region.

By rail: a fast service operates from London to Holyhead in Anglesey; change at Chester for minor stations along the North Wales coast. The beautiful Conwy Valley Line runs south into the park from Llandudno Junction to Blaenau Ffestiniog. Access by train to Aberdovey, Harlech, Barmouth and other towns along the park's south-west coast is from Shrewsbury in Shropshire.

By bus: National Express operates a regular service to towns along the North Wales coast – including Conwy, Bangor and Caernarfon – from London, Birmingham, Manchester and Liverpool. Crossville operates an hourly service along the same route from Chester. Local bus schedules are generally available at Tourist Board Offices or park information centres. Alternatively, send a self-addressed envelope to Bus Gwynedd, County Planning Department, County Council Offices, Caernarfon, Gwynedd, T:0286 4121.

WHERE TO STAY
Snowdonia's principal towns provide a full range of self-catering and serviced accommodation. Llanberis, Bethesda and Conwy lie just outside the park's northern boundary. Blaenau Ffestiniog and Betws-y-Coed serve the central area, while Harlech, Dolgellau and Bala are among the southern centres for

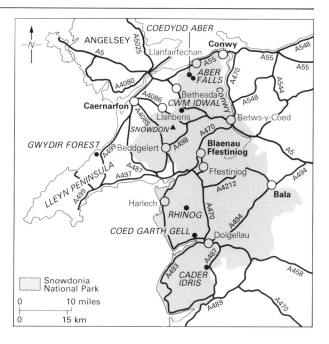

accommodation. *Wales Where to Stay* and *Wales Bed and Breakfast*, published by the Wales Tourist Board, include useful sections on Snowdonia. In conjunction with the Wales Tourist Board, National Park Information Centres produce lists of local accommodation, including camping and caravan sites; they also operate a telephone bed-booking service. There are 7 centres:

The Wharf, Aberdyfi, Gwynedd; T:065472 321.

High Street, Bala, Gwynedd, T:0678 520367.

The Royal Oak Stables, Betws-y-Coed, Gwynedd, T:06902 665/426.

High Street, Blaenau Ffestiniog, Gwynedd, T:0766 830360.

The Bridge, Dolgellau, Gwynedd, T:0341 422888.

High Street, Harlech, Gwynedd, T:0766 780658.

Oriel Eyryri, Llanberis, Gwynedd, T:0286 870636.

Youth hostels: there are 15

hostels within the park or just outside its boundaries at: Rhos-y-Gwaliau (T:0678 520215); Nant Gwynant (T;076686 251); Capel Curig (T:06904 255); Corris (T:065473 686); Ffestiniog (T:076676 2765); Harlech (T:0766 780285); Bethesda (T:0248 600255); Dolgellau (T:0341 422392); Llanbedr (T:034123 287); Llanberis (T:0286 870280); Dolwyddelan (T:06906 202); Penmaenmour (T:049 623476); Nant Gwynant (T:0286 870428); Conwy (T:0492 531406); Rhyd Ddu (T:028685 391). For a leaflet and further information contact YHA Area Office, 12 Wynnstay Road, Colwyn Bay, Clwyd, T:0492 531406.

WHERE TO GO
Snowdonia has no obvious centre. It falls into several regions, each with its own attractions, which are most conveniently approached from the following towns:

Beddgelert: at junction of A498 and A4085 to the south of Snowdon. Forest walks and climbs to 2,566-ft (783-m) Moel Hebog and summit of Snowdon. Can be congested with traffic in summer.

Bethesda: slate-quarrying town on the A5, just outside northern boundary of park. Good access from here to the Carneddau Range and Carnedd Llewelyn, at 3,484ft (1,062m) the park's second highest mountain.

Betws-y-Coed: major centre at the junction of the A5 A470, 21 miles (34km) south of Llandudno Junction. Extensive walks and beautiful waterfalls in the surrounding Gwydyr Forest. Information T:06902 665.

Dolgellau: on the A470, 10 miles (16km) east of Barmouth. Centre for climbing Cader Idris, for the Coed y Brenin Forest 6 miles (10km) to the north and the craggy Arans to the east. Information, T:0341 422888.

Harlech: west coast town on the A496. Access from here to the Rhinog Range and the coastal flats. Information, T:0766 780658.

Llanberis: 7 miles (11km) south-east of Caernarfon on the A4086. Principal centre for climbing Snowdon itself, by rail or by the gentle, 5-mile (8-km) Llanberis Path to the summit. Also convenient for access to the Glyder Range immediately to the east. Information, T:0286 870636.

The nature reserves in Snowdonia include:

Cader Idris: NCC NNR, best visited on the Llyn-y-Cau route from Minfford village, 7 miles (11km) from Dolgellau on A487. NCC permit required to visit enclosed woodland on reserve.

Coed Garth Gell: wooded river gorge; access on footpath off A496, 3½ miles (6km)

138

from Dolgellau. Excellent displays on local natural history at Penmaenpool Information Centre, 1 mile south across Afon Mawddach.

Coedydd Aber: wooded river valley; access from Aber village on A55, 5 miles (8km) east of Bangor; nature trail. Permit required for areas off rights-of-way. NCC leaflet.

Cwm Idwal: cliffs and glacial lake; access from footpath running south from Ogwen Cottage Mountain School on A5, 5 miles (8km) south of Bethesda. Nature trail. NCC leaflet.

Rhinog: craggy, heather-covered moorland and mountain 5 miles 98km) east of Harlech. Access on footpaths leading off unclassified roads in Cwm Bychan or Cwm Nantcol. NCC leaflet.

ACTIVITIES

Walking: the independent mountain walker will be in expert hands if he adds a copy of W. A. Poucher's *The Welsh Peaks* to the 4 OS Outdoor Leisure maps that cover the park. There are many other usueful guides, however, including *Wales Walking*, published by the Tourist Board and leaflets on individual routes produced by the park information service. The FC also produces leaflets for the walker. Contact FC Aberystwyth (T:0970 612367) or the Visitors' Centre in Gan Ilwyd (T:03414 666) or Betws-y-Coed (T:06902 665).

Guided Walks: during July and August the park authority offers a number of undemanding day and half-day walks, starting at various centres throughout the park. Full details are published in the *Snowdonia Star*, the park's newspaper-style information sheet – or ring the park information service (T:0766

Glyder Fach rises above the waters of Llyn Bochlwyd amid a jumble of frost-shattered boulders

770274).

Climbing: Snowdonia offers some of the most challengiing and popular climbing in Britain. The inexperienced mountaineer should associate himself with one of the following centres which will

provide equipment and expert instruction:

Outdoor Odyssey, 8 Blaen y Odol, Llanberris, Gwynedd, T:0286 870155. Year-round courses in climbing.

Geoff Arkless Mountaineering, St Katherine's, Church Walks, Llandudno, Gwynedd, T:0492 70329. Courses include rock climbing, winter mountaineering and scrambling.

Plas y Brenin, National Centre for Mountain Activities, Capel Curig, Betws-y-Coed, T:06904 280. The largest climbing centre in Britain. Year-round courses in hill walking, orienteering and mountain leadership, as well as in rock climbing.

Fishing: there is good fishing, both coarse and game, to be had in many of Snowdonia's lakes, rivers and reservoirs. Only Lake Bala, the largest natural lake in Wales, is controlled by the park authority. It contains 14 species of fish, with perch, roach, pike and trout frequently taken. For further information and a descriptive leaflet, contact the information centre in Bala (T:0678 520367) or the lake Warden (T:0678 520626). For fishing in other waters, enquire at local tackle shops or purchase *The Welsh Angling Guide* from the Welsh Water Authority, Cambrian Way, Brecon, Powys.

Field studies: Snowdonia National Park Study Centre, Plas Tan-y-Bwlch, Blaenau Ffestiniog, Gwynedd LL41 3YU, (T:076685 324). Courses include natural history and ecology, geology, photography, painting, mountain walking and archaeology. Open 50 weeks a year.

FURTHER INFORMATION
Snowdonia National Park Office, Penrhyndeudraeth, Gwynedd LL48 6LF, T:0766 770274. For information about activities organized by the park authority.

Snowdonia National Park Visitors' Centre, Y Stablau, Royal Oak Stables, Betws-y-Coed, Gwynedd, T:06902 665. The largest of the park's information centres, Y Stablau, features displays and information for both the FC and the RSPB; the centre also acts as an agent for the Wales Tourist Board.

Offa's Dyke Path

Offa, whose name is as grandly stamped on the pages of our early history as those of Alfred and Canute, was King of Mercia from AD757 to 796, and caused the bank and ditch to be built the 149 miles (238km) from Prestatyn in the north to the Sedbury cliffs on the Severn shore in the south. The frontier between the Saxon kingdom of Mercia and the cattle-raiding Welsh tribes forms the longest earthwork in Britain, and closely follows the present-day border between England and Wales.

The 168 miles (269km) of footpath along or close to the dyke was the fourth long distance footpath in Britain, opened in 1971 by Lord Hunt of Everest. Much of Offa's Dyke Path is waymarked; look for the upside-down acorn on signposts. Even so, you will need a compass for some sections of the route. This is no lowland ramble; prepare as you would for any rugged mountain trip. Although the border country is not as spectacular as Snowdonia or as spacious as the Cambrian Mountains, it does offer one of the least known parts of Wales, one which most visitors

---

WALKING IN SNOWDONIA

The uplands of Snowdonia offer a great variety of walks, most of which are well marked.

Make sure you are properly equipped, for there are a few places in Great Britain where the hill walker experiences such rapid changes of weather as in Snowdonia, where a fine sunny dawn may be replaced in a few hours by torrents of wind-lashed rain or shrouds of mist and low cloud.

Preparation is essential, and this includes obtaining local weather information from Llanberis (T:0286 870120). Be sure to have suitable footwear and clothing, maps, compass, whistle, food and drink.

Temperatures drop considerably at an altitude where snow can remain in some gullies until July. Wind speeds are much greater on the high exposed ground. Of further assistance are the information boards at the start of the main routes, while the National Park visitor centres will be pleased to provide advice.

A visit to Plas y Brenin, the National Centre for Mountain Activities at Capel Curig is a must for the walker, both novice and the more expert.

Be prudent and prepared, for in the often quoted words of Edward Whymper, 'negligence may destroy the happiness of a lifetime'.

Lastly if you do experience trouble, or see others in difficulty ring 999 and ask for the police.

pass through all too rapidly.

It is a dream land for geologists, a land of fossil beds laid down in an equatorial heat, of limestones now extensively quarried, of coal measures, Silurian mudstones, bands of Ordivician rock and pre-Cambrian grits. Such variety is reflected both in the scenery and the botanical gems to be found along the route, especially on the Breidden Ridge with its monument to Admiral Rodney, and at Corndon Hill, Long Mountain and Llanymynech, all close to where the Severn makes its massive bend east into England. Here plants like herb paris, parsley fern, hound's tongue, spring cinquefoil, blue-eyed grass and various orchids can be seen. Three great rarities may also be seen here: the western spiked speedwell, the sticky catchfly and the rock cinquefoil.

Before you go: the entire length of Offa's Dyke Path is covered from south to north by 7 OS Landranger Series Maps: Nos. 162, 161, 148, 137, 126, 117 and 116. As there is no discernible track along certain sections, the greater detail of the 1:25,000 scale series is useful. Alternatively, the Offa's Dyke Association publishes 9 strip maps of the entire route at 1 inch to the mile, increasing the scale to 1:25,000 where necessary. Two books – both called *Offa's Dyke Path* – provide detailed maps and background information; one is by John B. Jones (HMSO 1977), the other by C. J. Wright (Constable 1975). **Getting there:** the path can be joined at any road crossing along its route. Towns from which one would start to walk a section of the path are, from south to north:
Chepstow and Monmouth

The mountain spiderwort or Snowdon lily is found only in Snowdonia

(Gwent) for the scenic Lower Wye Valley, (see p.123).

Hay-on-Wye (Powys), 20 miles (32km) west of Hereford on B4350; approach on A438; easy access for section of path crossing the Black Mountains immediately to the south.

Knighton (Powys) on A488, 17 miles (27km) west of Ludlow (Shropshire); also a station on the Central Wales Railway from Shrewsbury to Swansea. Largest town on route; convenient for Radnorshire Hills to south and Shropshire hills to the north.

Llangollen (Clwyd) on A5, 11 miles (17km) north-west of Oswestry (Shropshire). Path leads north along splendid cliffs on way up to Clwydian Hills.

Prestatyn (Clwyd), 4½ miles (8km) east of Rhyl on A458; station on North Wales Railway from Chester. Clwydian Hills within a day's walk.

Where to stay: two useful publications list many bed and breakfast establishments: *Offa's Dyke Path Where to Stay List*, published by the Offa's Dyke Association and the *Bed and Breakfast Guide*, published by the Rambler's

Association, 1-5 Wandsworth Road, London SW8 2LJ. Youth hostels are situated at: Mountain Road, Chepstow (T:02912 2685); St Briavels, Lydney (T:0594 530272); Priory Street School, Monmouth (T:0600 5116); Capel-y-Ffin, Abergavenny (T:0873 890650); The School, Llandrindod Wells, (T:09824 367); Old Primary School, Knighton (T:0547 528807); The Mill, Craven Arms (T:05884 582); Tyndwr Hall, Llangollen (T:0978 860330); Holt Hostel, Mold (T:035285 320).

Further information: principal information centre and headquarters of the Offa's Dyke Association is at the Old School, West Street, Knighton, Powys, T:0547 528753/528529. Send a self-addressed envelope to the Correspondence Secretary for more information. Other Tourist Information Centres along the route are at High Street, Chepstow (T:02912 3772); Church Street, Monmouth (T:0600 3899); Mill Street, Knighton (T:0547 230202); Vicarage Garden Car Park, Welshpool (T:0938 2043); The Library, Oswestry (T:0691 662753); Town Hall, Llangollen (T:07456 860828); Scala Cinema, Prestatyn (T:07456 2484).

CHAPTER 6

Lowland Scotland

Crossing into Scotland from the Cheviot hills of Northumberland recently, I was struck by how quickly and perceptibly the feel of the country changed. The differences between England on one side of the border and Scotland on the other were subtle, and they were to be found as much inside one's own head as in the lie of the land. As an Englishman, I very soon felt as if I were in a different country; as indeed I was.

Sitting on top of a hill that had once been a defensible iron-age camp not far from the Roman army commando training base near Woden Law in the Scottish Lowland county of Borders, I tried to take my bearings among all those lonely green rolling hills and twisting valleys. This was Teviotdale; sheep country, and fox country too, with trout in the little streams and ring ouzel in the upper burns. The odd thing was that, though I was quite obviously to the north of the Cheviots, I now felt myself quite firmly in southern country. In the Cheviots my orientation had been instinctively towards London and the south. Here in the Borders it was towards the north, to Edinburgh and to the great rearing mass of the Scottish Highlands beyond.

The Lowlands of southern Scotland stretch from the border northwards to the great Highland Boundary Fault, which runs diagonally across the country from the Firth of Clyde in the west to Stonehaven on the east coast. Beyond that line lies the grandly wild and rugged world of the Highlands and

The play of sunlight and shadow on the depression known as the Devil's Beef Tub captures the essence of the undulating landscape of Lowland Scotland

142

the Islands – the most extensive wilderness areas in Britain from one point of view, and a neglected and underdeveloped colonial outpost from another.

There is no mistaking that the Highlands are high; it is less obvious that the Lowlands are low. Compared with lowland England, the Scottish Lowlands are high hill country. The Southern Uplands stretch east to west across much of the area south of the low-lying valley between the Firths of Clyde and Forth. In the eastern half of these uplands, in the border country dominated by the River Tweed and its tributaries, the hills are smooth and round and grassy. In the western half, especially in Galloway where the mountain called the Merrick rises to 2,764 feet (842 metres), the hills are more rugged and more Highland in character. Throughout their length, the Southern Uplands offer delightful hill walking through forests and over moors in weather that is generally finer than in the higher mountains to the north. The 212-mile (340-kilometre) Southern Uplands Way (see page 157) traverses the lot.

Though the interior of the Lowlands is really Scotland *sotto voce*, a curtain-raiser for the great show that booms out further north, the coastal perimeters are fine places in their own right, and of special interest to birdwatchers. To the west, the Solway Firth – a severe test for ornithological Rambos in the worst of winter weather – provides a haven for wildfowl in great numbers, best seen at the superb wildfowl reserve at Caerleverock. To the east, a succession of bird places are strung up the coast along the line of one of the major bird migration routes between Scandinavia and the Continent. These start at the great seabird colonies at St Abb's Head in Borders, where you will find the highest cliffs in eastern Scotland, and end with the sand flats and long shingle bars of Culbin Sands along a remote stretch of coastline on the Moray Firth in the Highlands, where seaduck, greylags and wading birds hole up for the winter in their thousands, and the north wind will have your guts for garters.

By all means set your sights on the wild splendours of the Highlands and Islands. But do give the Lowlands a whirl on your way there. They are worth every moment of the wild traveller and ornithologist's time.

GETTING THERE

By air: Edinburgh and Glasgow International Airports both have regular services from Europe, North America and the Middle East as well as from major centres within the UK. Prestwick Airport, 30 miles (50km) south of Glasgow, serves major North American cities. Domestic flights also serve Dundee's small airport.
By rail: there are direct routes or rapid connecting services to Glasgow and Edinburgh from all principal English and Welsh stations. Dundee is also

on the east-coast (Edinburgh) line.
By sea: two ferry services operate from Larne in Northern Ireland: Sealink to Stranraer and Townsend Thoresen to Cairnryan, both ports in Dumfries and Galloway.
By road: Edinburgh is served from the Midlands and South by the A1; Glasgow by the M6 as far as Carlisle, then the A/M74. The M8 connects Glasgow with Edinburgh.
By coach: a number of coach companies now run services to Edinburgh and Glasgow. For

local bus services, check at bus stations or tourist information centres in the area you wish to travel. You can expect to find public transport between most major settlements, but don't think that you are going to get anywhere quickly. And remember that more than anywhere else in Britain, Sunday in Scotland is a day of rest.

A particularly interesting way to travel is by post bus, generally a 4-seat van or an 11-seat minibus that carries passengers – as well as the post – to relatively isolated communities throughout the country. Apart from providing access to some of the remoter places mentioned in this book, post buses give you a valuable opportunity of literally rubbing shoulders with the people for whom Wild Britain happens to be home. The *Scottish Postbus Timetable*, updated annually, is available free from local post offices or tourist information centres.

WHERE TO STAY
Those who want to plan their accommodation in advance should refer to one of the Scottish Tourist Board's 4 useful publications; each under the general title *Scotland Where to Stay: Hotels and Guest Houses, Bed and Breakfast* and *Camping and Caravan Parks*. These publications are available by post from the Scottish Tourist Board, 23 Ravelston Terrace, Edinburgh EH4 3EU, T:031 332 2433.

Fully-equipped forest cabins for self-catering vacation homes can be rented from the FC, who also run well-provided camp and caravan sites. Contact the Public Information Division, FC, 231 Costorphine Road, Edinburgh EH12 7AT, T:031 334 0303.
Youth hostels: full details from *SYHA Handbook* and *Touring Map of Scotland*, available from SYHA, 7 Glebe Crescent, Stirling, FK8 2JA, T:0786 72821.
Outdoor living: Scotland has many camping and caravan (motor home) sites, but the walker may well find himself far away from such amenities. Remember that even in the wildest terrain, you are almost always on private land. Wild camping is not allowed on FC property, on National Trust for Scotland land, or in Nature Reserves. On private estates try to seek the landowner's

The crested tit, which feeds and breeds only in pine woods, welcomes the works of the Forestry Commission

permission – it will rarely be refused. Where this is not practicable, treat the land with consideration; leave no litter, carry a stove and use it with care.

ACCESS AND CLOSURES
Land trespass is not an offence in Scotland, but most land is owned or tenanted by people who try to earn a living from it. To prevent damage or disruption, access is controlled in the following seasons: deer stalking, 1 Sep–20 Oct; grouse-shooting, 12 Aug–10 Dec; lambing, Apr–May (no dogs should be taken on to grazings). If in doubt, enquire at local estate or nearest farmhouse. Your courtesy will be much appreciated and if access is restricted for that day you may be offered another route.

In restricted seasons you can still roam freely in areas held by the National Trust for Scotland. Many major cross-country routes in Scotland are safeguarded as public rights of way under common law,

including the 212-mile Southern Upland Way, which is waymarked from coast-to-coast by the Countryside Commission for Scotland. Rights of way, however, are not designated as such on OS maps as they are in England and Wales. The Scottish Rights of Way Society publishes 3 maps showing the principal rights of way: contact 1 Lutton Place, Edinburgh EH8 9PD, T:031 447 9242.

FURTHER INFORMATION
Information on 63 National Nature Reserves in Scotland, with details of nature trails, flora and fauna, can be obtained from the Nature Conservancy Council, 12 Hope Terrace, Edinburgh EH9 2AS, T:031 447 4784.

For details of nature trails and hides on the RSPB's reserves, contact the Royal Society for the Protection of Birds, 17 Regent Terrace, Edinburgh EH7 5BN, T:031 556 5624. Further information on reserves and wildlife conservation in Scotland can be obtained from the Scottish Wildlife Trust, 25 Johnston Terrace, Edinburgh EH1 2NH, T:031 226 4602.

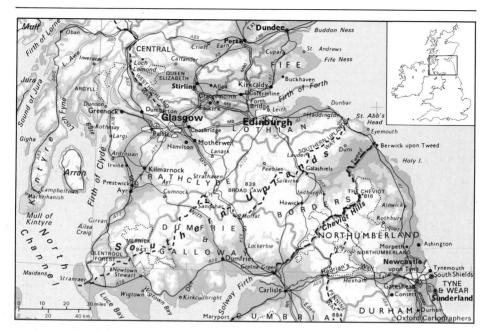

The Solway Coast

A long the shore of Galloway and Dumfries I came across an unexpected, unique corner of Scotland; a sunny south-facing coast with huge luminous skies, their light reflected on the calm waters of the Solway Firth, or at low tide on vast stretches of shining wet sand. But turn inland and you realize that typical Scottish scenes of moor and mountain are close at hand; the glaciers which formed this fertile coastal plain did not have far to travel.

Rising gently above the valley of the Cree to a height of 2,331 feet (710 metres), the Cairnsmore of Fleet, like the Merrick and most of the higher mountains in Galloway, is an intrusion of granite which has weathered better than softer surrounding rocks. It could not, of course, resist the great Scottish ice sheets, and erratic boulders of its pale grey granite can be found across the Solway Firth in Cumbria.

146

Much of the scenery is moorland rather than mountain, bleak expanses of purple moor grass and heather echoing to the melancholy cries of curlew and golden plover. It was the setting for Richard Hannay's desperate attempts to elude his evil pursuers in *The Thirty-Nine Steps*. To the east, however, especially from the valley of the Big Water of Fleet, the Cairnsmore presents a far more precipitous and dramatic mountainside. Ravens, becoming rare with the decline of sheep farming in south-west Scotland, find this a good place for carrion, sometimes that of an unfortunate feral goat.

Fringing the bays and estuaries along the Firth are the areas of merse or salt marsh. Many of these are extensions of the peat bogs formed by the rise and subsequent fall of the sea level at the end of the last Ice Age, the finest example being the merse of Lochar Moss with its magnificent wildfowl reserve at Caerlaverock.

The Caerlaverock National Nature Reserve covers over 20 square miles (50 square kilometres) of salt marsh and mud flats at the mouth of the Nith Estuary. The

With its rocky islands and inlets, Rough Firth is a distinctive feature in the otherwise sandy coast of Dumfries and Galloway

1,500-acre (600-hectare) Eastpark Wild-fowl Trust Refuge is splendidly equipped. The marsh is very treacherous and nowadays access is strictly controlled, for it has become one of the most important sanctuaries in Scotland, not only as a winter wildfowl refuge, but also as a prime example of an ecological niche that is fast disappearing elsewhere.

Chief attractions among the wildfowl are the barnacle geese. Up to 10,000 of them, the summer population of Spitsbergen, migrate *en masse* to the Caerlaverock merse. There is also a small but steadily growing flock of Bewick's swan, and other species that winter in good number include whoopers, pink-feet, greylags, wigeon, pintail and teal. Birds of prey often visit the reserve, and you may witness the menacing glide of a hen harrier or the stuttering flight of a merlin as it hunts low over the marsh.

In summer the glasswort and manna grass on the mud flats are bright with patches of sea pink and sea aster, which also

147

flourish among the red fescue grass and rushes of the marsh itself. The birds that breed here, mainly gulls and oyster-catchers, are not ones in need of protection; more care and attention is lavished on the colony of natterjack toads.

At the western extremity of the Solway Coast lies a strange, hammer-headed peninsula called the Rhinns, from the Gaelic *Roinn*, a promontory. At its southern tip, the Mull of Galloway, which points out towards the Isle of Man, there is a small RSPB reserve around the colony of cliff-dwelling seabirds. Here, at the 'Land's End of Scotland', your gaze will naturally wander out to sea. Jagged cliffs line the western side of the Rhinns which looks out across the North Channel to the Ards peninsula in County Down, while along Luce Bay on the eastern side stretches a procession of heathery dunes. In the middle of the broad bay stand the Scar Rocks, inhabited by gannets, which can often be seen fishing off the Mull.

BEFORE YOU GO
OS Landranger Map Nos. 82, 83, 84, 85.

GETTING THERE
By car: the A75 from Gretna to Stranraer is the main east-west artery, passing through Castle Douglas, Gatehouse of Fleet, Newton Stewart and Glenluce – and providing easy access by car to most parts of the Solway coast.
By coach: regular coach services link London and Birmingham with Stranraer, stopping at principal towns and villages along this route.
By train: trains run from Glasgow to Stranraer; Dumfries is on the Glasgow to Carlisle line.

WHERE TO STAY
This is a popular holiday area, where you are never far from accommodation. If booking in advance, write for the South West Scotland *Where To Stay* brochure from Dumfries and Galloway Tourist Board, Douglas House, Newton Stewart, Wigtownshire DG8 6DQ, T:0671 3401/2549. The Minnigaff Youth Hostel is in Newton Stewart (T:0671 2211).

WHERE TO GO
Caerlaverock (NCC) and Eastpark (WT): signposted access from B725, 8 miles (13km) south of Dumfries. Free access except to sanctuary area near Wildfowl Trust Centre. Beware of tides on the marshes and contact Warden before walking across over mudflats. The WT Centre is open daily 10 Sept–30 Apr; 3 observation towers and several hides. For further information contact the WT Centre, Eastpark Farm, Caerlaverock, Dumfriesshire DG1 4RS or the NCC Warden, Reserve Office, Tadorne, Hollands Farm Road, Caerlaverock, T:038777 275.
Criffel: rises to west of A710, 10 miles (16km) south of Dumfries. Easiest access from north east. Start on track to Ardwall, which leaves A710 1½ miles (2½km) south of New Abbey. OS Landranger Series Map No. 84.
Southerness Point and Mersehead Sands: 14 miles (22km) south of Dumfries an unclassified road leads south off A710 to Southerness Point. Drive to end of road. Good viewing at all sides. Geese and waders on Mersehead Sands, immediately west of Southerness Point, can best be viewed from A710 west of Coulkerbush.
Cairnsmore of Fleet: access from unclassified road off A75, 3 miles (5km) south east of Newton Stewart. Path leads to summit from Cairnsmore (OS Landranger series Map No. 83). Access to NCC reserve restricted. For details and further information contact the Warden, T:0557 4435.
Mull of Galloway: drive south from Stranraer on the A716 to Drummore, then take B7041 to the lighthouse on the headland. Unrestricted access.

FURTHER INFORMATION
Tourist information centres, from east to west: Dumfries (T:0387 53862); Dalbeattie (T:0556 610117); Castle Douglas (T:0556 2611); Kirkcudbright (T:0557 30494); Gatehouse of Fleet (T:05574 212); Newton Stewart (T:0671 2431); Stranraer (T:0776 2595).

THE EAST COAST

Few sounds in nature can compare with the beating of ten thousand pairs of wings as a flock of geese takes off from its winter roost. It may not feel so to you, as your fingers fumble to refocus your binoculars in a biting wind, but eastern Scotland, with its wide estuaries, shallow lochs and abundance of arable land, is the Côte d'Azur to the pink-footed goose.

The coast is also a popular winter resort for seaducks, grebes and divers, bobbing like flimsy coastal craft, dwarfed by the waves of the North Sea. But to them the sea is benevolent, not cruel; it is a different story for the crews of the fishing-boats and oil rigs who seek a living from the wealth beneath the same grey waves.

From the border to the Moray Firth, the coast retains an essentially lowland character. When the sea level rose at the end of the last glaciation and the narrow valleys in the west became flooded sea lochs, the tilt of Scotland kept the feet of her eastern mountains dry. The sea eventually settled at a less dramatic, but immensely varied coastline, subject to the same inexorable pattern of erosion and accretion that shapes the east of England.

St Abb's Head

Scottish Wildlife Trust Reserve

Perched like an animated black and white frieze, thousands of guillemots, razorbills and kittiwakes nest on the clifftops between the fishing village of St Abb's and the Bay of Pettico Wick, along with a fair number of fulmars, herring gulls and shags. The red sandstone of the Head and the offshore stacks is a volcanic intrusion thrust into the grey, gritty fabric of the Southern Uplands, and if you look at the neighbouring cliffs you can see the dramatic folds of the mountains revealed as clearly as in any geology textbook.

In the valley behind the Head an artificial lake has been created to refresh migrant waders. The edge of the lake has been planted with hawthorn and sycamore which already shelter a growing variety of woodland flowers and attract small migrants like yellow-browed, greenish and barred warblers.

Autumn is peak viewing time for birds of passage both onshore and off, where the rival attractions, best spotted from the lighthouse, include skuas, shearwaters and terns.
Getting there: from Coldingham, 11 miles (18km) north of Berwick-upon-Tweed, take B6438 to reserve. Walk from there along cliffs to lighthouse, or drive to car park at headland.
Access: unrestricted.
Further information: from Warden, Ranger's Cottage, Northfield, St Abbs, T:08907 71443. NTS leaflets available at car park.

The East Lothian Coast and the Forth Islands

Despite its proximity to Edinburgh and the paraphernalia of tourism, the shoreline at the entrance of the Firth of Forth supports an extraordinary wealth of wildlife. The landscape is dominated by North Berwick Law, a smooth cone of the same volcanic origin as the Bass Rock (see separate entry on p.150), whose famous gannets can be observed plummeting for fish along this stretch of coast.

The Forth Islands, closer inshore to the west of North Berwick, are important breeding colonies for seabirds such as razorbill, guillemot, cormorant and kittiwake.
Getting there: the A198 serves most of the coastline. Good bus service along the road between Edinburgh and North Berwick. Trains to North Berwick. **Where to go:** for birdwatching, from west to east:

Musselburgh; viewing from lagoon embankments east of River Esk. Parking west of race course off A1.

Gosford Bay; A198 runs along shore. Parking at Ferny Ness, 1 mile (1.6km) north of Longniddry on A198.

Aberlady Bay; see separate entry (p.150).

Gullane Point and Bay; Gullane is on A198, 5 miles (8km) west of North Berwick. Coastal car park and short walk to point.

Yellow Craig; access on minor road leading north from Dirleton, 2 miles (3km) west of North Berwick on A198.

Tantallon Castle; on coast 3 miles (5km) east of North Berwick. Access from A198 to Dunbar. Good coastal prospects from cliffs and castle. **Further information:** Tourist Information Offices, North Berwick, T:0620 2197 and Dunbar, T:0368 63353. East Lothian Tourist Board, Brunton Hall Musselburgh EH21 6AE.

Isle of May

NCC NNR

A small, cliff-girt island, only 140 acres (57ha) in area, in the mouth of the Firth of Forth. The island has been a major site for ornithological research since the early years of the century and the bird observatory has been here since 1934. The seabird colonies are busy and extensive, and increasing rapidly in numbers, but it is the bird migrations that cause all the excitement. At peak migration times strong east winds cause an extraordinary number of exhausted birds from a wide range of species to make a landing on this natural aircraft carrier. One October day in 1982, for example, 15,000 goldcrest settled on the island like a very pretty locust swarm. Some of the birds are rarities for Britain – scarlet rosefinch, Lapland bunting, red-breasted flycatcher, Sabine's gull and gyr falcon to name a few. The island is quiet in winter, with the notable exception of flocks of purple sandpipers and turnstones. Grey seals breed on the north coast and many unusual butterflies are blown here at times during migration.
Getting there: by sea on 1-hour boat voyage from Anstrithen, Crail or Pittenween; day trips run in summer. Contact Ian Gatherum, 27 Glenogil

Gardens, Anstrithen. **When to go:** May–Jul for seagull colonies; Apr–May and Aug–Oct for migrating birds. **Access:** at any time. **Where to stay:** the Bird Observatory offers basic self-catering accommodation for up to 6 people, usually for a week between April and October. Contact Isle of May Bookings Secretary, 9 Oxgangs Road, Edinburgh EH10 7BG, T:031 445 2489. **Further reading:** W.J. Eggeling: *The Isle of May: A Scottish Nature Reserve* (1985)

Bass Rock

Very small, privately owned, cliff-girt hump of rock rising to 300 feet (90m), 3 miles (5km) off North Berwick in the Forth Estuary. By origin an old volcanic plug, Bass Rock is famous for its gannets, 21,000 pairs of which throng the cliffs and summit of the island during the breeding season, hence the bird's Latin name – *Sula bassana*.
Getting there: by sea on daily summer boat trips round the island from North Berwick. Contact Bass Rock boatman, Fred Marr, 24 Victoria Road, North Berwick, T:0620 2838. **When to go:** May–Jul. **Access:** landing permit from Bass Rock boatman.

Aberlady Bay

Foreshore reserve of 1,439 acres (583ha) run by East Lothian District Council.

The bay is a striking example of how mud, sand and time, with the help of marram grass, glasswort and sea buckthorn, can create a whole series of new environments. The salt marshes and dunes are host to

flourishing communities of plants and mosses, and over fifty species of breeding birds, the most conspicuous being the boldly-patterned shelduck. As the duck is as brightly coloured as the drake, their nest must be extremely well concealed. In contrast, the eider duck with her drab speckled plumage can choose more exposed nest sites and rely on her own camouflage.

In winter, pink-footed geese and a few whooper swans roost on the flats, but to watch seaduck it is best to go to the east end of the bay. Round the point in Gullane Bay there are always common and velvet scoter and long-tailed duck, often accompanied by red-necked and Slavonian grebe. Regular waders on autumn passage include large flocks of dunlin and knot, with good numbers of scarcer species like bar-tailed godwit.
Getting there: Aberlady village is on the A198, 7 miles (11km) south west of North Berwick. Access to shoreline along footpaths. Aberlady Point to south west; Gullane Point to north east. Also good viewing from main road. **Facilities:** key to hide from warden. Car park ½ mile (1km) east of village. Free permits to park from Department of Leisure, Recreation and Tourism, Brunton Hall, Musselburgh EH1 6AE. **Further information:** Warden, 1–3 Craigielaw Cottages, Longniddry, East Lothian, T:0857 588.

Loch Leven

RSPB Nature Centre and NNR

The loch accounts for almost all the 3,946 acres (1,597ha)

of the National Nature Reserve, one of Britain's principal centres for wildfowl studies. Security is much tighter now than it was when Mary Queen of Scots escaped from Loch Leven's Castle Island. In summer there are boat trips to the ruined castle, but in the rest of the reserve strict measures are taken to prevent the public from disturbing the large population of nesting ducks.

The RSPB nature centre (with a reserve of 458 acres, 185ha) at Vane Farm is more accommodating, and if you follow their trail on the top of the Vane, you will not be disappointed. Below lies St Serf's Island, the moated refuge of mallard, tufted duck and wigeon with a noisy guard

of black-headed gulls. There is also a magnificent view of the horizon beyond the loch and the roofs of Kinross, where the rounded heather-clad Ochil Hills are the last lowland range before the wilder, grander landscapes of the Highlands.

Getting there: 12 miles (19km) south of Perth; immediately east of Kinross. Loch is encircled by main roads: A911 to north, B996 to west, B9097 to south. But access to shore is permitted only at Kirkgate Park, Burleigh Sands and Findatie. All are signposted.
Facilities: car park and RSPB nature centre with observation room at Vane Farm. Hide on lochside.
Further information: RSPB leaflet from centre. RSPB Warden, Vane Farm Nature Centre, by Loch Leven, Kinross KY13 7LX. T:0577 62355.

The Firth of Tay

The extensive sand banks and mud flats of this considerable estuary, which is contiguous with Tentsmuir Point and the Eden Estuary in Fife, has long been a major place for wildfowl and waders and the only internationally important site in Britain for eider.

Birds come here in their thousands, and successive waves of migrating geese may total 20,000 or more. But the mud flats are so vast that it is difficult to see birds even in these prodigious quantities, for when the tide is out, many birds at the water's edge are beyond the range of human vision. The gathering of eider for which the Tay is famous takes place at the mouth of the Firth, where the birds sit in great 'rafts' offshore from Abertay Sands, sometimes in extraordinary masses of over

The volcanic cliffs of St Abb's Head jut ruggedly into the North Sea at the edge of the Firth of Forth

15,000 birds.

The landscape and wildlife of the estuary is subject to considerable human pressures: wildfowling, holiday development, army firing and oil pollution from ships. But the area is big enough and the birds abundant enough to absorb these pressures for the time being, and in spring and autumn the flights of incoming geese are still a wonder to be seen.

Getting there: Perth and Dundee stand to west and east of estuary respectively. Access to north shore from A85 and B958; to south from A913.
Where to go: for birds, visit Buddon Burn, a small stream entering estuary mouth from the north. Walk east along shore from Monifieth. This is MOD land. Look for warning flags or check for access with information centres at Dundee or Carnoustie.

Tentsmuir Point

NCC NNR

The sandy headland at the mouth of the Firth of Tay is one of very few sites chosen for afforestation on the East Coast. Elsewhere in Fife the land has either been mined for coal or is valuable for agriculture. It is the rapidly-growing foreshore beyond Tentsmuir Forest, however, with its sands, dune heath and natural scrubby woodland that appeals more to the lover of wild places.

An enormous variety of flowers have colonised the dunes and scrub, attracting a number of attendant species of butterfly and moth. The National Nature Council Reserve includes the vast expanse of the Abertay Sands, which provide a winter roost for waders and geese and a handy resting place for common and grey seals.

Just off the Sands at the entrance to the Firth of Tay you may be lucky enough to witness one of the enormous flocks of wintering eider. Through their habit of sticking together in closely-packed armadas, the ducks have unfortunately been very vulnerable to oil pollution in recent years.

Getting there: an unclassified road leads east to the nature reserve from the B945, 2 miles (3km) south of Tayport. Several FC tracks give access to point and beach.
Access: open access. FC parking and picnic area at beach to south of reserve.
Further information: from Senior Warden (Peter Kinnear), T:0334 54038 (work), 0334 870358 (home).

St Cyrus

NCC NNR

Over 300 species of wild flowers bloom along the strip of sandy beach which runs 3 miles (5km) from the mouth of the North Esk to the headland of Milton Ness. This variety would be remarkable anywhere so far north, but is doubly so, because the reserve

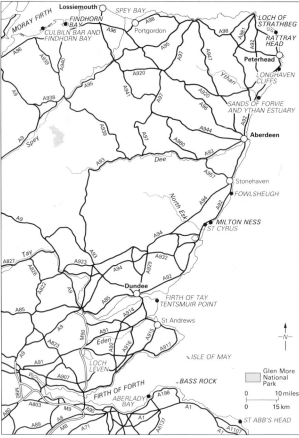

hardly extends any distance inland beyond the relict cliff.

On the dunes, the deep blue of the clustered bellflower is set off by cowslips and maiden pink. The grassy cliffs are equally colourful, providing food plants for a profusion of butterflies and moths and even sites for low-level nesters such as the grasshopper warbler. The many breeding seabirds include little tern, but their precarious colony does not enjoy the success of the herring gulls and fulmars.
Getting there: access to sands from village of St Cyrus, 5 miles (8km) north of Montrose on A92.
Access: south end of reserve closed during tern breeding season, May-Aug.
Further information: booklet from NCC/Hon. Wardens J. Richie (T:0674 85226), R. McElwee (T:0674 73308).

Fowlsheugh

RSPB Reserve

Three miles south of Stonehaven, the *heugh* (a Gaelic word for cliff) reaches a height of 200 feet (60m) and houses a typical restless, screaming, stinking colony of seafowl. As at similar colonies on the Scottish coast, the two most successful breeding species are those with apparently contradictory strategies: the kittiwakes, which cement their neat nests to the cliffs, and the guillemots, which build no nest at all. Other high rise tenants are razorbills, puffins and fulmars, with a number of shag and eider duck on the lower storeys.
Getting there: from A92, 4 miles (6.5km) south of Stonehaven, take minor road to Crawton. Park at end of road and walk north along cliffs. **Access:** unrestricted.

Further information: RSPB, Edinburgh.

The Sands of Forvie and Ythan Estuary

NCC NNR

The sight of terns hovering silently before plunging for fish gives so much more pleasure than that of gulls clamouring around mankind's refuse, yet everywhere, as man appropriates the seacoast, gulls multiply and terns take fright.

Here at this 2,516-acre (1,018ha) reserve at the mouth of the Ythan, man tries to stem the tide of his own making by encouraging Sandwich, common, arctic and little terns to breed, but it can be a heartbreaking business, especially when great and arctic skuas sabotage your good work. Another hazard is the sand, which can be blown by the wind to form new landscapes from one year to the next. The older dunes have become fixed under a cloak of heather and lichens, and in amongst them nest more eider duck than at any other site in the British Isles. You may even spot a rare king eider marking time among the non-breeding birds.

In winter the estuary is home to a flock of whooper swans, but most of the migrating geese move on southwards. Waders that can be seen feeding on the estuary usually include little stint, ruff, greenshank and spotted redshank, while large flocks of sanderling scurry back and forth at the edge of the waves.
Getting there: the A975 skirts the west bank of the River Ythan before crossing it near Newburgh, 14 miles (22.5km)

north of Aberdeen. Good observation points from main road. Access to Sands of Forvie NNR from B9003, which leaves A975 4 miles (6.5km) north of Newburgh. Forvie Centre, the NNR HQ is one the right of road.
Access: hide overlooking ternery at south end of sands, on spit to north of river mouth. Visitors are asked to keep to the footpaths in NNR.
Further information: NCC handbook. Warden, Little Colliston Croft, Collieston, Ellon, Aberdeenshire.

Longhaven Cliffs

SWT Reserve

These magnificent cliffs of flesh-coloured Peterhead granite stand just to the north of the Bullers of Buchan. At this famous freak of coastal erosion the sea rushes through an arch of granite into a kind of cauldron in the cliff-base.

The effects of the sea's violence can also be seen at Longhaven in the shattered stacks which are a favourite nest-site with the large population of herring gulls. Guillemots and kittiwakes take up their accustomed positions on the pitted cliff face, looking down on the stoic shag below, while the grassy slopes above provide plenty of burrows for puffins.

They also display a surprising variety of flowers, not only typical cliff-growing species like the lovely pale cream burnet rose, but also, in more sheltered places, incongruous spring carpets of bluebells fringed with bright clumps of primrose.
Getting there: drive south from Peterhead on A952. Access to cliffs on unclassified road about 2½ miles (4km) after turn for Boddam.

The Loch of Strathbeg

RSPB Reserve

At the centre of an RSPB reserve of 2,327 acres (942ha), this freshwater loch is the first landfall for thousands of wintering wildfowl. It was only at the beginning of the eighteenth century that it assumed its present shape and character; throughout the Middle Ages it had been a busy harbour.Finally the inlet from the sea near Rattray Head silted up, creating a shallow freshwater lagoon. The largest sand-dune slack in Britain, it still serves as a refuge from the rigours of the North Sea, but for geese instead of ships.

Among the incoming skeins of greylags and pink-feet in early autumn you may spot the barnacle geese which rest up here on their way to Caerlaverock. On the water of the loch, a large flock of whoopers presides nobly over the wintering mallards, tufted ducks and goldeneye, which are often joined by goosander and red-breasted merganser.

The reed beds and willow scrub of the marshlands provide cover for small birds like sedge- and willow-warbler. Inevitably this thriving and varied community draws its share of hopeful raptors, hen harrier, sparrowhawk and merlin, and a less welcome predator in the feral mink.

Watching the sea from Rattray Head, you are far enough north to count yourself unlucky if you do not spot all three species of diver, red-throated, black-throated and bird-spotter's holy grail, the great northern itself.
Getting there: access from village of Crimmond, midway

154

between Peterhead and Fraserburgh on A952. Without entering the reserve one can observe loch from unclassified Rattray road, leaving A952 just south east of Crimmond.
Access: permit required to enter reserve, which is on MOD land. Apply in writing to the Warden, The Lythe, Crimonmogate, Lonman, Fraserburgh AB4 4UB.
Facilities: Reception building. 2 hides overlooking loch and board-walk through fen woodland. **Further information:** RSPB leaflet.

Spey Bay

This long shallow bay between Lossiemouth and Portgordon in Grampian holds large numbers of seaduck including common, velvet and surf scoter, scaup, goosander and eider, as well as other birds such as red-throated, black-throated and great northern divers in autumn, and red-breasted merganser, purple sandpipers and commoner species. Common and arctic terns breed here, and common gulls may sometimes be seen on the beach.
Getting there: on foot along beach from Lossiemouth or Kingston, or for middle of bay drive to Speyslaw and walk to beach from there.
Access: at all times, except for Lossie Forest at back of beach (no cars, closed at times of fire risk) and firing range to west of Kingston.

Culbin Bar and Findhorn Bay

RSPB Reserve

Culbin Bar is the larger of two long spits of shingle lying off the mainland at Culbin Sands. The sands, as such, no longer

exist, having been transformed into Culbin Forest. There are those who disapprove of every conifer planted in Scotland, but at Culbin there are plenty of native Scots pine and a good sprinkling of birch.

Nor must we forget that the area was once a formidable 'desert', which had obliterated an entire community in one terrifying sand blow. Some will say that man created the desert in the first place, by pulling up the marram grass; but then again, the poor needed thatch for their houses. Conservation and social justice are often hard to reconcile.

The forest supports roe deer and birds as splendid as the capercaillie, the crested tit and the great spotted woodpecker, but true seekers of wild, natural beauty will head for the salt marshes enclosed by the Bar.

This somewhat melancholy landscape is enlivened by colourful splashes of sea pink. As you would expect, bird life is more abundant in winter with the arrival of seaduck, geese and waders, but arctic and common tern breed in the area and can be seen fishing off the Bar. In Findhorn Bay, you might even witness the most spectacular of all aerial fishermen, the peerless osprey.
Getting there: Culbin Bar: from A96 in Nairn a minor coastal road leads north-east along the dunes. Track to left in about 2 miles (3km) (at Kingsteps) lead to RSPB reserve. Be careful of tides on foreshore.
Findhorn Bay: from Forres on A96, 10 miles (16km) east of Nairn, take B9011 – the Kinloss Road. This leads along east side of the bay.
Access: unrestricted.
Further information: RSPB, Edinburgh.

THE SOUTHERN UPLANDS

Although formed during the same episodes of titanic pressure that gave birth to the Highlands, the Southern Uplands were folded from quite different rocks, Silurian sediments of grit and greywacke. In the few places where the rocks are still exposed, grey is the predominant colour, but only in the craggy outcrops of Galloway do you feel you are in the presence of mountains, although the height of the Merrick and other surrounding peaks is largely due to intrusions of hard-wearing granite.

As you travel east, the effects of aeons of wind, rain and above all, ice are clearly evident in the changing landscape. In the Lowthers and the Tweedsmuir Hills, the high moorlands are featureless tracts of grass and heather; then in the Borders you find gentle rolling hills between the dales of the streams that feed the Tweed.

Galloway Forest Park

This is the largest forest in southern Scotland: over 250 square miles (650sq km) controlled by the Forestry Commission. The conifers have not destroyed the beauty of the area's lochs and high peaks; there are also patches of unspoilt woodland and ancient peat bog.

It is easy to imagine you are a hundred miles further north when you see the Buchan Burn tumbling down its water-fall into Loch Troon, and the upper glen, its narrow gorges set in woods of sycamore and sessile oak, is spectacular. equally spectacular.

From Glen Troon trails set off in all directions. You can follow the Gairland Burn to Loch Neldricken and Loch Enoch with their silver sands of powdered granite, then on to the extraordinary relic of glacial erosion known as the Devil's Bowling Green. The bowls are the hundreds of erratic boulders that a melting glacier left strewn on a flat clearing of ice-scarred rock. At Silver Flowe 470 acres (190ha) of bog vegetation are

If you prefer clear mountain air to blanket bog, head north from the Bruce Monument above Loch Trool for the Range of the Awful Hand, a group of five peaks, which includes the Merrick, at 2,764ft (842km) the highest in southern Scotland. **Getting there:** via A712 and A714 from Dumfries. **Further information:** the FC guidebook *Galloway Forest Park* is available from the FC Regional Office, 21 King Street, Castle Douglas DG7

The Grey Mare's Tail cascades over the lip of a hanging valley on the north-west side of Moffatdale

1AA, T:0556 3626. Tourist Information Centres at Newton Stewart (T:0671 2431) and Dalmellington (T:0292 550145).

Ken-Dee Marshes

RSPB Reserves
NTS Wildfowl Refuge

The damming of the River Dee between New Galloway and Castle Douglas in Dumfries and Galloway has created Loch Ken, and a flood plain of marshes

In winter, some 300 Greenland white-fronted geese visit the valley, along with a thousand greylags and bean geese, whooper swan and several species of duck. Hen harriers, merlins, peregrines, buzzards and sparrowhawks hunt here; great crested grebe, redshank, curlew and goosander are among the birds that breed in the marshes and loch. The RSPB runs 2 reserves totalling 325 acres (132ha) on Loch Ken, and the NTS has a 1,300-acre (526-ha) wildfowl refuge near Threave Castle.
Getting there: for Threave Wildfowl Refuge, turn off A75 at Kelton Mains Farm or Lodge west of Castle Douglas and continue along footpaths to 4 observation points overlooking river and marshes. RSPB Reserves at Kenmure Holms and the Black Water of Dee can be viewed from A762, A713 and offshoots. **Access:** Threave Wildfowl Refuge open Nov-Mar only. RSPB reserves cannot be entered except by written arrangement with the Warden (Ray Hawley), Midtown, Laurieston, nr Castle Douglas, Dumfries and Galloway DG7 2PP. **Further information:** from RSPB or Warden, NTS or Warden at Threave Wildfowl Refuge, Kelton Mill, Castle Douglas.

156

Ailsa Craig

An isolated, dome-shaped rock over 1,100ft (335m) high but only 1 mile (1.6km) in diameter, occupying an isolated position in the Firth of Clyde 10 miles (16km) off Girvan on the Ayrshire Coast, Ailsa Craig is a basal remnant of an ancient volcano. This is the Clyde's most important seabird station: 70,000 seabirds nest on its 500-ft (150-m) high vertical cliffs, half of them gannets.
Getting there: boat trips from Girvan, on A77 south of Ayr, can be arranged with Mr McCrindle, T:0465 3219. These generally include a three-hour stay on the island. Those wishing to camp on Ailsa Craig should contact the owner, the Marquess of Ailsa, on 0655 6646. **Facilities:** a little short grass. **Further information:** Tourist Information Centre, Girvan, T:0465 4950.

Tweedsmuir Hills

This is Lowland country *par excellence*; high lowlands and nationally important landscape with long walks over peat and turf and heather. Often you will find you have only sheep and the occasional curlew or raven for company. At 2,754 feet (840m), Broad Law is the second highest point in southern Scotland, but it is a quick undemanding climb and can be reached easily from Tweedsmuir, St Mary's Loch or even Loch Skeen.

If you are making for Peebles, steer north-east via Dollar Law and Dun Rig to the head of the charming valley of Glensax. There you can join the rough track that

follows the burn gently down to the Tweed just to the east of your destination.
Getting there: from Tweedsmuir on A701 an unclassified road crosses hills to meet the A708 at Cappercleuch. A number of tracks lead into hills from A701. **Further information:** Tourist Information Centre, Moffat (T:0683 20620).

The Grey Mare's Tail and Loch Skeen

NTS Reserve

This is not the only waterfall in southern Scotland to recall the fate of Tam O'Shanter's steed, but it is by far the highest and really does hang like a silver tail. The exaggerated glacial furrow of Moffatdale left many hanging valleys along its sides; the waterfall itself is 200ft (61m) high, but the Tail Burn has to descend 700ft (213m) before it reaches Moffat Water.

Up at Loch Skeen, where the burn begins its cascade, we find another classical feature of glacial erosion, a corrie partially dammed by moraine. The whole dramatic scene can be better appreciated from the superb ridge water between Bodesbeck and Herman's Law, south of the road.
Getting there: falls are situated west of the A708, 10 miles (16km) north-east of Moffat. **Further information:** from summer Ranger at information centre.

The Southern Uplands Way

This 212-mile (341-km) route was dictated more by

PRECAUTIONS FOR WALKERS

Nobody should set off into the wilds without a compass and 1:50,000 Ordnance Survey map and a knowledge of how to use them. But the true wilderness walker will also make a mental map as he or she goes:

1 At regular intervals take a sighting, i.e. visually line up three or more landmarks (conspicuous trees or rocks). This is to avoid walking in circles, which most people do because one leg takes longer strides than the other.

2 If you want to return the way you came, look back often and mark turns in the path with rocks. The same section of path looks different when seen from the opposite direction.

3 Use other senses as well as sight to mark your bearings: distinctive sounds like rushing water, the sea, church bells, cattle or sheep; and strong smells like pine forests, meadow flowers, ocean breezes.

4 Use trees to tell direction. Green moss-like algae grows on the shadier side of a tree or facing the prevailing wind. Trees growing in the open may have more leaves on the sunnier, i.e. southern, side.

What to wear

Walking boots or very strong shoes with moulded rubber soles are essential. Shoes with smooth rubber or leather soles can be lethal. Clothing should be warm and windproof – the weather in the Highlands can change extremely rapidly and a fine day turn almost instantly to storm.

A hill-walker dressed for the hills in summer can expect to wear: woollen jersey, warm long trousers (tweed or other wool mixture), anorak or windproof jacket, woollen socks, walking boots or shoes.

In addition you should carry a rucksack containing spare clothing consisting of extra jersey, gloves, woollen cap, cagoule (or other waterproof protective clothing), together with food, map and compass, rope and guidebook, torch and whistle (in case of emergency flash or whistle six times, wait one minute, then signal again), first aid kit and plastic bivi-bag to crawl into if you are stuck on a mountain.

---

expediency than by history or the lie of the land. From Portpatrick in the Rhinns of Galloway to Cocksburnpath on the Berwickshire coast, the majority of the valleys lie across your path, and the hills are often high moorland blanketed in mist.

The Way passes through the Galloway Forest Park, where it joins up with the Forestry Commission's trail along the southern side of Glen Trool; it then skirts Loch Dee and the Clatteringshaws Reservoir.

At St John's Town of Dalry you turn north east to follow the course of the Water Ken, but it is a tough hill walk with fine views across the valley to the Cairnsmore of Carsphairn. There follows a two-day hike across the Lowthers, from Sanquar to Beattock via Wanlockhead, the highest village in Scotland. The highest point on the Way is reached at about 2,330 feet (710m) beside the radar-station on Lowther Hill.

You do not enter the basin of the Tweed until the following day on the splendid middle section of the Way between Beattock and St Mary's Loch, when, after following an old drovers' pass below the threatening crags of Loch Fell, you emerge into the delightful valley of Ettrick Water. The final laps of the Way give you a chance to take things easily, as you stroll along meandering rivers neatly fringed with pine, birch and willow, enjoying frequent glimpses of the three peaks of Scott's beloved Eildon Hills.

Before you go: buy the 2-part official guide: *The Southern Uplands Way* by Ken Andrew (HMSO). Each book – Volume I (west) and Volume II (east) – comes with its own 1:50,000 route map.

The route is indicated throughout with brown waymarkers carrying the CC's stylized thistle-in-a-hexagon motif. Unless you are a fell runner, expect to spend at least 10 days on the route. **Where to stay:** there are hotels, bed and breakfast accommodation and campsites at Portpatrick. Along the route, 4 bothies offer basic shelter. Wild camping is not encouraged. **Further information:** Dumfries and Galloway Tourist Board, Douglas House, Newton Stewart, Wigtownshire, T:0671 2549. Scottish Borders Tourist Board, Municipal Buildings, High Street, Selkirk, T:0750 20555.

CHAPTER 7

Scottish Highlands and Islands

I first entered the enchanted world of the Scottish Highlands in the company of Gavin Maxwell, an eloquent champion of wild places, who was returning to his West Highland retreat at Camusfeàrna (which he was to make famous in his idyllic *Ring of Bright Water*) after the death of his first otter. It was at Camusfeàrna that I first saw the ghostly glimmering of the Northern Lights, the Aurora Borealis, draped across the night sky in the direction of Greenland, and first witnessed the mysterious coming of the elvers, which arrived at the waterfall at Camusfeàrna in teeming millions after crossing the Atlantic all the way from the distant Sargasso Sea.

It was from here that I climbed Ben Sgreol, my first Munro (as climbers call any Highland peak over 3,000 feet, 915 metres high), and from its scree-flanked summit above Camusfeàrna caught my first view of the grey shapes of the Outer Hebrides far to the north-west beyond the snow-covered Cuillins of Skye. I came back to this coast often in subsequent years, once to winter here, once to sail around its lochs and islands, sometimes to revisit Camusfeàrna after the death of Maxwell and his otters.

I recall vividly my most recent return. Thick sea fog had delayed and then diverted my flight up to Inverness. By the time I reached Camusfeàrna on the west coast it was well past midnight – but an enchanted, breathless night of

The contrast between Highland and Lowland Scotland is shown in bold relief in this sub-polar winter view from the Cairngorms

crystalline clarity. A brilliant full moon hung over the Sound of Sleat, casting a wan glow over the brooding hills of Skye and a glassy ocean that seemed to stretch motionless to the very edge of the world.

It was October, but still warm, and I flung open the shutters of the small croft by the beach to catch all the sounds and ghosts of the night – the listless flop of the waves on the sand, the distant cataract roar of the waterfall above the burn, in spate after an autumn of incessant rain, the kraak of a solitary heron stalking fish in the moonlight at the edge of the tide, a seal singing softly in the bay below the croft, the plaintive, child-like voice rising and falling like a phantom lullaby in the dark.

The next day, miraculously, was as warm and blue as high summer. I followed the tracks of the wild sea otters barefoot over the crunching shell-sand and icy shallows to the otter islands where long before I had foraged for limpets and gulls' eggs to eat, and as I stumbled over the black rock and bladder-wrack the grey seal colony gathered to stare, snorting in the sunlight, and bobbing their flippers up and down on the bottom to catch a better view. But the day after that the wind was roaring in from the sea and the rain driving horizontally across the bay, so that the burn rose two feet in an hour and the fire spat and spluttered in the chimney piece.

The season advanced swiftly. Soon there was a first faint powder of snow on the high hills across the sound and an arrowhead skein of greylag geese came honking overhead on their southern migration, crossing swiftly from one horizon to another in a momentary vision of freedom and delight. On such days one forgot the times of discomfort and despair, when the air was saturated with salt spray and rain, and life seemed as sour and chill as the peat. One remembered instead the miraculous beauty of sunlit days over land and water – the two essential ingredients that mark the landscape of the Highlands and Islands as different from any other in Britain.

For long the traditional haunt of the vacationing sporting gentleman, the well-to-do stalker and grouser, yachtsman and angler, the Highlands and Islands are now host to a new breed of less privileged outdoor man: the backpacker, birdwatcher and hiker, and that phenomenon of the post-industrial era, the opter-out and wilderness man, among whom in past years I would have had to number myself.

The Highlands lie to the north of the rift valley that separates them from the Lowlands and Southern Uplands of Scotland. The dividing line, known as the Highland Boundary Fault or Highland Line, runs fairly sharp and straight north-cast from the Isle of Arran on the Clyde across Loch Lomond to Stonehaven on the North Sea coast. Beyond it lie some 13,000 square miles (33,670 square kilometres) of rugged, mountainous terrain; a unique and still largely unspoilt combination of loch, river, forest, moor and mountain.

The region boasts some 522 tops above 3,000 feet (915 metres), 12 above 4,000 feet (1,220 metres), 269 of them separate mountains known as Munros (after Sir Hugh Munro, a President of the Scottish Mountaineering Club, who listed them in 1891). The fantastically indented Highland coastline measures only 260 miles (418 kilometres) as the crow flies, but well over 2,000 (3,220 kilometres) as the seal swims, and the whole inchoate rock mass is sliced up by a series of long parallel transverse glens, of which Glen Coe and Glen Nevis are perhaps the best known, and one of which, the Great Glen, splits the Highlands diagonally into two dissimilar regions: the Grampians and the North West Highlands.

More than almost any part of Britain this is a region of extremes. It is possible to travel from one end to the other in comfort (if not *grande luxe*) without getting puffed or hungry or even (if you are cunning) wet, viewing the sublimest scenery from car park look-outs or the picture windows of waterside hotels. It is also possible to backpack for days across the wilderness of moor and mountain without crossing a road or encountering another human being or habitation of any kind; or be marooned for months on an Atlantic

The pine marten, at home in Scotland's native pines, also thrives amid imported Sitka spruce

islet with only the seals and the skuas for company and only what you have brought with you for food and shelter – lost to the world not only in space but in time. Between these extremes of *gran turismo* and pure wilderness survival are many permutations of experience in the great Scottish outdoors. These are yours to choose.

GETTING THERE

By air: there are 5 commercial airports in this area. Inverness is the main one and provides the most useful air access, with onward travel by road or rail. British Airways, Dan-Air and Loganair make regular daily flights, with restricted weekend services. Inverness is 80 minutes' flying time from London (Heathrow) 40 minutes from Edinburgh and Glasgow.

British Airways fly daily (except Sunday) to two airfields in the Outer Hebrides: Stornoway (Isle of Lewis) via Inverness or Glasgow and Benbecula from Glasgow. Loganair flies to Barra in the Outer Hebrides from Glasgow daily except Sunday (planes land on beach so tides affect timetable: check with operator); and to Broadford on Skye from Glasgow, weekends Jun-Sep (restricted winter service, T:041 889 3181).

By train: the east coast route

to Inverness is served by direct trains from London (Euston and King's Cross) by day and night, and from Edinburgh, Glasgow, Aberdeen and points *en route*. Inverness is also a direct motorail terminal from London and Crewe. From there the slow but marvellous Highland line crosses Scotland to Kyle of Lochalsh on the West Highland coast (three times daily, not Sundays).

The west coast route to Mallaig via Glasgow and Fort William is served by a direct overnight sleeper service from London (Euston).

Alternatively you can travel to Mallaig from Glasgow (Queen Street) via Fort William and enjoy the splendid West Highland Line by day (steam locomotives and courier-serviced observation cars in summer). There is no motorail service on the western route; use motorail terminals at Stirling, Perth or Inverness.

From Mallaig the ferry services of Caledonian MacBrayne run out to the islands of the Inner and Outer Hebrides, including Skye.

By bus or coach: a number of companies run express coach services to and from Scotland, and coach, bus, minibus and postbus services in the Highlands and the Islands. The *Scottish Postbus Timetable*, an invaluable companion for the remote adventurer, is available free from post offices or tourist information centres.

By car: main road motoring along principal approach routes to the region can be as good as elsewhere in the UK, but in the mountains even the main roads are narrower than normal, twist a good deal and climb long gradients. Minor roads are often single-track, with numerous hump-backed bridges, blind corners and wandering sheep. Petrol stations are often far apart and nearly all are closed on

161

Sunday, so fill up as opportunities offers.

WHERE TO STAY
Hotels: high-class hotels and the wilderness experience may seem incompatible, but there are many who value their evening comforts after a rugged day on the hills. The mixture of the two is in the grand old Highland tradition of the Edwardian sporting gentleman – and any fool can be uncomfortable.

For a complete list (over 2,000 entries) see the Scottish Tourist Board's *Where to Stay – Hotels and Guest Houses.* See also Hotels and Guest Houses listed in the following *Where to Stay* publications of the Scottish Highlands and Islands Tourist Board: *Sutherland; Ross and Cromarty; Inverness, Loch Ness and Nairn; Oban and Lorne; Outer Hebrides; Isle of Skye and South West Ross.*

The Scottish Tourist Board also publishes information on hotels offering shooting and stalking, and special amenities for children, the elderly and the disabled.
Bed and breakfast and self-catering: the *Where to Stay* publications listed above also include bed and breakfast accommodation on farms, houses and crofts, as well as self-catering accommodation in houses, crofts and purpose-built log cabins or wooden lodges.

See also the complete list in the Scottish Tourist Board's *Where to Stay – Bed and Breakfast and Self-Catering Accommodation in Scotland.*
Forest cabins: fully equipped forest cabins for self-catering holidays in Scotland's forest areas can be rented weekly from the *Forestry Commission Cabins and Holiday Houses* (Forestry Commission, 231

Corstophine Road, Edinburgh).
Youth hostels: hostels run by the Scottish Youth Hostel Association for youths of any age up to 80 are scattered throughout the Highlands and Islands. Full details from *SYHA Handbook* and *Touring Map of Scotland* (from Scottish Youth Hostel Association, 7 Glebe Crescent, Stirling FK8 2JA, T:0786 72821).
Outdoor living: for a full list of over 350 camping and caravan parks in the Highlands see the Scottish Tourist Board's *Camping and Caravan Parks.* Lay-bys are for meal breaks only, not overnight stops.

In remote areas there are few restrictions on wild camping. But you should always ask if you want to camp near habitation or on someone's land, and there are certain areas – in nature reserves or Forestry Commission Land, for example, or near youth hostels or certain mountaineering club huts – where camping is not allowed. It is illegal to light an open fire in the Scottish countryside without the landowner's permission. Once a fire is started it may get down into the peat and burn for years. Carry a stove and use it with care.

ACTIVITIES
See LOWLAND SCOTLAND fact pack (p.144).

FURTHER INFORMATION
Highland and Islands Development Board, Bridge House, 27 Bank Street, Inverness IV1 1QR. Information on holidays. Runs Tourist Information Centres in many towns.

MOUNTAIN BOTHIES

As an alternative to pitching a tent, walkers can sometimes find shelter in a mountain bothy. These old farm-workers' stone huts may either be derelict or maintained by the Mountain Bothies Association, among others. Bothies are remote and provide little else but shelter, so you have to bring everything with you.

You should respect the Bothy Code:
1 Seek the owner's permission to use a bothy.
2 Keep parties small (three or four).
3 Keep fires small.
4 Leave the bothy in better condition than you found it.
5 Leave no litter, burn or bury all rubbish.
6 Lay in fuel and kindling for the next user.
7 Add unused stores to the food cupboard – but safe from vermin.
8 Do not damage the structure.
9 Put out the fire when you leave.
10 Secure windows and doors when you leave.
11 Observe sanitary precautions and safeguard the water supply.
5 Sign the visitor's book.

For further details contact Mountain Bothies Association, 7 Church Avenue, Burnside, Glasgow G73 5BX, or the New Members Secretary, 26 Rycroft Avenue, Deeping St James, Peterborough, Cambridgeshire.

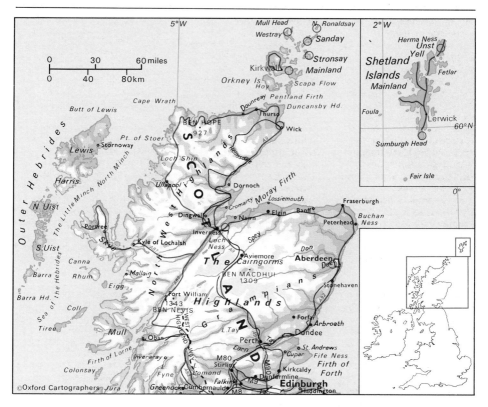

THE SOUTHERN HIGHLANDS

The Southern Highlands extend northward from the line of the Highland Boundary Fault as far as Loch Rannoch. To the west they are bounded by the Atlantic, with its deeply riven seaboard, great sea lochs and peninsulas; and to the east by the Tay-Tummel valley, one of the two main gateways into the Highlands, the other being Loch Lomond. Along the southern edge of this region the country is lower than further north, but offers a greater variety of scenery and a more beautiful landscape of mountain, wood and water.

To the north the mountains roll towards Loch Rannoch in ranges of greater and greater height, almost reaching 4,000 feet (1,220 metres) on Ben Lawers. Seventy of the tops are more than 3,000 feet (915 metres), 46 of them Munros, but the mountains here are mostly rounded and grassy, with few cliff faces to note except on the Cobbler at Arrochar. With its sea coast, lochs, forests, moors and accessible hills this attractive region has much to offer wild traveller and naturalist alike.

Argyll Forest Park

Occupying 100 square miles (260sq km) of rugged Highlands between Loch Eck and Loch Lomond, the Argyll Forest Park encompasses an amazing diversity of habitats, from seashore to mountain top. It successfully combines commercial forestry, natural history and recreational activities: anything from rock climbing to orienteering, canoeing and subaqua exploration of the underwater caves of Loch Long.

Basking shark, grey seal and sea otters frequent the Clyde sea lochs that intrude deep

163

into the forest area, and crabs, shrimps, sea scorpions, sea slugs, sea lemons, sea anemones and other creatures of the sea shore inhabit the inter-tidal zone.

Less than half the park has been afforested. Semi-natural mixed woodlands survive in the glens and along the shore of Loch Eck and in spring and summer they are full of the song of woodland birds and carpeted with primroses, bluebells, violets and wood anemones, while ferns and mosses thrive in the temperate, rainy climate of the coastal area.

Above the forest line, bare hills of grassy moorland stretch upwards to a maximum height of nearly 3,000ft (915m) in the 'Arrochar Alps' in the north of the forest park. The crags and corries of the highest summit, Ben Arthur (2,891ft, 881m), popularly known as the Cobbler, draw many enthusiastic hill walkers and climbers.
Before you go: OS Landranger Series Map No. 56. **Getting there:** from A83 take B828 for Loch Goll or A815 for Loch Eck and Loch Long. Arrochar and Tarbet, a station on the Glasgow-Fort William line, is just outside the park's north-east border. **Where to stay:** Dunoon, to the south of the park, has a wide range of serviced accommodation. See the Dunoon and Cowal Peninsula Tourist Board brochure, available from the Information Centre, 7 Alexandra Parade, Dunoon, Argyll, T:0369 3755. The Forestry Commission runs the Ardgartan campsite, by the A83, 2 miles ((3km) south west of Arrochar. **Further information:** *Argyll Forest Park Guide* from FC offices or Tourist Information Centres: Dunoon (T:0369 3785), Tarbet (T:03012 260).
164

Loch Lomond

National Scenic Area, includes NNR

The largest freshwater lake in Britain, Loch Lomond occupies a deep channel gouged by glacial ice. At Balmaha near its southern end, it is bisected by the Highland Boundary Fault, which marks the beginning of the Highland region. North of this fault the loch narrows and deepens like a fjord crowded in by looming mountains to north, east and west.

To look up Loch Lomond from the southern end is to stare at one of Scotland's scenic glories: a shining ribbon of water that disappears among the distant mountains, luring you onwards towards an interior promising magic and mystery. The eastern shore is the less spoilt; there is no road beyond Rowardennan, and to continue north you must take the WEST HIGHLAND WAY (see p.189) into the Craigroyston hills and beyond.

Alternatively the walker can strike out east over one of the wooded trails that crosses the vast Queen Elizabeth Forest Park to Aberfoyle and the Trossachs, or take the track that leads to the summit of Ben Lomond. The most southerly Munro in Scotland, Ben Lomond is an easy, popular climb offering from its summit a tremendous panorama over Loch Lomond, Ailsa Craig and the Arran Hills, the Paps of Jura, Ben More on Mull, Ben Nevis and Ben Lawers.

The National Nature Reserve is situated in the south-west corner of Loch Lomond, where it occupies more than 1,000 acres (405ha)

of wood, water, shore and fen on five islands and marsh on the mainland. Fine oakwood flora and fauna, unusual fishes such as a freshwater herring called the powan, swamp and fen with rich wetland vegetation round the mouth of the River Endrick, and wintering wildfowl and waders in a cast of thousands.
Before you go: OS Landranger Series Map No. 56.
Getting there: the A82, which clings to Loch Lomond's west bank, is the main Glasgow-Inverness road. Regular coach service. Trains from Glasgow to Balloch at the south end of the loch; stations on Glasgow-Fort William line at Tarbet and Ardlui in the North. Access to the quieter east bank is on the B837 from village of Drymen. This road stops half way along the length of the loch. Bus service to Balmaha only. The B829 from Aberfoyle leads to Inversnaid at the north-east end of the loch. An 11-seater postbus operates daily along this route. A pleasant way to reach the east bank is by boat. Steamer from Balloch to Inversnaid and other points; T:0389 52069 for information. Ferry from Inverbeg across to Rowardennan. **Where to stay:** accommodation of all ranges, but book ahead in the holiday season. *Where-to-stay* brochure from Loch Lomond, Stirling FK8 2LQ, T:0786 70945. Tourist Information Centres at Balloch, T:0389 53533 and Tarbet, T:03012 260. Youth hostels at Arden (nr Balloch); Inverbeg, T:043686 635 and Rowardennan, T:036087 259. T:043686 635 and Rowardennan, T:036087 259. **Facilities:** fishing permits for Loch Lomond and its rivers available locally from boatyards and many hotels. Boat hire from Balmaha,

Luss, Balloch, Drumkinnon and Ardlui. Fishing map from Loch Lomond Angling Association. Canoeing: Rowardennan Youth Hostel is centre for Scottish Hostellers canoe club.

Further information: excellent map of the loch (4 inches to the mile) is produced by Cuillins Yacht Charters, The Flat Afloat, Ardlui, Dumbartonshire. Primarily for sailing, it includes useful information on travel and recreation in the area.

Inversnaid

RSPB Reserve

North-east of Loch Lomond the ground rises steeply through deciduous woods to a rocky ridge and moorland beyond. The loch is a migration route for wildfowl and waders, making this an ideal site for the RSPB reserve. Buzzards nest in the woods and crags; blackcock on the slopes; dipper, grey wagtails and common sandpiper along the shore of the loch and the burns. The 'wildness and wet' of Inversnaid was celebrated by Gerald Manley Hopkins in a marvellous poem.

Getting there: via B829 west from Aberfoyle, then minor road north to reserve. Alternatively, by ferry from Inveruglas on west bank: phone Inversnaid Hotel (T:087 786 223) for arrangements. **Access:** at all times along West Highland Way, which follows the loch shore. **Further information:** RSPB or summer Warden (Mike Trubridge), Garrison Cottage, Inversnaid, Aberfoyle, Central FK8 3TU.

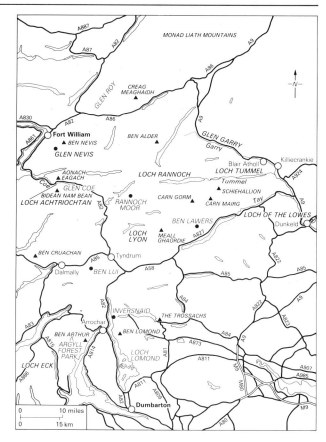

Ben Lui

Includes NCC NNR

Ben Lui is at its most beautiful under bright winter snow. It rises to an elegant, 3,708ft (1,130m) conical summit north of Loch Lomond, the main peak of a group of four Munros on the Perthshire-Argyllshire border. Its high north-east corrie offers serious mountaineers a classic climb, while gentler souls can traverse all 4 mountains in about 10 hours on a route of moderate difficulty between Tyndrum and Dalmally.

From the summit of Ben Lui you can see across to Ben Nevis and all the way to Ben More on Mull. The northern cliffs of Ben Lui are outstanding for their rich mountain flora and an area of some 2,000 acres (800 ha) is now a National Nature Reserve. Anyone proposing to visit the reserve should notify the Warden at NCC, Balloch.

Before you go: OS Landranger Series Map No. 50.

Getting there: Ben Lui rises above the A82 between Crianlarich and Dalmally. Tyndrum and Crianlarich are stations on the Glasgow-Fort William line; Dalmally is on the Oban line. Good bus service along A82.

The most popular ascent leaves the A82 1½ miles (2.5km) east of Tyndrum. Follow the rough track to where it ends past Canonish Farm. Then head along one of the ridges to the summit. This is a moderately strenuous climb of about 6 miles (9.5km). A shorter, rougher ascent can be made from the north west, near Dalmally. **Where to stay:** Dalmally, Tyndrum, Crianlarich. Accommodation listed in *Holidays* brochure published by Loch Lomond, Stirling and Trossachs Area Tourist Board. Youth hostel in Crianlarich (T:08383 260). **Further information:** NCC Reserve Warden, John Mitchell (T:0360 60428). Tourist information, Tyndrum, T:08384 246. Scottish Mountaineering Trust Guide: *The Southern Highlands*.

Ben Lawers

NTS-NCC NNR

At 3,984ft (1,214m), Ben Lawers is the highest mountain in Britain south of Ben Nevis, and so nearly 4,000ft (1,219m) high that in the late C19th a cairn was built on the summit to enable climbers to scramble up to this magic number.

In winter, its long, easy, southern slopes make it good for skiing (fortunately without the usual commercial spoilation); there are good long walks to be had over Ben Lawers and the neighbouring Tarmachans; and its lime-rich metamorphic schists make it Britain's finest mountain for flowers, especially post-glacial arctic-alpines. The moles of Ben Lawers are particularly

166

hardy and adventurous, burrowing upwards to ever greater heights.
Before you go: OS Landranger Series Map No. 51.
Getting there: via unclassified road leaving A827 5 miles (8km) north-east of Killin. Car park and information centre 2 miles (3km) along this road.
Where to stay: youth hostel at Killin (T:05672 546). **Access:** open access to all NT land, mainly south of principal summits. Nature trail, audio-visual programmes, ranger service. **Further information:** booklet and leaflets from information centre. Ranger-naturalist David Marden (T:05672 379).

Atholl

National Scenic Area

Atholl is the name of the large, elongated area that stretches along the line of the River Tay from south of Dunkeld, where the Lowlands give way to the Highlands, northwards to beyond Blair Atholl, hereditary seat of the Dukes of Atholl for more than 7 centuries.

Three rivers flow down this valley through the hills: the Garry, the Tummel and the Tay. Both the Garry and the Tummell have been badly affected by hydroelectric development, but on the inaccessible higher slopes lie areas of interest to naturalist and hill walker alike. From the large estate at Blair Atholl right of way tracks lead through Glen Tilt across wild country to Deeside and through Glen Bruar across no less wild country to Speyside: major expeditions requiring proper gear and true grit.

There are two important

reserves in the area. The SWT Reserve at Loch of the Lowes covers 242 acres (98 ha) of loch with fringing woodland and marsh in a hilly Highland setting east of Dunkeld. The Loch is most famous for its ospreys, which have nested here off and on since 1969, and can be seen between early April and August; and also for its grebes (great crested, Slavonian and little).

The RSPB reserve at Killiekrankie stretches from the gorge of the River Garry through oakwoods, pasture and birchwoods to crags and heather moorland nearly 1,000 ft (300m) above. Woodland birds include redstart, crossbill and buzzard, while black grouse and whinchat inhabit the moorland, and raven and kestrel the crags. With luck you might see golden eagle and peregrine, too. The wooded gorge of the adjacent Pass of Killiekrankie (part of the Loch Tummel National Scenic Area) is NTS land, and worth visiting for its birds, flowers and geology.
Before you go: OS Landranger Series Map Nos. 43, 44, 52, 53. **Getting there:** the main road through Atholl is the A9 from Perth. For Loch of the Lowes, turn off A9 at Dunkeld and take A923 in direction of Blairgowrie. For Killiekrankie, turn off A9 just north of Pitlochry and continue on B8079. **Access:** at Loch of the Lowes, restricted to south shore, hide, visitor centre (Apr-Sep) and car park at west end. Free access at all times to Killiekrankie RSPB reserve, but on waymarked trail only. Access to NTS property is unrestricted.

Rest and Be Thankful, a quaintly-named pass at the head of Glen Croe, is far from restful in winter when fierce winds tear through it

Further information: RSPB Warden (Martin Robinson), Balrobbie Farm, Killiekrankie, Pitlochry PH16 5LJ. NTS visitor centre open Easter to September. Leaflet and handbooks from Loch of the Lowes Centre, Dunkeld, Tayside, T:03502 337.

Glen Lyon

Part of the Loch Rannoch-Glen Lyon National Scenic Area

Glen Lyon is deeply entrenched between the high mountains of Meall Ghaordie (3,410ft, 1,039m) and Ben Lawers (3,984ft, 1,214m) to the south and Carn Gorm (3,377ft, 1,029m) and Carn Mairg (3,419ft, 1,042m) to the north. Loch Lyon descends through wild bare mountain country to Meggernie Castle, where the landscape becomes gentler and more sylvan. Every bend in the river offers a fresh view of river, wood, mountain and meadow. At the Pass of Lyon, the river hurls itself through a rocky, beech-screened gorge before opening out to the civilized world around Fortingall.
Getting there: from B846, 5 miles (8km) west of Aberfeldy, an unclassified road leads the full length of Glen Lyon to the power station at Loch Lyon. A daily 11-seater postbus goes up the glen as far as Gallin.
Where to stay: youth hostel at Killin, 7 miles (11km) south of glen (T:05672 546).
Where to go: for climbs in the area, see *The Southern Highlands* (Scottish Mountaineering Trust).
Further information: Tourist Information Centres at Killin (T:05672 254) and Aberfeldy (T:0887 20276).

Rannoch Moor

NCC NNR

Rannoch Moor is a 1,000-ft (300-m) high plateau whose rotted granite was ground flat by the last batch of Ice Age glaciers to leave 60 square miles (150sq ft) of nothing but peat bogs, lochans, pools, puddles and blanket bog.

But Rannoch Moor is far from lifeless. There is the wildlife all about you: red and roe deer, dunlins, greenshanks, ducks, divers, plovers and other birds of moorland and water, and a luxuriant spread of boggy plants like bog myrtle, bog asphodel, cotton grass and sphagnum moss.

Rising like islands on the watery horizon lie the surrounding mountains: stand by Loch Ba in the west and you can stare eastward across one of the wildest terrains in Scotland, all the way to the exquisite cone of Schiehallion, which rises to 3,547ft (1,081m) in the far distance like some volcanic islet on the ocean's rim.

To the north lies Loch Rannoch, with Rannoch Forest on its northern flank and the Black Wood of Rannoch on its southern slopes. In this important remnant of the old native pinewoods of Scotland, the last wolf in Britain met its end. Now a Forest Nature Reserve of nearly 6,000 acres (2,430ha) where pine marten, wildcat, capercaillie and golden eagle still thrive.
Before you go: OS Landranger Series Map Nos. 41, 51.
Getting there: A82 Callander-Ballachulish road flanks the west of the moor. To the east, the B846 from Aberfeldy ends

at Rannoch Station, a stop on the Glasgow-Fort William line. Buses to Rannoch Station from Pitlochry.
Where to stay: hotel at Rannoch Station. Limited bed and breakfast accommodation in immediate vicinity. Information centre at Aberfeldy (T:0887 20276) will assist. Youth hostel at Loch Ossian, 9 miles (14.5km) north east of Rannoch Station (no roads; access on foot or by train to Corrour Station 1 mile (1.6km) away). Kilvrecht campsite in Rannoch Forest.
Where to go: Rannoch Forest: access from unclassified road leaving B846 at Kinloch Rannoch and following south side of Loch Rannoch. 3 picnic sites. Waymarked walks. Fishing and boating on Loch Rannoch. **Access:** stay on footpaths during deer stalking season. In Rannoch Forest keep to forest tracks. Access to NCC reserve is restricted. **Further information:** for NCC reserve contact the Warden, Gordon Wright, on T:0577 64439 (work)/63543 (home). FC information from campsite warden or Forest Office.

Loch Tummel

National Scenic Area

Stretching westwards from the Pass of Killiekrankie and presenting upland sylvan scenes rather than a wild mountain landscape, the famous Queen's View (a favourite spot for Queen Victoria) enjoys a marvellous outlook over Loch Tummell westward to the cone of Schiehallion (3,547ft, 1,081m). The Forestry Commission owns an area of 17,000 acres (6,880ha) of mixed woodland

and lochs on the north side of Loch Tummel, Tayside. Woodland birds include capercaillie and goldcrest.

Getting there: south of the B8019, 3 miles (5km) west of its junction with A9 at Garry Bridge in the Pass of Killiecrankie. An unclassified road from Pitlochry runs along the southern shore of the loch.

Where to stay: youth hostel, Pitlochry (T:0796 2308).

Where to go: Queen's View: on B8019, 4 miles (6.5km) west of Garry Bridge.

Linn of Tummel: NTS wooded valley. Car park on B8019 at Garry Bridge.

Forest of Tummel: mainly to north of loch. Waymarked walks and picnic places.

Further information: leaflet from FC. Booklet from Killiecrankie visitor centre (NTS) on A9.

The sea eagle, until recently extinct in the British Isles, has now been reintroduced on Rhum

THE CENTRAL HIGHLANDS

The Central Highlands, which are confined by the Great Glen to the north and west, Strath Spey and Glen Garry to the east, and Rannoch to the south, cover a smaller area than the Southern Highlands but contain double the number of mountain tops; the Black Mount Hills, Ben Alder, Creag Meaghaidh, Ben Cruachan, the Monadh Liath mountains and big Ben Nevis, the tallest of the British peaks. These massive lumps, with their sensational corries and enormous cliffs, offer some of the best rock, snow and ice climbing, and the finest ridge walking in Britain. Magnificent glens such as Glen Nevis, Glen Coe and Glen Etive thread through this mountainous region, with extensive wilderness areas in the hinterland.

Glen Coe

NTS NNR

Glen Coe is a spectacular mountain wilderness of precipitous summits, towering, cloud-hung rock faces and deep gullies. A tourist road runs through the bottom of the glen bearing its busy caravanserai of summer holidaymakers, but up in the wilds of the surrounding hills,

Glen Coe is not a place to be trifled with. Only the foolhardy would venture out to walk or climb without proper preparation; the local mountain rescue team is one of the most experienced in Britain.

The visitor from the south approaches the Glen by way of Black Mount, with the desolation of Rannoch Moor stretching far to the east. Viewed from the Moor, it is the mountain of Buchaille Etive Mor (3,353ft, 1,022m) that dominates the landscape to the north-west. A rocky gateway called the Study forms the entrance to the Glen, an ice-worn valley which lies betweeen the 6-mile (9.5km) ridge of Aonach Eagach and the spurs of Bidean nam Bian, at 3,766ft (1,148m) the highest mountain in Argyll.

169

Between sheer walls of volcanic rock, the River Coe rushes westwards over foaming cataracts and through limpid pools to the stiller waters of Loch Achtriochtan. Precipices and waterfalls tower above the flats of the lower glen; this is climbing country *par excellence*.

Glen Coe was the appropriately spectacular location of the notorious massacre of the Macdonalds by the King's soldiers in 1692. There is little shelter for wildlife here, though red deer, golden eagle and peregrine can occasionally be seen, and there is a rich mountain flora on the most inaccessible cliffs.
Before you go: OS Landranger Series Map No. 41. SMT Guide *The Central Highlands*.
Getting there: the A82, which runs through glen, is main Glasgow-Fort William road. Consequently, good coach service. **Where to stay:** Clachaig Hotel is in the glen and welcomes campers on surrounding land. Bed and breakfast in Glencoe village. Youth hostel between village and glen (T:08552 219). Nearest tourist information centre in Balachulish (T:08552 296). **Further information:** NTS Information Centre (T:08552 307). Ranger-naturalist at centre or home (T:08552 311).

Ben Nevis

Ben Nevis, as almost everyone knows, is the highest mountain in Britain, heaving its great bulk up to 4,406ft (1,343m) above Fort William at the western end of the Great Glen. It is essentially a granite mountain ground down by ice and time, and

displays many of the typical features of a granite mountain landscape, including enormous corries with sheer cliffs that fall vertically for as much as 2,000ft (610m).

Walkers toil up to the summit in droves along the easy pony track way in summer – easy, that is, in terms of technical difficulty, but arduous in terms of fitness and stamina, for it is a long, 7-hour haul. With a mean monthly temperature below freezing, snow can fall on any day of the year and icy, howling winds buffet about the place most of the time.

If you are lucky and the cloud clears for a moment, and it will usually be only a moment, you will glimpse the ultimate mountain view in Britain, right across to the Irish hills 120 miles (193km) away, to the Hebridean Isle of Rhum 92 miles (148km) away, the Cuillins of Skye beyond it and, 77 miles (124km) away to the west, the Paps of Jura, not to mention other heights nearer to hand: Torridon, the Cairngorms, Ben Lawers and the Glen Coe peaks.

There are many other ways up Ben Nevis, most of them much more difficult. By far the best is by way of Glen Nevis, one of the most beautiful glens in Scotland. The middle section of this approach is almost Himalayan in character, with the river running clear and swift and the waterfalls streaming down from the cliffs above. From this glen you can stare up a continuous slope through 4,000ft (1,220m) of evolving landscape, up past alpine-like meadows to moor and rock. All you have to do is persuade

Glen Coe is best remembered for the massacre of 1692; today, its rugged beauty attracts more sporting visitors

your feet to follow where your eyes have gone – it's worth it. **Before you go:** OS Landranger Series Map No. 41. SMT Guide. **Getting there:** Fort William, the base for any exploration of the area is on the A82, 65 miles (105km) south west of Inverness. It is on the Glasgow-Mallaig railway line and is a principal stop for coaches from Edinburgh, Glasgow and Inverness.

From the south side of Nevis Bridge, close to the centre of town, an unclassified road leads along Glen Nevis. To north of Bridge another road is signposted to Ben Nevis Path. **Where to stay:** all ranges of accommodation at Fort William. Information centre will assist. Glen Nevis Hostel (T:0397 2336) is 2½ miles (4km) along Glen Nevis road.
Further information: Fort William and Lochaber Tourist Board, Cameron Centre, Fort William, T:0379 3781.

Glen Roy

NCC Reserve

Nearly 3,000 acres in extent, the reserve occupies the mountainous country between Glen Spean and Glen Mor. It is of primary importance for earth scientists on account of its series of Ice Age geological features, above all the so-called 'Parallel Roads of Glen Roy', which mark the successive shorelines of an ancient ice-blocked lake.
Getting there: from Roybridge, 3 miles (5km) east of Spean Bridge on the A86, take unclassified road north along Glen Roy. Good viewing of Parallel Roads in about 3 miles (5km).
Access: open all year round.

THE CAIRNGORMS AND EAST GRAMPIANS

This enormous mountain group comprises the whole of the north-east Highlands between the rivers Tay and Spey, some 2,200 square miles (5,700sq km) of high, wild, mountainous country. From the Pass of Drumochter in Glen Garry to the west, the main Grampian range stretches for some hundred miles to the coastal lowlands above Aberdeen to the east. About 20 miles (30km) east of Drumochter this range sends out a northern spur, a high granite range occupying 400 square miles (1,000sq km) of high mountain country north of the River Dee. This is the Cairngorms. To the south of the River Dee lies a semi-circle of high mountains which are usually referred to as the East Grampians, with Lochnagar (2,789 feet, 850m) in the Royal Forest of Balmoral taking pride of place.

The high, almost arctic plateau of the Cairngorms is dominated by the broad 4,000-foot summits of Cairn Gorm, Cairn Toul, Braeriach and Ben MacDui at 4,296 feet (1,309m) the second highest mountain in Scotland.

Cairngorm National Nature Reserve

Over 100 square miles of the Cairngorms is now a huge National Nature Reserve, the largest in Britain. The reserve straddles the Lairig Ghru and reaches to north and south of the high tops down to the pinewoods of the low ground. It thus presents to the visitor not only the grandeur and almost polar isolation of its awesome landscape but a wide range of Highland wildlife in a variety of habitats.

On the windswept, nearly arctic summits, the few flowering plants that can survive the regions of the climate include moss campion and wood rush. The high corries shelter highly local plants like mountain rock-cress, alpine speedwell and a few very rare plants like arctic mouse-ear and hare's-foot sedge. The moorland slopes are dominated by heather and deergrass; lower down are the native Scots pinewoods.

Most of the area has long been managed as deer forest. Roe deer frequent the woods and lower moors in small family groups, and reindeer, red squirrel, blue or mountain hare and all the carniverous animals of Scotland except the pine marten can be found here, among them the otter in the streams and lochs. Breeding birds of the pine forest include buzzard, black grouse, capercaille, crossbill, siskin and crested tit, while golden eagle and peregrine nest on the cliffs, and osprey have returned to breed after many years' absence.

Before you go: OS Landranger Series Map Nos. 36, 43, and 1:25,000 Leisure Map – *High Tops of the Cairngorms*. Remember this is high, exposed and potentially savage terrain. Observe the Mountain Code. Phone local weather forecasts from Kingussie (054 02 308) or Cairngorm (047 986 261). If in doubt, don't set out.

Getting there: there is no problem reaching the perimeter of the Cairngorms; the A9, A93 and A939 roughly define its perimeters. Within this area there are many tracks but little opportunity for the motorist to penetrate more than 2 or 3 miles into the mountains. Chair lift from car park below Cairn Gorm to top. Then prepare to walk. The Perth-Inverness railway stops at Kingussie and Aviemore. Coaches between Edinburgh and Inverness serve Aviemore and other centres along the A9. There are also services between Aberdeen and Braemar. **Where to stay:** accommodation of all kinds is easy to spot, but booking is essential in peak periods. The main tourist route along the A9 to the north of the region. Contact Scottish Tourist Board or local information centres, which will provide information and *Where to Stay* brochures. Youth hostels at Aviemore, Glenmore and Braemar. There are several mountain bothies throughout the area. Their location is clearly indicated on OS maps – Sinclair Hut, Corrour Bothy, Gean's Hut in Coire or Lochain of Cairngorm. The FC has a convenient campsite near Loch Morlich in Glenmore Forest. **Further information:** from NCC Wardens at Achnagoichan (T:0479 810287); Kinakyle (T:0479 810250); Woodlea

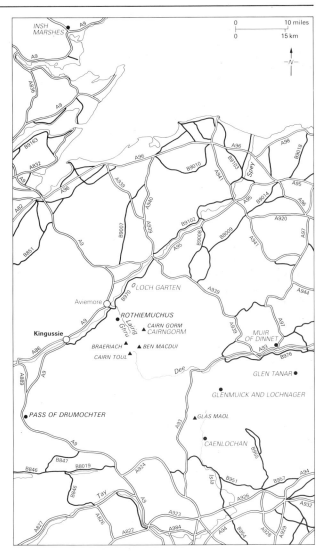

(T:05402 421); and Achantoul (T:0479 810477).

Insh Marshes

RSPB Reserve

These 2,000 acres (800ha) of wetland fen are situated in the flood plain of the upper River Spey between the Monadhliath and Cairngorm mountains. They are important for wintering wildfowl (including large numbers of whooper swans), breeding duck, greylag geese and waders. An impressive range of birds of prey have been seen here: buzzard, sparrowhawk, hen harrier, osprey, golden eagle, goshawk, marsh harrier, peregrine, kestrel and the

173

occasional merlin.

Other fauna include 17 species of butterfly (the Scotch argus most notably), 200 species of moth (Rannoch sprawler, Kentish glory, elephant hawk-moth), several species of dragonfly and the rare bee beetle: and roe deer, otter, badger and fox.

Getting there: off B970 to Insh village 1½ miles (2.5km) south-east of Kingussie. **Access:** every day except Tuesday. **Further information**: Warden (Zul Bhatia), Ivy Cottage, Insh, Kingussie, Highland PH21 1NT.

Rothiemuchus

This enormous private estate covers more than 30 square miles (75sq km) of lochs and hill ground between the Spey Valley and Braeriach in the middle of the Cairngorms. It contains very fine stands of native pine, as well as moorland and wetland with a good range of characteristic flora and fauna.

The beautiful Loch an Eilein (otters, brown trout, pike, eel, crossbills, buzzards and feeding osprey) is also part of the estate and can be explored along the nature trail. A large part of the estate lies within the boundary of the Cairngorm National Nature Reserve and 85% of the land is protected as sites of special scientific interest.

Getting there: to visitor centre at Inverdruie on B970 south of Aviemore. **Access:** all year, but in forest keep to waymarked paths; open access to Cairngorms above tree line except during period of deer cull (Sep-Oct), and calving (May-Jun), when visitors should keep to specified hill routes. **Further information:**
174

leaflets from Rothiemuchus Estate Office, Dell of Rothiemuchus, by Aviemore, Invernesshire PH22 1QH, T:0479 810647.

Loch Garten

RSPB Reserve

This reserve in Speyside, Highland, occupies nearly 3,000 acres (1,200ha) of the Abernethy Forest, a remnant of the ancient Caledonian Forest and now the largest area of natural woodland in Britain. These great old northern pinewoods are a national heritage, but it is Loch Garten's famous ospreys that are one of the great conservation success stories. After half a century's absence from Scotland a single pair of ospreys came to Loch Garten in the 1950s to breed. Every spring since then ospreys have returned from their winter quarters in Africa to nest in their Loch Garten eyrie.

Seventy-two other birds breed here and a remarkable total of 144 species have been recorded (some of them rare), 260 moths, 18 butterflies, 11 dragonflies; and otter, wild cat, pine marten, red deer, red squirrel, badger, fox, and a wide variety of northern pinewood plants.

Getting there: turn off B970 at Boat of Garten and follow signpost to reserve at Loch Garten. **Access:** ospreys are in Statutory Bird Sanctuary; access confined to waymarked paths leading to observation post (open mid Apr-Aug). Rest of reserve accessible at all times. **Further information:** for booklet, send a stamped addressed envelope to the Warden (Stewart Taylor),

Grianan, Nethybridge, Highland PH25 3EF, or from RSPB Edinburgh.

Glen Tanar

NCC NNR

Occupying over 10,000 acres (4,000ha) of woodland and moorland on the Glen Tanar Estate south of the River Dee, this is the finest and most easterly remnant of the ancient Caledonian Forest, with large spreads of splendid native Scots pine of great age, and natural regeneration on an extensive scale. Typical pinewood flora and fauna includes crossbill, siskin and capercaillie, red squirrel, wild cat, otter, fox and mink.

Getting there: to Glen Tanar Estate at Braeloine, south of B976, almost 6 miles (9.5km) east of Ballater. **Access:** at any time on waymarked paths on old drove roads. Access off paths by permit only, apply Glen Tanar Estate Office. **Further information:** NCC or Glen Tanar Estate, Braeloine, nr Ballater, Grampian.

Glenmuick and Lochnagar

SWT Reserve by agreement with the Royal Estate, Balmoral

The reserve covers 6,355 acres (2,572 ha) of mountainous terrain and lochs, with the stark, boulder-strewn slopes of Lochnagar rising abruptly from the shores of Loch Muick: the highest point of a range of hills forming an almost continuous 9-mile (14.5km) plateau. Lochnagar

is remarkable for the sheer granite cliffs of its gigantic, ice-sculptured corries and the vast expanse of purple heather on its hillsides in August.

This is wild country by any standards, the world of running deer, soaring eagles, swooping peregrine. In winter it feels like Alaska, but in summer you can see adders and lizards basking by the trail on sunny days. The luxuriant flowers of the corries are the region's scientific treasure: red campion, globeflower, Alpine willowherb and various saxifrages, as well as alpine lady fern and parsley fern. You might even see bird rarities like honey buzzard and wry neck.

Before you go: OS Landranger Series Map No. 44. **Getting there:** turn off B976 at Bridge of Muick and follow road to Spittal of Glenmuick. Proceed from car park on foot. **When to go:** May-Sep for birds and flowers, Nov for deer. **Where to stay:** accommodation in Ballater, including youth

hostel (T:0338 55227). **Access:** at all times. Visitor centre and ranger service at Spittal; a variety of trails, some rough, some easy, lead from here to Loch Muick, Lochnagar and Glen Cova. **Further information:** Ranger or Balmoral Estates Office.

Caenlochan

NCC NNR

The reserve covers 9,100 acres (3,680ha) of wild mountain country centring on the head of the River Isla and stretching east as far as Glen Cova mountains. This is a difficult place to get to and involves some rough walking in rugged terrain. But it is the real McCoy – who was McCoy? – with red deer in great numbers on the corries and summits, and blue hare and foxes, and golden eagles

Sunlight plays on the Grampian moor between Clattering Bridge and Bridge of Dye

wheeling over the glens, and many ptarmigan, golden plover, dunlin and ring ouzel. **Before you go:** OS Landranger Series Map Nos. 43, 44. **Getting there:** Glas Maol (3,502ft, 1,067m), the area's highest mountain, rises to the east of A93 – in the Cairnwell Pass – between Blairgowrie and Braemar. Climb it from the highest point on the main road. The area has an attractive back door at the head of Glen Cova, reached on the B955 north from Kirriemuir. There is a daily (except Sundays) bus service along this road.
Where to stay: tourist information in Kirriemuir will assist with accommodation (T:0575 74097). Glendoll Youth Hostel at head of Glen Cova (T:05755 236).
Access: to nature reserve restricted June-20 Oct. Contact NCC, Edinburgh.

THE NORTH-WEST HIGHLANDS

The cataclysmic landslip of the Great Glen cleanly slashes Scotland in two. This flooded fault stretches diagonally from Inverness on the east coast to the Isle of Mull on the west. Incorporating the deep waters of Loch Ness in its 76-mile (107-km) course, the Great Glen is the most stupendous geological feature in Britain. Beyond it lies the wild world of rock and water of North-West Scotland; the wettest, windiest, oldest and least populated part of Britain. It is also a very complex region. From Moidart to Cape Wrath the west coast is a confused mixture of old rocks and new volcanic ones, a wild jumble of ancient gneiss, old sandstone and the weathered lava flows and eroded granites of the volcanoes. The Torridonian mountains of Wester Ross jut to 3,000 feet (900 metres) straight out of the sea. The wastes of west Sutherland, a so-called 'wet desert' scoured bare by the Ice Age, stretch soilless and treeless to the edge of vision.

The coast, where the Atlantic rollers thunder against the sheer cliffs and off-shore islands with an impact measured at three tons per square foot, is wild and indented, and fiercely glaciated sea lochs like giant fjords gnaw deep into the heart of the rocky landscape. Amid this grandeur and desolation signs of human settlement are few: only here or there an isolated cottage where a crofter wrests a living from the meagre soil.

SCOTTISH PLACE NAMES

Aber *river mouth*	Eilean *island*
Aird, ard *height, promontory*	Fionne, fyne *white, shining*
Allt *stream*	Garbh *rough*
Aonach *ridge*	inch, innis *island*
Auch, ach *field*	Inver *river mouth*
Ban *white*	Kil *church, burial place*
Beallach *pass*	Knock *knoll*
Beg, beag *little*	Kyle *firth, strait*
Ben, beinn, bheinn *mountain*	Lairig *pass*
	Liath *grey*
Breac, vrackie *speckled*	Linn, linne *pool*
Cairn, carn *hill*	Meall, mheall *rounded hill*
Cnoc *hill, knoll*	Mor, more *big*
Coire, corrie *mountain valley, or hollow*	Na, nam, an *the, of, of the*
	Ru, rhu, row, rudha *point*
Creag *crag, rock*	Sgurr *peak*
Dearg *red*	Stob *peak*
Druim, drum *ridge*	Strath *broad valley*
Dubh *dark, black*	Tarbet, *isthmus*
Eaglais *church*	Uamh *cave*
	Voe *narrow bay*

Ardnamurchan, Moidart and Morar

National Scenic Area

These three West Highland peninsulas overlook the Small Isles, forming a coastal landscape of tremendous variety and interest. To the south lies Loch Sunart and the remote Morvern peninsula, whose interior consists entirely of moorland and low hills; to the north the wild, uninhabited mountain country of the Morar peninsula is split almost in two by the trackless 10-mile (16-km) length of Loch Morar, the deepest inland water in Britain.

The coastal fringe is made up of several subsidiary areas, each different in character but complementary to the others: the rocky, indented coastline of northern Ardnamurchan; the sandy bays and moss of Kentra; Loch Moidart's sheltered, intimate landscape of wooded islands, sand, rock and water; the wooded shores, rocky promontories and heather-covered islets of Loch Ailort and Loch nan Uamh; and the silver sand beaches of Morar backed by 5 miles (8km) of machair overlooking the Sound of Arisaig and the Isle of Eigg.

It was on the beach where the Borrodale Burn flows into the Loch nan Uamh that Bonnie Prince Charlie landed in July 1745 to raise his rebellion, and departed thence 14 months later after its failure. With its looming hills and mountains, its ever-changing western light, its gigantic flaming sunsets behind the isles, this is a magical part of the Highland world, inaccessible by road, but a joy on foot.

There is an NCC-FC reserve of native woodland on opposite sides of Loch Sunart – oak on the north bank, ashwood on the south. The main scientific interest is the range of rare and local species of mosses, lichens and leafy liverworts which flourish luxuriantly in the high humidity of the area.

Lacking really high and dramatic peaks this area attracts few climbers and hill walkers. However, the traverse of the Rois Bheinn ridge of Moidart from Rois Bheinn (2,895ft, 882m) across the mountains of Loch Shiel to Glenfinnan, a high-level walk of 18 miles (29km) across a rough and trackless wilderness, must count as one of the finest hill walks in Britain, offering considerable variety and marvellous views. An experienced walker should

allow 9 hours, and be prepared for wind and rain. **Before you go:** OS Landranger Series Map Nos. 40, 47, 49. **Getting there:** A861 leaves the A830 18 miles (29km) south of Mallaig at Lochailort in South Morar. It winds south along the coast, through Moidart, giving access to the shores of Loch Ailort and Loch Moidart. At Salen it turns east, keeping to the north shore of Loch Sunart. The B8007, which leaves the A861 at Salen, gives access to the Ardnamurchan peninsula. Lochailort is a station on the Fort William to Mallaig line. **Where to stay:** bed and breakfast and hotel at Lochailort, Arisaig, Morar, Mallaig and other places in the area. *Where to Stay* brochure from Fort William and Lochaber Tourist Board, Cameron Centre, Cameron

Square, Fort William PH33 6AJ, T:0397 3781. **Where to go:** Loch Sunart NNR. Access to Ariundle Wood from A861 north of Loch Sunart. Travelling west, turn right at Strontian, then right again at sign of Ariundle. Nature trail. Fine waterfall. Leaflet from FC office at Strontian. Access to Glen Cripesdale section of reserve is by permit only. Apply NCC. Rois Bheinn Ridge. Access to Rois Bheinn along west slope from Roshven on A861, at mouth of Loch Ailort. For route details of climbs in the area consult *The Western Highlands* by the Scottish Mountaineering Trust. See also *The Knoydart and Morar Passes*, a map produced by the Scottish Rights of Way Society. **Further information:** Tourist Information, Salen, T:096785 622.

Knoydart

The first time I set eyes on Knoydart was from nearly 3,200 feet (975 metres) up on the top of Ben Sgreol one blindingly frosty sunlit blue day in midwinter. I had climbed up the mountain in Wellington rubber boots and a peat-digger's donkey jacket, starting literally at sea level on the beach at Sandaig Bay and following the line of a very steep burn for much of the way. When I eventually got to the top, and looked about me in that dry, crystal light, the view took me completely by surprise.

Skye, and the whale-backed hump of Rhum, and the blue shapes of the Outer Isles; all that I had expected. But I was quite unprepared for the view over the mountains of the hinterland. To north, east and south stretched a seemingly limitless wilderness devoid of human habitation; under its cover of pristine snow it looked

more like a mountain range in Siberia, certainly unlike anything I had ever seen in Britain up to that time.

Much of this wild and crackling landscape I saw from Ben Sgreol belonged to a remote region called Knoydart, which stretched away from the far shore of the deep, dark loch called Loch Hourn below me. I was intrigued by this unexpected wilderness, and I resolved to set foot there as soon as the opportunity offered.

So one still, early spring day in late March I launched the dinghy into the bay, and after picking up a friend from the south at Glenelg jetty, set course for the Knoydart shore. My friend had brought a bottle of excellent Glenfiddich malt whisky to help the voyage along, so to speak, and we steered a giddy course down the Sound of Sleat, before abruptly grounding on the boulder shore by the Croulin Burn on the north side of Knoydart.

I teetered ashore. It was a very hallucinatory sort of day. Above the high spring tide line lay an abandoned croft whose owner, an old and reclusive fisherman, had recently died. Now there were deer in the overgrown garden, two hinds in his tumbledown parlour and a very proud, heavily antlered, seriously lame stag out on the rough track that led over the hill and far away. I followed the limping stag into the silent interior over the rough, bouldered ground, and at length stood alone in a bowl of rocks, above which wheeled the silhouette of a buzzard on stiff flared wings, and beyond which soared a horseshoe of summits and behind them a high, extremely precipitous, solitary peak: Ladhar Beinn (3,343 feet, 1,019 metres).

I was so mesmerized by the curiously primordial magic of this wild place that in subsequent years I tried to buy some sort of dwelling there: croft or bothy or ruin, I didn't mind. Only much later did I discover that Knoydart was ruled by a very autocratic and feudal Laird who rigorously repelled all intruders; and this was one reason why Knoydart had remained for so long a wilderness backwater, unvisited, unknown and unsung. All this has now changed, however, following the death of the Laird.

The Rough Bounds of Knoydart is the old name for this wild and isolated peninsula of mountains and glens to the north of Morar between Loch Nevis and Loch Hourn. It is an apt name, for though strictly speaking it refers only to the coast, which is both trackless and exceedingly rough going on foot, it could serve just as well for the interior, where no road goes and precious few people either.

Loch Hourn, on Knoydart's northern frontier, is one of the most gaunt and melancholy of all Scottish sea lochs, and so hemmed in on both sides by mountains above 3,000 feet (900 metres) that it is virtually sunless – hence, perhaps, its name, which means Hell Loch. By contrast, Loch Nevis (Loch of Heaven), bounding Knoydart to the south, has an open and sunny aspect, but like Loch Hourn it penetrates deep into the mountains, and together

The typically Highland scenery of Loch Blain lies at the landward end of Ardnamurchan

these two sea lochs serve to emphasize Knoydart's sense of extraordinary remoteness and apartness.

Five main glens and passes open up Knoydart to the wild traveller. Shepherds' and stalkers' tracks lead through these glens, and you would be well advised to stick to them as far as possible, because away from them Knoydart is rugged indeed. The tracks, which are rights of way, provide convenient access to Knoydart's three Munros – Ladhar Bheinn (pronounced Larven 3,343 feet, 1,019 metres), the most westerly Munro on the British mainland, with one of the most spectacular corries ringed by 100-foot (30-metre) vertical cliffs; and to the east the peaks of Luinne Bheinn (3,083 feet, 940 metres) and Meall Buidhe (3,107 feet, 947 metres).

The only two settlements on Knoydart are at Barrisdale Bay on Loch Hourn and at Inverie on Loch Nevis. There is a good long walk you can do across the rugged and mountainous country between the two via Ladhar Bheinn – distance 22 miles (35km), time 11 hours, but you will have to try and connect with the evening mail boat from Inverie to Mallaig or you will be stranded for the night, and the local factor will be very vexed with you.

BEFORE YOU GO
OS Landranger Series Map No. 33.

GETTING THERE
The determined motorist can penetrate a part of this remote area from the A87 via two winding and precipitious unclassified roads. One leaves the main road at Loch Garry, 5 miles (8km) west of Invergarry, ending at the head of Loch Hourn (Kinloch Hourn). The other leaves the A87 at Shiel Bridge by the head of Loch Duich and goes via Glenelg and Arnisdale to Corran on Loch Hourn.

Easier access by boat from Mallaig. Thrice weekly mail boats (Mon, Wed, Fri) stop at Inverie and Tarbet, hamlets on Loch Nevis. Contact Bruce Watt Cruises, The Pier, Mallaig, T:0687 2233 or 'Western Isles', East Bay, Mallaig, T:0687 2320. Bruce Watt Cruises also operates excursions into Loch Hourn.

A 4-seater postbus makes a daily trip (excepting Sundays) to Arnisdale on Loch Hourn from Kyle of Lochalsh. Another postbus service links Invergarry with Kinloch Hourn 3 times a week.

WHERE TO STAY
Bed and breakfast accommodation Mallaig. Hotel at Tomdoun, 20 miles (32km) east of Loch Hourn. Youth hostel: Ratagan, near Shiel Bridge, T:059981 243. Two area tourist boards cover this region and produce *Where to Stay* brochures: Fort William and Lochaber (south and central), T:0397 3781 and the Isle of Skye and South West Ross (north), T:0478 2137. There are 4 self-catering vacation houses and an inexpensive walkers' hostel on the estate. Inverie House takes bookings for parties of 7 or more. Enquiries to Estate Office, Knoydart Estate, Mallaig, T:0687 2243.

WHERE TO GO
For the walker there is rough, trackless going across the peninsula's beautiful mountains. Ladhar Bheinn (3,343ft, 1,019m) is accessible from Inverie on north shore of Loch Nevis. On any excursion into this remote region, carry an authoritative guide book: *The Western Highlands*, produced by the Scottish Mountaineering Trust, covers the area thoroughly. *The Knoydart and Morar Passes*, a simple map of the area, is published by the Scottish Rights of Way Society, 1 Lutton Place, Edinburgh, EH8 9PD. Remember that most of this area is 'deer forest'. In late summer or autumn enquire whether deer stalking is in progress.

ACTIVITIES
A recent change in ownership has altered the face of Knoydart. From an unknown and impenetrable wilderness, it is rapidly becoming an upmarket, high-profile wilderness, with the cost of killing a deer about the same as what most people spend on a new car. Fishing is excellent and slightly less expensive than stalking (enquiries to Estate Office – above), but the budget-minded visitor will leave his blood-lust at home and go walking.

FURTHER INFORMATION
Tourist Information Centres, Shiel Bridge, T:0599 81264; Mallaig, T:0687 2170.

Loch Arkaig to Loch Quoich

Inland from Knoydart, between the National Scenic Areas of Kintail to the North and Loch Shiel to the south, lies a vast tract of uninhabited mountain country that must count as one of the wildest and least tamed areas in Britain. It has no name, this rugged, almost trackless muddle of peaks and glens, but it is bounded immediately to the west by the wild lands of Knoydart and Morar, and far to the east by the definitive divide of the Great Glen, and it incorporates the lonely inland lochs of Arkaig and Quoich (pronounced Kooich), and between them one of Scotland's remotest and most dramatic mountains, Sgurr na Ciche, rising in sharp and perfect symmetry to a height of 3,410ft (1,039m).

This exciting wilderness has one other distinction – it is one of the wettest places in the British Isles, with an average annual rainfall of up to 159ins (404cm) recorded at Kinlochquoich, and fine days counted on the fingers of your hands. This makes an expedition to the interior a more than unusually serious undertaking, for not only are there no roads, but there are no bridges also, and as the burns can rise extremely rapidly in sudden floods, and entire hillsides stream with water, you may have to make long detours, thus adding considerably to your allotted time, and even leaving you stranded in the wilds overnight.

The trek from Arkaig to Quoich takes you cross-country from south to north. But five rights of way radiate through the mountains from Strathan, the stalker's cottage at the head of Loch Arkaig, and instead of following Glen Dessarry towards the north, you could follow Bonnie Prince Charlie's escape route eastwards down the boggy track through Glen Pean to Morar (and the Hebrides), thus accomplishing an east-

west crossing of this Highland outback. But in such a free-ranging landscape, you can head off in any direction you like, an ocean voyager over the peat and rock and the morained and hummocked ground where your Ordnance Survey is your lodestone and evening star.

Before you go: OS Landranger Series Map Nos. 33, 34.

Getting there: this wild area lies immediately west of the A82 between Spean Bridge and Invergarry. For Loch Quoich, take the A87 from Invergarry. A minor road to the left in about 5 miles (8km) follows Glen Garry and leads to the north shore of Loch Quoich. For Loch Arkaig leave the A82 at Spean Bridge. The B8004 and B8005 lead to a minor road that clings to the north shore of Loch Arkaig. Spean Bridge is a station on the Glasgow-Fort William Line. A 4-seater postbus operates Mon, Wed and Fri from Invergarry to Kinloch Hourn, passing Loch Quoich. **Where to stay:** accommodation at Spean Bridge, Invergarry and Fort Augusta. Hotel at Tomdoun, 6 miles (10km) east of Loch Quoich. *Where to Stay* brochure from Fort William and Lochaber Tourist Board, Cameron Centre, Cameron

Square, Fort William PH33 6AJ, T:0397 3781. Youth hostel at South Laggan, 3 miles (5km) south of Invergarry, T:08093 239. **Where to go:** Sgurr na Ciche (3,410ft, 1,039m), the area's highest mountain, requires a long hike up Glen Dessarry from where the road ends at the west end of Loch Arkaig. **Further information:** Tourist Information, Fort Augustus, 7 miles (11km) north of Invergarry, T:0320 6367.

Kintail
From Gaelic *Caen da Shaill*, the head of two seas

National Scenic Area

To the north of the wild areas of Knoydart, Loch Quoich and Loch Arkaig and immediately to the south-west of Glen Affric lies another superb piece of the wild West Highland jigsaw puzzle. This is the National Scenic Area of Kintail, consisting of three long mountain ranges terminating round the head of

The wildcat is one of Scotland's most elusive predators

Loch Duich – Beinn Fhada, the Five Sisters of Kintail, and the Cluanie Forest, which culminates in the summit known as the Saddle.

All these ranges have peaks in excess of 3,300ft (1,006m), and Sgurr Fhuaran (one of the Five Sisters) is over 3,500ft (1,067m). Together they present a mountain scene of imposing grandeur, with the pinnacles of the Saddle dominating Glen Shiel and the beautifully elegant peaks of the Five Sisters – among the sheerest grassy mountains in Scotland – forming a very majestic background to the head of Loch Duich, especially when viewed from the high mountain pass of long views in the West Highlands.

These mountains, only a few miles from the western sea, form the watershed of mainland Scotland, and the glens which thread between them from Loch Duich are short, steep and deep, with rivers and burns which tumble headlong from the ridges and corries of their upper reaches over waterfalls and through alder-fringed pools down to the green pastures of the lower glens.

Thus one of the highest waterfalls in Britain, the spectacular Falls of Glomach, plunge nearly 350ft (107m) down a narrow ravine into a savage cauldron in wild, rugged and remote mountain country above. Loch na Leitreach, north of Beinn Fhada, which can only be reached after a long, rough walk from Morvich.

Kintail is the epitome of the West Highland scene, and for naturalist and hill walker alike it is a land of delights. Herds of red deer and wild goats roam through the area and the varied flora on its grass slopes includes such notable species as fragrant orchid, butterfly

182

orchid, pale butterwort and mountain azalea. The area offers three very fine long mountain walks. The first, a 14-mile (22.5-km) traverse of moderate difficulty, along the Five Sisters Ridge, starting at the Cluanie Inn and ending about 10 hours later near Shiel Bridge, takes up most of a long and arduous day but offers from the top of Sgurr Fhuaran one of the finest views in all Scotland, with the whole of the Inner Hebrides, all the Outer Hebrides between Harris and Barra Head, and the mainland peaks between Assynt and Ben Alder laid out around you. The second walk is along the South Kintail Ridge, which runs parallel to but further west than the first, and contains no less then seven Munros in 8 miles (13km) – a delightful, relatively easy traverse of about 7–8 hours starting at the Cluanie Inn and ending at the battlefield of Glen Shiel, where the Redcoats fought the Jacobites in 1719. The third walk is over the Saddle of Glen Shiel, starting and ending at Shiel Bridge. This walk takes about 7 hours and is very fine, but since it entails crossing rocky and exposed sections, it is not recommended for the inexperienced.

Before you go: OS Landranger Series Map No 33.

Getting there: easy access to Loch Duich and to the mountains along both sides of Glenshiel from the A87 – the Invergarry to Kyle of Lochalsh road – which bisects this scenic area. Buses from Edinburgh, Glasgow and Inverness, bound for Skye, run along the A87.

Where to stay: accommodation at Shiel Bridge and Dornie. Inn at west end of Loch Cluanie. Morvich caravan and campsite (NTS) on River Croe near

Loch Duich (T:059981 354). Youth hostel: Ratagan, Kyle – 1 mile from Shiel Bridge (T:059981 243). *Where to Stay* brochure from Isle of Skye and South West Ross Tourist Board, Portree IV51 9BZ, T:0478 2137. **Facilities:** NTS Visitor Centre at Morvich farm, off A87 3 miles (5km) north-east of Shiel Bridge. Resident ranger naturalist. Guided walk service. Fishing in River Croe. Permits from NTS visitor centre. **Further information:** NTS ranger-naturalist Alan Whitfield, Morvich Farm (T:059981 219).

Glen Affric

National Scenic Area and FC Reserve

Glen Affric is a long glaciated valley with steep sides and a broad floor containing a roaring river and two substantial lochs. The lower slopes of the hills are covered in one of the most beautiful of all the remnants of the native Caledonian Forest, with many fine old trees, a good sprinkling of birch and rowan and a canopy open enough to allow heather and bilberry to carpet the hummocky ground.

By contrast, the high ground of the upper glen is stark moor and mountain, and it is here you may see the red deer which have been banished from the pinewoods as part of a forest regeneration programme. A few roe deer still inhabit the woods, along with the pine marten, wild cat, badger and fox. There is a thriving population of crossbill, capercaille and black grouse; and fungi galore.

A walk along the high mountain ridge which forms the northern boundary of

Glen Affric NSA takes you across Scotland's main watershed from east to west via Carn Eighe, the highest mountain north of the Great Glen. You begin at Loch Beinn a'Mheadhoin, not far from Affric Lodge, and end at the Alltbeithe Youth Hostel at the western end of Glen Affric, or at the Cluanie Inn if you prefer. It is a very long, tough mountain traverse of some 26 miles (42km), including 6 Munros, and it will take a fit and experienced mountain walker up to 14 hours hard slog – albeit in some of the wildest and remotest and most wonderful Highland scenery in Scotland.
Before you go: OS Landranger Series Map Nos. 25, 33.
Getting there: from the village of Cannich on A831, 27 miles (43km)south west of Inverness by road, an unclassified road is signposted to Glen Affric. Sparse bus service to Cannich from Beauly and Inverness. Also access on foot from Cluanie Inn on A87, to south of Glen Affric, or from Croe Bridge to west. **Where to stay:** bed and breakfast and hotel at Cannich. Remote youth hostel at Alltbeithe in Glen Affric. Another hostel in Cannich, T:04565 244. Accommodation brochure from Inverness, Loch Ness and Nairn Tourist Board, 23 Church Street, Inverness IV1 1EZ, T:0463 234353. **Where to go:** Long Ridge walk to north of Loch Affric, including twin peaks of Carn Eighe (3,877ft, 1,182m) and Mam Sodhail (3,862 ft, 1,177m), the highest mountains in North West Highlands. Access on track from north shore of Loch Beinn a'Mheadhoin. Distance to Cluanie Inn – end of traverse – 26 miles (42km). A' Chralaig (3,673ft, 1,120m) and Sgurr nan Conbhairean (3,634ft, 1,108m) – mountains

An eerie mist settles on Glen Affric, obscuring the view of Loch Beinn a'Mheadoin

to south west of Glen Affric – are short climbs from A87 east of Cluanie. Full details in Scottish Mountaineering Trust's *The Western Highlands*. **Facilities:** most of Glen is in Affric Forest (FC). 4 car parks, picnic sites beside river and lochs. Short waymarked walks start from picnic areas. Fishing permits available from FC office.
Further information: FC guidebook from Forest Office Cannich, Invernessshire.

Strathfarrar

National Scenic Area
NCC NNR

Glen Affric is the most southerly of the great glens which feed into Strathglass and the Beauly River. The other two, Glen Cannich in the centre and Glen

Strathfarrar to the north, have been spoilt in part by hydroelectric schemes, with the exception of the lower middle stretch of Strathfarrar.

The reserve covers some 10,000 acres (4,000ha) of native Scots pinewood: the largest surviving remnant of the ancient Caledonian Forest in this part of Scotland. The best pine stands are on the south side of the River Farrar at Coille Garbh, where some massive specimens may be up to 300 years old. To ensure the continuation of these pinewoods a regeneration programme is under way which is scheduled to last a hundred years.
Before you go: OS Landranger Series Map No. 26. **Getting**

there: access on a minor road leading west off A831 7 miles (11km) north-east of Cannich. No access for cars past Leishmore on this road – about ½mile (1km) – without a permit from the gatekeeper's cottage. **Where to stay:** Cannich and Beauly provide bed and breakfast accommodation. Youth hostel at Cannich (T:04565 244). **Where to go:** NCC Nature Reserve stretches along glen from gatekeeper's house at Leishmore in the east to near Loch Beannacharan in the west. **Further information:** leaflet from NCC. Warden at Eilean Aigas Bungalow, Hughton, by Beauly (T:046374 310).

'Human beings need primeval nature to re-establish contact now and then with their biological origins; a sense of continuity with the past and with the rest of creation is probably essential to the long-range sanity of the human species.'

Rene Dubos:
So Human An Animal

Wester Ross

National Scenic Area

North of Glen Carron the landscape undergoes an abrupt change from West Highland character to Northern Highland. Between Applecross and Assynt in Wester Ross there are sandstone mountains of immense antiquity and extraordinary shape; between Assynt and Cape Wrath in Sutherland a vast and desolate wilderness of rolling moor from which scattered mountains rear like monoliths. Wester Ross has often been described as the last great wilderness in Scotland. This is not precisely true, for the area is threaded with roads and dotted with villages; but by and large you will find some of the sublimest sea, loch and mountain landscapes in the Highlands, and extensive pockets of wilderness as pristine as any in Britain.

To traverse the whole length of this superb back of beyond, from the lowering crags and vertiginous corries of the Applecross Forest in the south west to the piranha-teeth ridges of An Teallach in the north east, is to explore a cross section of mountain scenery which can be rivalled in few other parts of the British Isles: Ben Damph, Beinn Eighe, the Torridon group and especially Liathac – 'the most soaring mountain in the north' – Ben Alligin, Slioch, a'Mheadhoin, Mullach Coire Mhic Fhearchair, Beinn Lair, Ben Dearg Mhor, and An Teallach, whose eastern corrie is one of the great natural sights of Scotland.

The area has much else to offer beside the ragged grandeur of the highest peaks – gentler, lusher parts, where woods of oak, birch and Scots pine soften the lower slopes around inland lochs of serene and breathless beauty. Going south to north the main components are the Applecross Forest, the Ben Damph Forest, the Torridon Mountains, Loch Maree, the Letterewe Forest, the Fisherfield Forest, the Strathnasheallag Forest (where An Teallach rises) and along the coast the sea lochs of Torridon, Gairloch and Ewe and the broader expanse of the beautiful Gruinard Bay, with their beaches, headlands, isles, inlets and wooded slopes, their incomparable outlooks across the water to Skye and the Outer Hebrides, their marvellous synthesis with the mountains that soar from the vast hinterland that lies behind them.

From Loch Torridon to Loch Maree

stretches a truly vast, truly wild expanse of mountain territory. Few roads penetrate the interior of this peninsula, and there are few signs of human habitation; this is a trackless refuge for rare and sensitive species such as the peregrine and golden eagle. Most of the area lies within the Gairloch Conservation Unit, a landowners' co-operative for the management of the large herds of red deer which roam these parts. Much of this land is privately owned, with restricted access during the stalking season between September and November, but two major areas – Torridon and Beinn Eighe – are held for the nation by the National Trust for Scotland.

Torridon is the huge wilderness either side of Glen Torridon and Upper Loch Torridon, offering some of the oldest mountains on earth, with 18 tops above 3,000 feet (900 metres), six of them Munros. To the south, the wild country of the Ben Damph and Coulin Forests between Glen Carron and Glen Torridon, where the going is almost as rough as Knoydart, rise some dozen mountains to which access can be gained from Achnashellach or Annat along a network of old stalking tracks and rights of way.

To the north of Glen Torridon lies the Torridon range proper, with its fine triplet of peaks: Ben Dearg (2,995 feet, 913 metres); Ben Alligin (3,232 feet, 985 metres), with its vast views down the coast between Capes Wrath and Ardnamurchan; and the 3,456-foot (1,053-metre) mass of ancient sandstone known as Liathac (pronounced Leeagach), a narrow five-mile (8-kilometre) long ridge bearing no less than seven tops in its short length.

Beinn Eighe has seven summits. The highest (Ruadh Stac Mor, 3,314 feet, 1,010 metres and Sail Mhor, 3,218 feet, 981 metres) are just on the boundary of the reserve. The remaining four (the highest is Sgurr Ban, 3,188 feet, 972 metres) lie on the long jagged ridge which dominates the southern half of the reserve. This fine mountain and moorland habitat is rich in associated fauna: pine marten, wild cat, otter, fox, red and roe deer, golden eagle, peregrine, merlin and buzzard can all be found here. The mountain tops are clothed with a fine carpet of alpine vegetation and there is a spectacular high-altitude traverse for climbers as well as good low-altitude trails for ramblers. The ancient rocks contain the oldest fossils in Scotland.

BEFORE YOU GO
OS Landranger Series Map Nos. 19, 24, 25. SMT Guide *The Northern Highlands*. The *Scottish Peaks* by W.A. Poucher (Constable).

GETTING THERE
One main road winds through Wester Ross. Starting as the A896 on Loch Carron, it cuts north to Shieldaig on Loch Torridon, then angles north-east past the Torridon Forest and Beinn Eighe. At Kinlochewe it becomes the A832, veering north-west along the shore of Loch Maree, then changing direction again at Gairloch as it circles clockwise past Loch Ewe, Little Loch Broom and An Teallach to join the A835 12 miles (19km) south of

Ullapool. A few roads lead off this north-south artery towards tiny communities on the coast.   Kyle of Lochalsh, directly south of Wester Ross is the nearest station, linking the area by rail with Inverness.

WHERE TO STAY
Gairloch is the principal centre for accommodation, but there are a surprising number of guest houses and self-catering accommodation in the region. Write for the *Where to Stay* brochure from Ross and Cromarty Tourist Board, Information Centre, Noreth Kessock, Inverness IV1 1XB, T:046373 505. Youth hostels at Craig (very remote on north shore of Loch Torridon, T:044587 284) and

Carn Dearg (near Gairloch, T:0445 2219).

FURTHER INFORMATION
Tourist Information Centre, Gairloch, (T:0445 2130).

Ben Wyvis

NCC NNR

If you have slogged over the superb wilderness areas of Wester Ross and still have an appetite for more, you can always try Easter Ross. Here Ben Wyvis, an isolated plateau measuring 6 miles by 3 (10km by 5), sprouts 9 tops above 3,000 ft (1,000m) in an ocean of moor. The National

Nature Reserve is outstanding for its carpet of moss heath, the most extensive in Britain. **Before you go:** OS Landranger Series Map Nos. 20, 21, 26. **Getting there:** the A836, running north from Inverness, crosses the eastern edge of this region; the A832/835 from Inverness to Ullapool skirts the south. No main roads reach the interior but a few tracks provide access. **Where to stay:** Strathpeffer for Ben Wyvis. Youth hostel, Strathpeffer, (T:0997 21532). **Where to go:** Ben Wyvis – 6½ miles (10.5km) due north of Strathpeffer – can be climbed from the A835 to the west (about 4 miles, 6km) or from Loch Glass from the north east. **Further information:** leaflet from NCC.

Coigach to Assynt

National Scenic Area

In the northernmost corner of Ross and Cromarty, between Little Loch Broom and Eddrachillis Bay, lies a rugged and spectacular landscape the like of which cannot be found elsewhere in Britain; a vast, flat, hummocky sea of gneiss, from which rise a few steep, widely scattered peaks. They are not as high as they seem; Ben More Coigach, for example, is only 2,438ft above sea level, while Stac Polly, its summit ridge shattered into little pinnacles and great cascades of scree like some geological Armageddon, barely clears 2,000ft (610m). Even the extraordinary sugar loaf of Suilven is dwarfed by many less celebrated peaks in the Highlands.

All these peaks are made in whole or in part of old Torridonian sandstone and

hugely shaped by erosion. Coigach in the far north of the area is almost entirely sandstone. Quinag, in the far north, has a bed of gneiss up to 2,000ft, but 7 sandstone tops, the highest 2,651ft (808m) above the sea. Ben More Assynt (3,273ft, 998m), across in Sutherland to the east, is composed largely of gneiss, with great caverns in its limestone lower slopes.

Further north lie two other natural attractions. The first are the falls of Eas a' Chual Aluinn, the highest in Britain, where a little burn drops 658ft (201m) off a mountain, four times the height of Niagara. The second is the sea stack of the Old Man of Stoer, a sheer sandstone needle thought unclimbable till Don Whillans got to the top in 1966. **Before you go:** OS Landranger Series Map Nos. 15, 19. SMT Guide *The Northern Highlands*. **Getting there:** the A835 heads north-east from Ullapool, then joins the A837 and curves around west to Lochinver on the coast. Most of the Coigach/Assynt hills are encircled by this 35-mile (56-km) loop of highway; only Quinag, to the north, and Ben More Assynt, to the east, lie outside it. Buses run daily from Lairg to Lochinver and infrequently – summer only – from Lochinver to Ullapool. Another daily service connects Fiag Bridge with Kylesku. **Where to stay:** Ullapool, and Lochinver are the major centres for accommodation, but there are bed and breakfast and hotels scattered throughout. Information Centres at Ullapool, (T:0854 2135) and Lochinver, (T:05714 330) will assist. Youth hostels at Ullapool, (T:0854 2254); Achininver (nr Achiltibuie); Achmelvich (nr Lochinver, T:05714 480). **Further**

information: Ross and Cromarty Tourist Board, Information Centre, North Kessock, Inverness IV1 1XB, T:046373 505. Sutherland Tourist Board, The Square, Dornoch, Sutherland IV25 3SD, T:0862 810400.

Ben More Coigach

SWT-RSNC Reserve

Set amid the spectacular mountains of Coigach and overlooking the Summer Isles at the mouth of Loch Broom, this is a huge wild place of rock, bog and rolling moorland. It rises in the south from sea level to the summit ridge of Ben More at 2,438 ft. (743m); in the north it is bounded by a chain of large lochs, beyond which lies Inverpolly NNR.

Typical north-west Highland fauna to be found here includes red deer, roe deer, pine marten, wild cat, badger, otter and seals; golden eagle, peregrine, raven, black grouse, greenshank, eider, red and black-throated divers and barnacle geese. **Before you go:** OS Landranger Series Map No. 15. **Getting there:** minor road to Achiltibuie leaves the A835 at the Old Drumrunie Lodge, 9½ miles (15km) north of Ullapool. This runs along the north-east boundary of the reserve, but a chain of lochs and burns makes access from here difficult. Continue on this road, which leads through Achiltibuie and Polglass, to gain access to the reserve – and to Ben More Coigach itself – from the south west. A daily minibus service runs between Ullapool and Achiltibuie. **Where to stay:** bed and breakfast and self-

The summit of Suilven is a popular goal for backpackers setting out from nearby Lochinver

catering vacation accommodation in Achiltibuie. Information Centres in Ullapool or Lochinver will assist.
Further information: leaflet from SWT-RSNC Ground Officer, 132 Polglass, Achiltibuie-by-Ullapool, Ross and Cromarty.

Inverpolly

NCC Reserve

This enormous, uninhabited wilderness covers some 27,000 acres (11,000ha) of magnificent moor, mountain, woodland, lochs, bogs, seashore and islands, and contains the spectacular peaks of Stac Polly, Cul Mor (2,786ft, 844m) and Cul Beag (2,523ft,769m). No roads enter Inverpolly and few tracks cross the undulating plateau of wet moorland and blanket peat.

Red deer, otter, wild cat, pine marten and badger inhabit these wilds; 104 species of birds have been recorded here; and in the scattered fragments of surviving birch-hazel woodland a rich ground cover thrives. But Inverpolly is best known for the rocks at Knochan Cliff, a classic site in the history of geology.
Before you go: OS Landranger Series Map No. 15. **Getting there:** reserve is bounded to the east by A835. A minor road, which leaves the A835 at Drumrunie, gives access to Stac Polly and the south of the reserve; another unclassified road leads north to Lochinver along the reserve's western boundary. **Where to stay:** Lochinver, Achiltibuie and Ullapool provide serviced accommodation. Youth hostels at Achininver (nr Achiltibuie) and Achmelvich (nr Lochinver, T:05714 480). No camping on reserve.
Further information: leaflet NCC. Wardens at Knochan Cottage (T:085484 234) or Strathpolly (T:05714 204).

Inchnadamph

NCC Reserve

Covering 3,200 acres (1,300ha) of moorland and

187

limestone plateau, between Loch Assynt and Ben More Assynt, the reserve is famous for its caves, swallow holes, underground streams and the best limestone pavements in Scotland. The caves above Allt nan Uamh have revealed the bones of brown bear, arctic fox, reindeer, lynx and lemming which inhabited this part of Scotland at the end of the last Ice Age, as well as evidence of Stone Age occupation.

Today, of course, the fauna is much reduced: red deer, wild cat and mountain hare, red grouse, ring ouzel and twite. But the reserve is well-known for its rich and varied flora: mountain avens, holly fern, globe flower and serrated wintergreen, which flourish on the limestone outcrop. **Before you go:** OS Landranger Series Map No. 15. **Getting there:** reserve lies to east of A837, just south of Inchnadamph Hotel. Daily Lairg-Lochinver bus service passes reserve. **Where to stay:** all ranges of accommodation in Lochinver. Hotel at Inchnadamph. Youth hostel at Achmelvich (nr Lochinver, T:05714 480). No camping on reserve. **Where to go:** Ben More Assynt (just north of reserve): access from Inchnadamph Hotel, then cross country up Glen Dubh. Various routes to summit. Return trip 6–7 hours. **Access:** all visitors to reserve are asked to contact the Honorary Reserve Warden, Stronchrubie, Inchnadamph, T:05712 208. In deer stalking season (15 Jul–15 Oct), visitors should also contact Assynt Estates (T:057 14 203). **Further information:** leaflet NCC. Tourist Information in Lochinver (T:05714 330).

North-West Sutherland

A huge, empty and rugged region of more than 2,000 square miles (5,000 sq km) but less than 20,000 people, containing 2 National Scenic Areas

This is a remarkably wet and windy part of the world, and arctic in appearance in winter, and I remember vividly how I was blown backwards by fierce winds from Cape Wrath when I tried to fly along the craggy northern coast of Sutherland in a light aircraft out of Orkney.

Much of the interior is a marvellous, uninhabited tundra of moorland and bog. Partly forested in ancient times, it is now spattered by innumerable lochs and lochans and criss-crossed by a complex network of peaty streams. This is the land called the Flow Country, which stretches all the way to Caithness in the east and contains much of the world's surviving bogland.

No less exciting are the peripheries of this British Lapland. In north-west Sutherland you can see the highest cliffs in mainland Britain (921 feet, 281m) at Clo Mor, near Cape Wrath, the great caves of Smoo, magnificent sea lochs like Eriboll (the deepest natural anchorage in Britain), and the silted Kyles of Tongue and Durness.

Isolated peaks such as Ben Hope (3,040 feet, 927 metres) and Ben Loyal (2,504 feet, 763 metres) in the north, and Foinaven (2,980 feet, 908 metres), Ben Arkle (2,580 feet, 786 metres) and Ben Stack (2,356 feet, 718 metres) which soar majestically out of the wilderness of the Reay Forest in the north west, provide superb climbs for hill walkers and refuge for the golden eagle, ptarmigan, dotterel, snow bunting, and blue hare. From the tip of Foinaven, you can look west over 120 square miles (310 square kilometres) of absolute desolation containing hundreds of glittering lochans.

Cape Wrath, the north-west corner of mainland Britain, enjoys no formal status, though it probably attracts more people than most places in the region by reason of the grandeur of its location.

A long, rough but exciting coastal walk has been devised between Cape Wrath and Kinlochbervie to the south. Sixteen miles (26 kilometres) in length and about eight hours in duration, it crosses sheer granite cliffs, skerries and stacks, wide bays of golden sand such as the mile-long Sandwood Bay, and trackless heather moorland and peat. Throughout its length, you are rarely out of sight or sound of the screaming birds and the booming Atlantic rollers.

BEFORE YOU GO
OS Landranger Series Map
Nos. 9, 10. Full details of the
climbs mentioned here in *The
Northern Highlands* (Scottish
Mountaineering Trust).

GETTING THERE
From Ullapool take the A835
and A894; the A838 then
leads up and around the north-
west corner. Trains avoid this
part of Scotland; nearest
stations are Inverness and
Kyle of Lochalsh. Buses from
Inverness connect with
services to most towns.

WHERE TO STAY
Despite its remoteness, this is
a popular tourist area. Write
for *Where to Stay* brochure
from Sutherland Tourist
Board, The Square, Dornoch,
Sutherland IV25 3SD, T:0862
810400. Youth hostels:
Durness (T:097181 244) and
Tongue (T:084755 301).

FURTHER INFORMATION
Tourist information centres in
Durness (T:097181 259) and
Bettyhill (T:06412 342).
Reserve leaflets from NCC.

Handa

RSPB Reserve

A very high island of 766 acres
(310ha) a few hundred yards
off the Sutherland coast in the
north-west Highlands,
bounded on three sides by
vertical sandstone cliffs rising
to over 400ft (120m). These
cliffs have weathered in layers
to produce ideal nesting ledges
for seabirds and in the
breeding season Handa is like
a spectacular multi-storey
bird-park, a wild, guano-white
tenement block of busy,
unruly, noisy, squalor-inclined

guillemots, black guillemots,
fulmars, razorbacks,
kittiwakes, puffins, shags and
gulls – most easily and
impressively seen on the Great
Stack of Handa.
   The interior of the island
consists of rough pasture,
heather moor, peat bogs and
six lochans. The moorland has
been colonised by arctic and
great skua, and the moorland
flora is enlivened in the
damper parts by orchids, bog
asphodel, pale butterwort and
royal fern. Red-throated
diver, shelduck and eider
breed on Handa. Grey seal
and various species of whale
and dolphin can sometimes be
seen offshore.
Before you go: by sea on boat
service which operates daily
(except Sun) from Tarbet on
the mainland opposite.
1 Apr–10 Sep. The boatman is
William MacRae, Scourie,
(T:0971 2156). **Access:** at all
times, but keep to the
waymarked path and take
extra care on the cliff-top.
Where to stay: camping or
bothy for RSPB members
only. Contact RSPB,
Edinburgh. **Further
information:** leaflet from
RSPB Edinburgh, or contact
RSPB Summer Warden, c/o
Mrs A. Munro, Tarbet,
Foindle, near Laing,
Sutherland IV27 4SS.

West Highland Way

Scotland's finest national long-
distance path starts in
Milngarvie, north-west of
Glasgow, and runs for 95
miles (153km) across an
increasingly wild and rugged
interior of the Southern and
Central Highlands of Fort
William below Ben Nevis. The
way follows the eastern side to
Loch Lomond, goes over the

slopes of Ben Lomond to
Crianlarich, then across the
western side of Rannoch Moor
and past the mouths of Glen
Etive and Glen Coe to
Kinlochleven, whence it
follows an old military road
over the slopes of the
Mamores and across wild
country in the Ben Nevis
range to its journey's end. A
terrific walk, but a very tough
one at times.
Before you go: OS Landranger
Series Map Nos. 64, 57, 56,
50, 41. The CCS's official
guide, *The West Highland Way*
by Robert Aitken comes with
a separate 1:50,000 map.
Alternatively, use *A Guide To
The West Highland Way*
(Constable) by Tom Hunter,
who developed the route.
Getting there: Glasgow and
Fort William, the end points
of the route, are linked by the
A82 and the Glasgow-Mallaig
railway. One or other of these
arteries follow the path for
much of the way, providing
opportunities to join or leave
the route at various places
along the way.
Where to stay: The West
Highland Way calls for careful
preparation since there is little
chance of finding a nearby pub
for shelter, a shop for a loaf of
bread or a farmhouse for
unbooked accommodation.
There are only 2 youth hostels
along the way, at
Rowardennan and
Crianlarich, as well as one at
each end: budget-minded
walkers should be prepared to
camp. Accommodation details
are included in the CCS's
invaluable free leaflet.

Scotland:
The Islands

At one time when I was travelling the West Highland coast, I was told a story about Squeaky Harris, a Hebridean ferry steamer skipper now long dead, who was renowned throughout the islands as one of the truly eccentric salts of the sea.

It seems that on one memorable voyage through the channel of the Minch separating Skye from the Outer Hebrides, Squeaky's little ship was overtaken by a particularly thick Hebridean sea fog. Though Squeaky's navigational aids were rudimentary, he knew these waters like the back of his whisky locker, and his old tub juddered onwards at full-ahead, straining at every rivet – to the mounting alarm of a naval Admiral who happened to be a passenger on board.

At length, unable to conceal his anxiety any longer, the Admiral decided to go up to the bridge and check the situation for himself. Squeaky was profoundly unimpressed by the sudden appearance of all this gold braid in the middle of his holy of holies.

'Get øff my ploody pridge, you ploody pugger,' he squeaked in his high-pitched Hebridean voice.

The Admiral explained as tactfully as he could that he was merely interested in the course they were steering and would love to have a peep at the charts.

'Well, if it's charts you're after, Admiral, I've got some somewhere here or hereabouts,' squeaked Squeaky. He finally found a dog-eared pile of old sea maps, and laid them out for the Admiral's perusal; the South China Sea, the Malacca Straits, the Mozambique Channel, and at last the Minch. The Admiral stared in horror at the chart and, pointing with quivering finger at a cluster of black dots strewn right across the steamer's bow, loudly exclaimed: 'What on earth are *those*?'

Squeaky peered at the chart, first with one eye, and then with another, and after due deliberation declared: 'Well, Admiral,

if those are rocks we're puggered for sure. But if they are what I think they are, which is fly shit, then we'll be as right as rain.'

And he gave a great puff and blew away the fly shit rocks and the sand banks of accumulated dust and reefs of old tobacco ash and gave a great hoot on the ship's siren as his battered old tramp ploughed on through the fog at an unabated full-ahead amid the scream of seagulls.

This story tells us a lot about the isles. About the island weather, for instance, and the preoccupation with the sea; about the exoticness of travel in those parts (clearly we are not off Bournemouth or even Cromer), and the sheer hazardry of adventuring into this wild, watery North West Frontier of the European continent.

What the story does not convey is the sheer magic of Scottish island-going, the bewitchment these places work on all those who venture among them. There is the ever-changing beauty of those vast skies and long, empty seas, and the wonderful pellucid light which has been compared with the light of the Greek islands. And there is the extraordinary aural clarity: for miles across the water I have heard the stags roaring from among the hills of Skye, and from far out in the bays the snort of a grey seal surfacing to breathe.

There is, too, the sense of primordiality: the soaring cliffs, the winter hurricanes, the Northern Lights. I recall the long, marvellous skeins of geese migrating south over Eilean Bhan at the first dust of snow on the Cuillins of Skye; the time I was thrown across the galley of a boat when we ran full tilt into the dreaded maelstrom of the Corryvreckan off the Isle of Jura; flying backwards before a storm-force westerly when I tried in vain to fly out of Orkney by light aircraft; and sleeping rough on a tiny island beach one spring, listening in the dark to the crooning of the seals and the murmuring of the surf and the strange cries of the distant birds in the vast, starlit, mind-expanding Hebridean night.

Sandaig Bay, on the edge of the Sound of Sleat that separates Skye from the mainland, looks out towards Eigg and the Western Isles

THE INNER HEBRIDES

The windswept islands of the Hebrides, the half submerged edge of the continent of Europe, consist of about 550 islands divided into two parallel archipelagoes called the Inner and Outer Hebrides, which stretch for 240 miles (386km) along the western coast of Scotland. Fewer than 70 of them are inhabited, some of them only by lighthouse keepers. The total population of the Hebrides amounts to little more than 30,000, making this one of the most deserted regions in Europe. Some of these islands are mere pinpricks in the ocean; others are more substantial places, such as the islands of Islay, Jura, Mull and Skye in the Inner Hebrides.

Islay
Pronounced 'Eye-lee'

A large island off the south-west coast of Jura, and the most southerly island of the Inner Hebrides. Though the Paps of Islay struggle up to more than 1,600ft (490km) in the south-eastern corner, the island is mostly low-lying and the scenery rather tame. However, Islay has a lavish variety of habitats – woods, scrub, moorland, cliffs, dunes, machair, sea- and fresh-water lochs, rivers, marshes and farming land – and this is good for the birds.

The RSPB has a big reserve at Loch Gruinart in the north of the island, but that is not the only place to watch some spectacular species – along the cliffs of the Oa in the south, for example, you may see golden eagle, peregrine and chough, and peregrine and chough again by the cliffs of the Rinns in the west. But it is the geese which have pride of place, and for these you go to Loch Gruinart.
Before you go: OS Landranger map 60. **Getting there:** daily car ferries from Kennacraig on Kintyre to Port Ellen and Port Askaig. Enquire Caledonian MacBrayne, Ferry Terminal, Kennacraig, T:088073 253.

Daily (except Sundays) air service from Glasgow to Islay. Enquire Loganair, T:041 889 3181. **Where to stay:** accommodation brochure from Tourist Information or Mid Argyll, Kintyre and Islay Tourist Board, The Pier, Campbeltown, Argyll, PA28 6EF, T:0586 42056. **Further information:** Tourist Information Centre, Bowmore, Isle of Islay, T:049681 254.

Jura
From the Gaelic meaning 'deer island'

A large, mountainous island (and National Scenic Area) to the south of Mull, 28 miles (45km) long and 8 miles (13km) wide, for the most part barren and uninhabited, and overrun by red deer, which outnumber the human population of 200 by ten to one. Unlike lava-layered Mull, Jura is made of hard quartzite rock which rises dramatically in the south of the island to form the three attractive but desolate peaks of the Paps of Jura, which as their name suggests resemble three teat-tipped breasts, each bosoming the sky to a height of more

than 2,400ft (732m).

Much of the island is trackless, and much of the interior consists of bog and scattered lochans, which makes exploration of Jura's remarkable west coast no task for tenderfoots.
Getting there: a regular car ferry leaves Kennacraig on Kintyre for Port Askaig on Islay; journey time 2 hours. Contact Caledonian MacBrayne Ltd, Ferry Terminal, Gourock PA19 1QP, T:0475 3755. From Port Askaig take the short car ferry crossing to Feolin in Jura. Western Ferries (Argyll) Ltd, Kennacraig, Argyll, T:049684 681. **Further information:** Information Centres at Tarbert, Loch Fyne (T:08802 429) and Bowmore, Isle of Islay (T:049681 254).

Scarba, Lunga and the Garvellachs
National Scenic Area

Lying off the north coast of Jura, the small, rocky conical island of Scarba is part of a National Scenic Area which includes the neighbouring islets of Lunga and the Garvellachs (the holy 'Isles of the Sea' or 'Rough Islands'). Tidal races rip between these islands, notably through the narrow sound between Scarba and Jura – the Gulf of Corryvreckan – where the funnelling of the fierce, 9-knot, Atlantic tide over the uneven sea bed produces a celebrated whirlpool which can give small boats a nasty time (as I discovered when my boat ran into it with an impact that threw me and a pan of baked beans from one side of the galley to the other).

The tiny uninhabited Garvellachs, which blaze with wild flowers in summer, are the site of the earliest

Christian settlement in
Britain, dating from AD542 –
two decades before St
Columba reached Iona.
Getting there: boat trips to the
islands leave from Cullipool
on the Isle of Luing. Access to
Luing by road from the A816
south of Oban. Contact
L. MacLachlan, T:08524 282.
Access: for permission to
camp on Scarba, T:8524 210.
For Lunga contact Major
Brian Johnson-Ferguson,
Solway Bank, Canonbie,
Dumfriesshire. For the
Garvellachs, contact the Rt.
Hon. Eddie Gully, Dunmore
Farm, Easedale, Argyllshire.

Mull

A large, rainy, beautiful
island, part Hebridean in
character, part West
Highland, Mull was the centre
of violent and prolonged
volcanic activity in the
Tertiary period. For millions
of years vast waves of lava
poured out and settled in
layers which at one time were
up to 6,000ft (1,830m) thick.
These layers weathered into
the terraced landscape which
is characteristic of much of
Mull today. Mull is fertile and
forested, but there are plenty
of wild places south of the
narrow neck of land between
Salen and Loch na Keal.

The west coast is deeply
indented with lochs and
spattered with rocks and islets,
while inland the high tableland
rises to 3,169ft (967m) on Ben
More, the highest mountain in
the Hebrides outside of Skye
and the haunt of red deer,
blue hare and golden eagle.
The ascent of the Ben More
ridge takes about 4 hours of
relatively straightforward, airy
going with fabulous views as
far away as the Barra Head

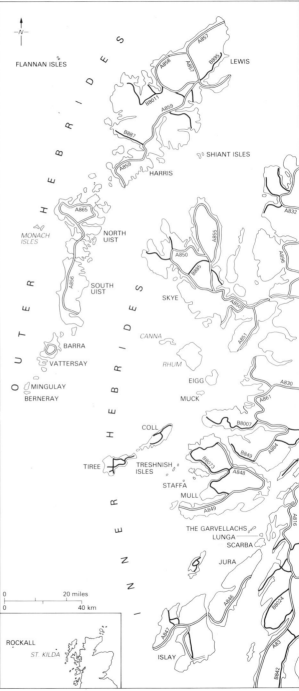

A winter stag party of red deer forage amicably, the rivalry of the rut forgotten until next autumn

light, 60 miles (96km) away.

More mountains rise up in the south east, while to the south west of Ben More, in the hinterland north of Loch Scridain, lies the wilderness of the Ardmeanach peninsula which can only be explored on foot. At the seaward tip, embedded in the basalt cliffs of Rubha nah-Uamha, stands the cast of a 40ft (12m) fossil tree – 'McCulloch's Tree' – engulfed by lava 50 million years ago and viewable only at low tide.

Along the southern shore of the island's longest peninsula, the Ross of Mull, stretches a wild, little-visited sea coast of columnar basalt cliffs and numberous caves where no road goes. This is a fine island for the wild traveller, offering plenty of wildlife interest, too – dolphins and basking shark off-shore, otters on the sealochs, seabirds along the coast, and fascinating rocks and fossils for the geologist and petrologist.

Before you go: OS Landranger
194

Series Map Nos 47, 48, 49.
Getting there: year round car ferry from Oban to Craignure; summer pedestrian ferry from Kilchoan to Tobermory. Contact Caledonian MacBrayne Ltd, Oban (T:0631 622859). Charter flights to Mull can be arranged with Loganair at Glasgow Airport (T:041 889 3181).
Where to stay: brochure from Oban, Mull and District Tourist Board, Boswell House, Argyll Square, Oban, Argyll PA34 4AN, T:0631 63122. **Where to go:** Ben More is most frequently climbed along its north-west ridge. Access from B8035 south west of Salen. See *Islands of Scotland* by Scottish Mountaineering Trust.
Further information: tourist Information Centres at Oban (T:0631 63122) and Tobermory (T:0688 2182).

Staffa

Tiny lava island like a tilted black block 6 miles (10km) off the west coast of Mull. Staffa is famous for the rock

formations at the entrance to Fingal's Cave, a huge gap in the cliffs, 60 feet (18.5km) high and over 200 feet (61m) deep, where the basalt lava has cooled and cracked into perfect hexagonal columns similar to those at the Giant's Causeway in Northern Ireland. When rough seas pound into the cave, the roar reverberates all over the island – a sound that inspired the motif for Mendelssohn's *Hebridean Overture*.
Getting there: twice-daily boat trips from Iona with over an hour on the island. Contact D.R. Kirkpatrick, Seaview Cottage, Isle of Iona, T:06817 373. Also trips from Ulva Ferry, Isle of Mull, including stop at Lunga on the Treshnish Isles. Contact B.J. and J.D. Burgess, Castlecroft, Tobermory, Isle of Mull, T:0688 2165. Caledonian MacBrayne run twice-weekly trips from Oban to Iona, which include a close look at Staffa from the sea. Contact Caledonian MacBrayne, Oban (T:0631 62285). **Further information:** Tourist Information, Tobermory (T:0688 2182).

Rhum (or Rum)

From the Gaelic *I-Dhruim*, 'Isle of the ridge'

NCC Reserve
UNESCO Biosphere Reserve

ι̕ι̕ι̕

I first came to this great, whale-backed lump of an island on a MacBrayne steamer one wild and storm-tossed day in March half a lifetime ago, when gannets were hurtling about the sky like flying crucifixes and floating 'rafts' or Manx shearwaters rose and fell in the sea swell like flotsam from a mid-Atlantic wreck.

The impression of Rhum from the sea on such a day was daunting: huge cliffs girt the island's wild coast; volcanic mountains, pyramidal and black, rose straight from the sea; and an extraordinary turreted Gothic edifice, an incongruous red in colour, stood four-square on the shore.

When I enquired if I could land I was informed that the island was a strictly private estate where no uninvited visitors were allowed to set foot. Today all that has changed. The island now belongs to the Nature Conservancy Council, and is used for wildlife conservation and ecological research. Visitors are welcome provided they respect these aims.

Rhum is one of the Small Isles at the northern end of the Inner Hebrides chain, a group which also includes Skye, Eigg, Muck and Canna. The island sparkles best in summer. Winters are mild but fiercely windy, relentlessly rainy and, with only eight resident families, screamingly lonely. There are no public roads or public transport on Rhum, so all journeys round the island have to be made on foot. Four valleys radiate from the island's low-lying centre and rough tracks follow each of the valleys to former settlements, all except Kinloch in ruins. One track leads north over heather-clad moors to the sands of Kilmory, another east down the nature trail to Kinloch, another south-west to the storm beach at Harris Bay and another west to the long green slopes of Guirdhil.

There are also pony trails from the Harris track to the massive scree buttress of Bloodstone Hill above the west coast and from Kinloch southwards past the great 666-foot (203-metre) sea-cliff of Welshman's Rock to the canyon of the Dibidil River and Papadil Loch, the southernmost point of the island, where bare treeless slopes are dominated by the towering cones and peaks of the Cuillins of Rhum.

The Rhum Cuillins, the weathered teeth of an extinct volcano, provide some of the best ridge walking in Britain. All the peaks but one have evocative Norse names bestowed in the days when they served as landmarks for passing Viking ships: pyramid-shaped Askival – the highest at 2,663 feet, 812 metres) – Hallival, Barkeval, Trollaval, Ainshval, Ruinsival. The exception is Sgurr nan Gillean, a Gaelic name. All can be climbed by non-climbers with a modicum of puff and will-power. The reward is a vast panoramic view over the Outer Isles and the Cuillins of Skye – one of the finest in the Hebrides.

Rhum's striking landscape of glens, lochs, corries and razor-ridged mountains was shaped by the Ice Age. The native forest that followed the Ice Age was largely felled by early settlers, but the vegetation and wildlife of the cliffs and mountain summits has been little disturbed.

The flora thrives in a rich and fascinating variety due to the island's oceanic position and wide range of soil types and growing conditions. Specialized plant communities exist in a series of distinct ecological systems: alpine, moorland, woodland, grassland, wetland and coastal. Rhum is an island of flowers, and 427 species have been counted there. Across the brilliant summer machair one can wade knee-deep in them. Relic native woodland of stunted birch, rowan, holly, hazel, aspen and oak survives in ravines and crags and protects a woodland flora of wood sorrel, wood anemone, wild hyacinth, ferns and other shade-loving plants.

Bird life is abundant on Rhum, where around 200 species have been recorded. A huge and uniquely high-altitude breeding colony of 130,000 pairs of Manx shearwaters is one of the island's ornithological specialities. The birds make their nesting burrows in the loose soil on the highest terraces of Askival and Hallival, whence the flightless fledglings must shuffle down the mountainsides and hurl themselves off the cliffs to reach the open sea, where they will spend the rest of their lives.

Another speciality is the convocation of eagles: several pairs of golden eagles breed regularly on Rhum, and in 1981 a pair of sea eagles, reintroduced from Norway, occupied a nest site for the first time since the species became extinct on the island in the early years of the century. Modest colonies of guillemots, razorbills, fulmars and kittiwakes nest on the southern cliffs, and common and Arctic terns, black-backed and herring gulls, puffins, black guillemots and shags on scattered promontories.

The wild animals most commonly seen on Rhum are the red deer, numbering about 1,500 in large free-ranging herds on the open hill ranges. Other wild animals include the feral goat, grey seal, common seal, otter, brown rat, pygmy shrew, pipistrelle bat and Rhum mouse. The wealth of butterflies to be found makes the island a lepidopterist's paradise.

BEFORE YOU GO
Map: OS Landranger Series Map No. 39.
Guidebook: SMT Guide *The Islands of Scotland: Rhum* by Hamish Brown (Cicerone Press).

GETTING THERE
A year-round scheduled passenger and mail ferry service from Mallaig to Rhum and the other Small Isles is provided by the Caledonian Macbrayne steamer MV *Lochmor*. Advance bookings from Ferry Terminal, Gourock (T:0475 34664/6) or same day from The Pier, Mallaig (T:0687 2402). Trains to Mallaig from Glasgow and Fort William connect with the ferry.

WHERE TO STAY
Accommodation on Rhum is limited and consists of a hotel and hostel in Kinloch Castle; a self-contained cottage, three bothies and a campsite in Kinloch; and two mountain bothies. Individuals and groups should apply to the Chief Warden, White House, Kinloch, Isle of Rhum (T:0687 2026).

ACCESS AND CLOSURES
No pets or cats may be taken on to the island. Visitors wishing to stay overnight must make prior arrangements with the NCC, or report to the Chief Warden at the White House, Kinloch. As Rhum is a National Nature Reserve some areas may be restricted from time to time. A map showing these areas is displayed outside the White House or the castle each morning. The entire island is closed to visitors around the first week of May (deer census) and the first week of August (stalkers' training course).

ACTIVITIES
Shopping: there is a post office and a public telephone on Rhum but no bank, pub, papers, TV or general store. Visitors should aim to bring their own supplies, including food if they are not staying at the hotel. Some shops in Mallaig will deliver supplies by prior arrangements.
Climbing: applications for rock climbing must be made in advance, by Climbing Club secretaries, to the Chief Warden. There is no rescue service on the island, so parties should not number less than 4 and must be prepared to carry out their own rescue operation in the event of an accident.

FURTHER INFORMATION
Regional Officer, Nature

Conservancy Council, Caledonia House, 63 Academy Street, Inverness, T:0463 39431.

Muck

From the Gaelic for 'pig' (meaning sea-pig or porpoise)

The most southerly of the Small Isles, Muck is a small, low green island, covering only 2 ½ square miles, nearly treeless and very exposed. Like Eigg, however, it enjoys some of the most fertile soils in the Hebrides. A mass of black volcanic rock dykes swarm up the west coast. The whole island is run by Mr and Mrs Laurence MacEwen and provides an interesting insight into communal Hebridean living, as well as an excellent, relatively untrodden island platform from which to admire the beauties of the sea of the Hebrides and all its denizens. **Getting there:** by sea on Caledonian MacBrayne ferry from Mallaig. There is a 1-mile road – Muck 1 – from Port Mor across to the Atlantic coast. **Access:** at all times. **Where to stay:** guest houses or camping near sandy beach on west coast. Bring your own supplies. **Further information:** Mr Laurence MacEwen, Gallnach, Isle of Muck, T:0687 2362.

Canna

NTS Reserve and SSSI

The most westerly of the Small Isles, Canna is inhabited by about 30 people, covers 3,785 acres (1,532ha) and is largely given over to farming; it has been referred to as 'The Garden of the Hebrides'. There are good walks along the cliffs, where you can see breeding seabirds like puffins, razorbills and Manx shearwaters, and various birds of prey, including the sea eagle from nearby Rhum.

Both Canna and its subsidiary island of Sanday are made up of ancient lava flows which can be clearly seen in the 400-ft (122-m) columnar basalt cliff face in the northern part of the island and in the basalt reefs and platforms along the coast. The rich iron deposits in Compass Hill deflect the compasses of passing ships. **Getting there:** on Caledonian MacBrayne ferry from Mallaig. **Access:** at all times. No safe access between cliffs and shore. Access to Sanday at low tide or by footbridge. **Where to stay:** camping only. No shop. **Further information:** leaflets from NTS or Canna Post Office.

Eigg

Eigg is a naturalist's paradise. This small, privately owned and actively crofted island 12 miles (19km) from the mainland to the south-east of Rhum measures only 5½ by 4 miles (9 by 6km), yet it contains no less than seven SSSIs and three nature reserves run by the SWT.

Like many islands of the Inner Hebrides, Eigg is overlaid by sheets of lava which poured from volcanic eruptions on nearby Rhum and other places in tertiary times. A large part of the island consists of a plateau of basalt over a platform of Jurassic limestone, edged by high escarpment cliffs. The exception is the Sgurr, at 1,300ft (396m) the highest point and dominating feature of the island, a volcanic outcrop of black pitchstone which cooled to form hexagonal columns. The narrow ridge of the Sgurr extends for 2 miles (3km) to the north west across rough country containing two lochs and 11 lochans, and from the summit on a clear day you can look out over Rhum, the Cuillins of Skye, the Outer Hebrides, Muck, Coll, Tiree, Mull and Ardnamurchan.

Much of the hinterland is heather moor, but woodland, bog, marsh, loch, flower meadow, seashore and cliff face provide a variety of alternative habitats for a wealth of island wildlife. 68 species of bird breed on Eigg, including golden eagle, long-eared owl, short-eared owl, red-throated diver, raven, buzzard and Manx shearwater. **When to go:** May to July. **Getting there:** by sea on Caledonian MacBrayne ferry from Mallaig. There is only one road – a Land Rover track from the port of Galmisdale to the small village of Cleadale. Local 'taxis' available – enquire at pier tea shop. **Access:** at all times to the island. Permit only to the SWT reserves around the Sgurr, Beinn Bhuide and above Laig Farm. SWT walks (3 to 10 hours) for day visitors. **Where to stay:** available locally, but is rather expensive. Camping is possibly by the Singing Sands. Only one store, in Cleadale – open irregularly, so bring your own supplies. **Further information:** for permits and walks contact SWT Warden (John Chester) via post office or pier tea shop, Eigg.

Skye
From the Norse *Sku-o*, 'Island of Cloud'

Skye is the largest and most northerly of the islands of the Inner Hebrides. Measuring 60 miles (96 kilometres) in length and covering some 670 square miles (1,735 square kilometres), Skye retains its island character in spite of the rolling expanse of high moorland and the mass of ridge-backed Cuillin mountains that give its hinterland a Highland flavour. It is one of the most heavily crofted areas in the Highlands and Islands, with crofted land along much of the coast and much of the high ground inland given over to grazing.

Nowhere on Skye are you ever more than 5 miles (8 kilometres) from the sea, for a dozen or so sea-lochs reach deep into the land, bringing their share of the sea creatures for which these waters are famous: the killer whale and basking shark, porpoise and dolphin, grey seal and sea otter, and seabirds of great variety, from the Manx shearwater that skim an inch or two above the waves to the great sea eagle on a visit from neighbouring Rhum, soaring in leisurely orbit high above the water.

The mountains of Skye are wild and grand. There are three main groups – the Black and Red Cullins in the south of the island, and the Trotternish in the north. The Cuillins are essentially ramparts of granite and gabbro, the Trotternish a huge heap of solidified lavas. Cuillins is a Norse word meaning keel-shaped ridge, and the main ridge of the Black Cuillins – the highest and ruggedest of the Skye hills – forms a spectacularly pinnacled seven-mile (11-kilometre) horseshoe around Loch Coruisk. Reaching 3,257 feet (993 metres) at its highest point on Sgurr Alasdair, it offers the mountain walker 10,000 feet (3,050 metres) of ascent in a landscape of immense diversity.

Fortunately, the highest peak with the grandest views – Sgurr Alasdair – can be reached relatively easily by ordinary walkers from Glen Brittle via the Great

Stone Shoot of Coire Lagan. But the real magic of these hills are their infinite changes of mood in capricious weather, from stormy Wagnerian melodrama to ethereal mist-hung mystery.

By contrast, the Red Cuillins, to the north and east of the Black Cuillins, are composed of granite – hence their name. They are considerably lower than their black neighbours, and their highest summits – Glamaig and Beinn na Caillich – only reach 2,542 and 2,403 feet (775 and 732 metres) respectively. For the most part these are rounded, scree-covered hills, offering next to no rock-climbing.

The rocks of the Trotternish hills, on the other hand, assume fantastical shapes that require fantastical climbs. The basalt lava of this part of Skye has slipped and eroded to form a castellated landscape of towers and spires. Round the rim of a corrie unique in Scotland the 160-foot (50-metre) pinnacle of the Old Man of Storr rises weirdly from a rock plinth in the company of a number of lesser pinnacles. At the north of the Trotternish group a natural rock fortress called the Quiraing, guarded by a hundred-foot (30-metre) high natural obelisk called the Needle, looms out of the mist and rain like the ramparts of an ancient lost basalt city.

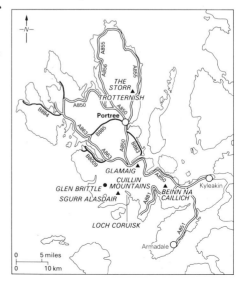

The jagged basalt pinnacles of the Storr on Skye have been a landmark since the first prehistoric settlers ventured to the Hebrides

BEFORE YOU GO

Map: OS Landranger Series Map Nos. 24, 24, 32, 33, 39.
Guidebook: serious hill walkers should consult *The Island of Skye* by the Scottish Mountaineering Trust.

GETTING THERE

By boat: car ferries leave the mainland ports of Mallaig and Kyle of Lochalsh for Armadale and Kyleakin on Skye (trips of 25 and 5 minutes respectively). Contact Caledonian MacBrayne, Kyleakin (T:0599 4482) or Armadale (T:04714 248).
By car: approach Mallaig on A830 via Fort William and Kyle of Lochalsh on A87 via Invergarry.
By train: take the West Highland line from Glasgow to Mallaig or the beautiful Kyle line from Inverness to Kyle of Lochalsh.
By bus: daily services run from Glasgow.

WHERE TO STAY

Complete listing in the Isle of Skye and South West Ross *Where to Stay*, available from Tourist Information Centres. Youth hostels at Armadale (T:04713 260), Broadford (T:04712 442), Glenbrittle (for the Cuillins, T:047842 278), Kyleakin (T:0599 4585) and Uig (T:047042 211).

WHERE TO GO

Two regions of Skye have been designated as National Scenic Areas. These are the Cuillin Hills in the south west and the Trotternish peninsula in the north east. The Cuillins are most easily approached from the junction of the A863 and A850, at the Sligachan Hotel 9½ miles (15km) south of Portree, or from Glen Brittle on a minor road leaving the B8009 1 mile (2km) south-east of Carbost.

The Old Man of Storr is a short walk from a car park on the A855 7 miles (11km) north of Portree; 10 miles (16km) farther north along the A855 a group of remarkable pinnacles overlook Staffin Bay. Quick access to the Quiraing, as the area is known, from a minor road that cuts across the peninsula to Uig.

Walkers looking for something challenging but low

could try one of Britain's most unusual long-distance walks – the circumambulation of the coast of Skye, which, with all its ins and outs, measures between 600 and 1,000 miles (960 and 1,600km).

FURTHER INFORMATION
General enquiries by post to Isle of Skye and South West Ross Tourist Board, Meall House, Portree, IV51 9BZ. Year-round Tourist Information Centre at Portree (T:0478 2137). Other centres (May–Sep) at Broadford (T:04712 361), Kyle of Lochalsh (T:0599 4276) and Shielbridge (T:059981 264).

The sturdy Soay sheep is found on several Hebridean islands

THE OUTER HEBRIDES

Stretching from Barra Head in the south to the Butt of Lewis in the north, the Outer Hebrides or Western Isles lie 50 miles (80 kilometres) from the West Highland coast. These outer islands wear two faces. Their windward western sides are fringed with dazzling white beaches of shell sand that stretch, island after island, for a hundred miles and are lapped in fine weather by a crystalline sea of exquisite peacock colours. Behind the beaches lie the sand dunes, and behind the dunes the machair that is the Western Isles' greatest glory. In spring and summer it is carpeted with a marvellous multicoloured tapestry of wildflowers, whose scent is so strong that it can be smelled on ships far out at sea. Their eastern sides are a total contrast, covered by infertile peat bogs up to 20 feet (32 metres) deep and dotted with rocks and innumerable lochans of brown acid peat.

The Hebridean sea is the haunt of marine creatures of all kinds, from the giant killer whales, dolphins and basking sharks of the open sea to the grey Atlantic and common seals of the great nurseries on the Treshnish Islands and the humble acorn barnacles, sand mason worms and hermit crabs of the tidal rock pools.

Barra

Only two of the 20 islands at the southern end of the Outer Hebridean chain are still inhabited – Barra and Attersay (the latter only tenuously). Barra itself, the

main island of the group, noted for its sand beaches and rich machair, is now a focus of tourism, and its machair has suffered considerable degeneration.

South of Barra, however, you will find some of the

loveliest, loneliest desert islands in the British Isles, and some of the most wondrous seascapes in the Hebrides. One of the largest, Mingulay, a mere 1 mile by 2, was inhabited until the early years of this century, but is now the realm of the puffins, kittiwakes and guillemots that crowd its soaring 800-ft (244-m) cliffs. The southernmost of them all, Berneray, which sprouts a lighthouse 580ft (177m) up on the sheer cliffs of land's end at Barra head, is the anvil for some of North Atlantic's most punishing hammer blows – seas that can throw fishes on to the very top of the high headland, and roll a 42-ton block of solid gneiss a distance of several feet.
Before you go: OS Landranger Series Map No. 31. **Getting there:** car ferries operate between Oban and Castlebay on Barra. Contact Caledonian MacBrayne, Oban, T:0631 62285. A once-weekly service connects Castlebay with Vatersay. Contact ferryman O.A. Macneil (T:08714 307). There is no regular service to Mingulay and the other southern islands, but

excursions can be arranged from Castlebay with Barra boatmen, including Mr MacLein, T:08714 339. **Where to stay:** for local accommodation enquire tourist information, Castlebay, T:08714 2 336. Camping is possible on Mingulay.

North and South Uist

The Uists have much to offer the wild traveller and itinerant naturalist. These islands are as yet relatively unspoilt by modern tourism, and possess two nature reserves of importance. The long, white, shell sand beaches of the Atlantic coast, and the sweetly perfumed summer machair behind them, are one of the glories of the Western Isles, and the machair supports the densest population of breeding waders in Britain.

The beautiful machair coast of South Uist stretching down the western side of the island from Stilligarry to the southern tip is as fine as anything in the Outer Hebrides and has won accolades as a National Scenic Area. The eastern side, by contrast, is peaty and mountainous, and the highest peak, Beinn Mhor, rears its summit more than 2,000ft (610m) above the sparkling (or, as often as not, lowering) sea. Beneath the southern slopes of Beinn Mhor, which is a good place to watch out for golden eagles, lies the National Nature Reserve of Loch Druidibeg.

North Uist is a large, low, virtually treeless island of lochs and marshes, machair and seashore. The east coast of North Uist (and of

Benbecula beyond) is a littoral (and literal) chaos, a maze of channels, skerries and islands, almost inacessible except by boat, and almost uninhabited except for the small ferry port of Lochmaddy – the whole wild bomb-burst scene a classic example of land drowned by the sea when the ice cap thawed at the end of the last Ice Age.

Only in its north-west corner does the North Uist coast rise significantly above the level of the sea. Between Griminish Point and Balranald there are cliffs and geos and great rock arches, as well as more of those dazzling white shell-sand beaches and peacock-coloured, clearwater bays that are so characteristic of the western shores of the Hebridean islands. North Uist is an important place for wintering and migrating birds, and at Balranald there is a nature reserve, one of the two reserves in the main Outer Hebrides island chain.

Before you go: OS Landranger Series Map Nos. 18, 22, 31. **Getting there:** BA has daily (except Sunday) service from Glasgow to Benbecula. Car ferries operate between Oban and Lochboisdale in South Uist. North Uist is 30 miles (48km) by road on the A865 – a causeway now connects the islands. Another car ferry runs a triangular route between Lochmaddy in North Uist, Tarbert in Harris and Uig in Skye. Contact Caledonian MacBrayne Ltd, Ferry Terminal, Lochmaddy, T:08763 337. **Where to stay:** *Where to Stay, What to Do* brochure available from Outer Hebrides Tourist Board, 4 South Beach Street, Stornoway, Isle of Lewis PA87 2XY, T:0851 3088. Youth hostel, Lochmaddy, North Uist, T:08763 368. **Further information:** Tourist

Information, Lochmaddy, North Uist, T:08763 321 and Lochboisdale, South Uist, T:08784 286.

Monach Isles

National Nature Reserve

A group of small, low-lying islets of sand-swamped reef, 8 miles (13km) south-west of Hougarry Point, North Uist, the Monachs are remarkable for their wealth of machair wild flowers and important grey seal nursery. Barnacle and white-fronted geese winter on the islands, and a variety of wading birds can be seen on the sandy shores.

Inhabited till 1942, the Monachs now provide a night stop for passing lobster fishermen and summer grazing for sheep. A thriving population of feral cats keeps down the less thriving population of breeding terns. **Getting there:** by small boat; enquire Grimsay Post Office for boat hire. **Access:** restricted. Permit from North Uist Estate Office (T:08763 329) and NCC Warden, Loch Druidibeg, South Uist.

Lewis and Harris

Lewis is the largest and most northerly of the Outer Hebrides. The southern half of Lewis is known as Harris, separated from the main bulk of Lewis by a line of bare hills and a wilderness of moors, lochans and deer forest. North Harris is joined to South Harris – almost an island in its own right – by a narrow isthmus, no more than half a mile (1km) wide.

Though Lewis and Harris – sometimes collectively called the Long Island – share the same continuous coastline, they present very different faces to the world. Lewis is for the most part bare, treeless and flat, a waste land of featureless blanket bog where the peat is up to 13ft (4km) thick in places. The wild traveller can squelch for miles over the island's peaty horizons without encountering another soul.

The coast is an almost perfect reverse image of the moorland interior: a splatter of innumerable sea rocks and islets strewn across a waste of water, a haunt of birds and sea creatures, at its finest at Loch Roag and the Great Bernera peninsula and between Valters and Mangersta. To traverse this coast on foot, from (say) the north-west roadhead at Brenish in Lewis to the south-west roadhead at Hushinish in North Harris, is no mean feat of Hebridean exploration, for there is no formal route, indeed no track at all, and you pick your own way across the wilds, pushed far inland by the long sea lochs of Tamanavay and Resort.

Harris is more spectacular than Lewis. The hills of North Harris are the highest in the Outer Hebrides, reaching 2,622 ft (800m) on the peak of Clisham. Though hardly comparing in grandeur with the loftier crags of Skye, the high ground of Harris is well endowed with space and solitude, and yields rewarding views towards Cape Wrath in the north east and the Cuillins in the south east and the dramatically massed outlines of St Kilda, 50 miles (80km) away on the skyline in the far distant west.

The interior of Harris is badland – dead, empty, infertile. But its coast is a gem. The south-east side overlooking the Little Minch is rocky and deeply indented, a steep gneiss desert with 20 bays in a 12-mile (19-km) stretch between Tarbert (the chief port and town of Harris) and Renish Point, and densely populated little clachans at the heads of the inlets.

The north-west coast of South Harris is a gentler, more exquisite place; a succession of sandy bays and white deserted beaches backed by grassy dunes and a flower-scented machair, dominated by the high hill of Chaipaval on Toe Head. From the 1,200-ft (366-m) summit of Chaipaval one can look out over the shallow, green and turquoise, island-scattered channel of the South of Harris, which separates Lewis and Harris from the rest of the Outer Hebrides, the Uists and Benbecula. At Callanish, near the west coast of Lewis, stands the finest prehistoric monument in the Hebrides, a stone circle of great gneiss monoliths with a Neolithic burial cave in the centre.

Before you go: OS Landranger Series Map Nos. 8, 13, 14, 18.
Getting there: daily BA flights (except Sundays) link Stornoway, Isle of Lewis, with Inverness and Glasgow. Charter flights can be arranged with Loganair Ltd, Glasgow Airport, Abbotsinch, Renfrewshire, T:041 889 3181.

Caledonian MacBrayne operate a daily car ferry service (except Sundays) between Ullapool and Stornoway, Isle of Lewis. There is also a vehicle ferry from Uig on Skye to Tarbert, Isle of Harris. Contact Caledonian MacBrayne, The Ferry Terminal, Gourock PA19 1QP, T:0475 33755. Local offices: Stornoway, T:0851 2361 and Tarbert, T:0859 2444. **Where to stay:** most serviced accommodation to be found in Tarbert, Isle of Harris, or Stornoway, Isle of Lewis. Both towns have Tourist Information Centres that will assist. Alternatively, write for the *Where to Stay, What to Do* brochure from the Outer Hebrides Tourist Board, 4 South Beach Street, Stornoway, Isle of Lewis PA87 2XY, T:0851 3088. Youth hostel in Stockinish, Isle of Harris PA85 3EN; 7 miles (11km) from Tarbert.
Further information: Tourist Information Centres at Stornoway, Isle of Lewis (T:0851 3088) and Tarbert, Isle of Harris (T:0859 2011).

The Shiant Isles

The Shiants, a group of small islands 5 miles (8km) off the south-east coast of Lewis, are the northern outposts of Scotland's youngest rocks. The hexagonal columns of solidified basalt on the northern face of the Garbh Eilean are the most impressive examples of this curious rock formation in Scotland. Flowery and lush, with a large puffin colony, a substantial seal nursery and a lot of brown rats.
Getting there: arrangements can be made by boat trips to Shiant Isles from Tarbert and Scalpay, Isle of Harris. Contact N. MacLeod and Sons, Harbour View, Scalpay, T:085984 225.

Flannan Islands

These 7 small islands, also known as the Seven Hunters, and numerous skerries, lie 17 miles (27km) west-north-west of Gallan Head on west side of Lewis. All the islands are cliff-bound and rise sheer from the sea. The largest, Eilean Mor, is 39 acres (14ha) in extent and 228ft (70m) at its highest point. The islands are a favourite spot for grey seals and for a large variety of seabirds, most importantly Leach's petrel, which breeds in holes on the grassy top of Eilean Mor.

The lighthouse on Eilean Mor is one of the remotest in the world. In 1900 all three lighthouse-keepers mysteriously vanished in circumstances resembling the disappearance of the crew of *The Marie Celeste*. They were probably swept away by a freak wave.
Getting there: there is no regular boat service, and landing is difficult except at the lighthouse jetty. Prospective visitors should

Callanish on Lewis is set amid a classic Hebridean landscape of water and weathered stone

make their own arrangements for boat hire on Lewis.
Accommodation: none.
Further information: Northern Lighthouse Board.

North Rona
From the Old Norse *Roy-y* – seal island

NCC NNR

A green island one mile square, 44 miles (70km) north-east of the Butt of Lewis and the same distance north-west of Cape Wrath. With Sula Sgeir it forms the northern termination of the Outer Hebrides and is one of the remotest British islands ever to have been regularly inhabited. Continuous habitation finally ended in 1844 but the ruins of the old settlement can still be seen. Today the men of Ness bring their sheep to graze on the island every summer.

North Rona is one of the

most important breeding colonies in the world for the grey Atlantic seal: about one-seventh of the world's population congregates here, and some 2,000 pups are born here each year. The seal nursery is located on the only low, level ground along the coast, for the rest of it is cliff-bound, pierced by huge caverns and fringed by many stacks and rock arches and hidden skerries and reefs. The air is full of the booming of the great Atlantic rollers and the screaming of the innumerable gulls. North Rona boasts major colonies of Leach's and storm petrel, uncommon birds which only ever come ashore to breed.
Getting there: by sea by private charter with boatmen at Ness, Lewis. **Access:** landing permit required; apply Barvas Estates, c/o Smith's Gore, The Square, Fochabers, Morayshire. Please contact NCC Inverness prior to proposed visit. **Further information:** NCC Inverness.

ORKNEY

Only 6 miles (10 kilometres) from the Scottish mainland lie the Orkneys, some 67 islands, of which 21 are inhabited. Their intricate outline of firths and peninsulas is the consequence of the rise in the sea level following the melting of the Ice Age ice cap: if the present sea level fell by 120 feet (37 metres) Orkney would become a single island again. The land is for the most part low-lying, with the notable exception of the island of Hoy, where a great wall of red sandstone cliffs rise sheer to 1,140 feet, (348 metres), and in front of it a spectacular geological freak, a perpendicular pillar of rock 450 feet (137 metres) high known as the Old Man of Hoy sticks up out of the ocean.

Like Shetland, the Orkneys are strung out along the main bird route between Scotland and Scandinavia, and birds swarm over the islands in numbers worthy of Genesis. Two special groups are attracted to these islands: the Atlantic birds, the ocean wanderers that breed on the islands' cliffs; and the Scandinavian land birds, that use the islands as stepping stones on their great voyages between north and south.

Mainland

Mainland is the principal and most developed island of Orkney. Much of the interior moorland has been reclaimed for farming, especially cattle pasture, but sizeable areas still remain, along with their associated marshes, lochs and streams; and much of the coast, which includes the great naval anchorage and seaduck haven of Scapa Flow, is as pristine as ever.

The RSPB have established several reserves on Mainland. Mirsay Moors and Cottasgarth, in the north of the island, consist of rough, rolling heather moorland, with blanket bogs, marshes, lochans and streams. They are the home of two Orkney specialities that both need wide open spaces in which to hunt: the hen harrier and

short-eared owl. Merlin and Kestrel occasionally nest in the heather.

At the Loom, in north-west Mainland, the reserve occupies a marsh bordered by the Loch of Isbister. Greenland white-fronted geese come here in winter, and otters all year.

Marwick Head reserve runs along a mile of sheer cliffs on the north-west Mainland coast. The seabird colonies are the most spectacular on Mainland and the easiest to see anywhere in Orkney. The most numerous birds are guillemots (35,000) and kittiwake (10,000 pairs) and razorbill, fulmar, a few puffin, rock dove, raven and peregrine also nest here, while great and Arctic skua maraud up and down off-shore. Look out for thrift, sea campion and spring squill, and grey and common seals, too. Lord Kitchener was drowned off Marwick Head in 1916 when his cruiser struck a German

mine. A memorial stone stands on the cliff top, overlooking the wheeling, shrieking birds.

The Hobbister Reserve, by Waulkmill Bay overlooking Scapa Flow, incorporates heather moorland, bogs and fen, low sea cliffs and salt marsh. The diversity of habitat has produced a corresponding diversity of breeding bird species: hen harrier, short-eared owl, merlin, red grouse, red-throated diver, discreet little twite and many more.

Before you go: OS Landranger Series Map Nos. 5, 6, 7. For a list of maps, guides and general literature relating to Orkney, write to the Orkney Tourist Board, Broad Street, Kirkwall, Orkney KW15 1NX.

Getting there: Mainland is the first port of call for most visitors to the Orkneys. British Airways operate a direct service to Kirkwall Airport on Mainland from Aberdeen, Glasgow and Inverness, with connecting services from London, Birmingham and Manchester. Loganair fly from Edinburgh, Inverness and Wick. P&O car ferries sail daily (except Sun) from Scrabster, near Thurso, to the Mainland port of Stromness: journey time 2 hours. Contact P&O, Stromness (T:0856 850 655). A pedestrian ferry operates daily between John O'Groats and Lerwick, May–Sep: journey time 40 minutes (T:095581 353).

Where to stay: the Orkney Tourist Board publishes a full list. Youth hostels are at Stromness and Kirkwall (T:0856 2243). **Further information:** Information Centre, Broad Street, Kirkwall, T:0856 2856 and Ferry Terminal, Stromness (summer only), T:0856 850716. For information about RSPB reserves, contact RSPB Orkney Officer.

Hoy

From the Old Norse
meaning 'high island'

Hoy is the largest island in
Orkney after Mainland; it is
also the highest, rising to
1,577ft (481m) at Ward Hill
and 1,420ft (433m) on the
Guilag. While most of the
Orkney islands are green and
cultivated, Hoy is wild, rugged
moorland with a wilder,
ruggeder coast. The cliffs
soar sheer from the sea to
great heights – 1,140ft (348m)
at St John's Head for
example, and 450ft (137m) at
the immense pillar of rock
called the Old Man of Hoy.

Between Hoy and the
mainland of northern Scotland
swirl the fearsome waters of
the Pentland Firth, the worst
tidal race in the British Isles,
where Atlantic and North Sea
meet, sometimes with
turbulence severe enough to
send a boat to the bottom.

A very extensive RSPB
reserve occupies the north-
west part of Hoy around Ward
Hill. Large populations of
great and Arctic skuas breed
on this large moorland
plateau; kittiwake, shag, raven
and peregrine nest on the
cliffs, with small colony of
Manx sheerwater not far
away. Between Ward Hill and
the Guilag you may be lucky
enough to sight a golden
eagle; you should certainly see
mountain hare.
Getting there: daily passenger
ferry from Stromness
(Mainland) to Moness (Hoy),
or by car ferry from Houton to
Lyness. Taxis or hire cars
available; enquire at pier.
Access: at all times. **Where to
stay:** Hoy Inn at Moness.
Hostels at Rackwick and
outside Moness. **Further
information:** RSPB Warden

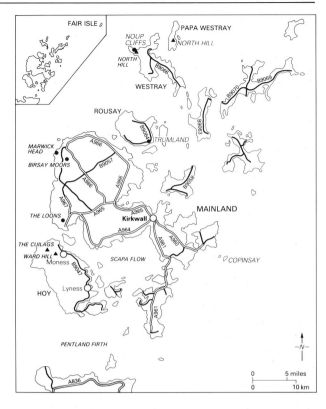

(Keith Fairclough), Ley
House, North Hoy, Orkney.

Copinsay

*RSPB James Fisher
Memorial Seabird Reserve*

Small, grassy island off the
west coast of Mainland, with
nearly a mile of vertical cliffs
where large colonies of
kittiwake, guillemots,
razorbill, fulmar and other
seabirds breed. On the north
coast, where the Old Red
Sandstone cliffs have been
eroded into a jigsaw of geos,
stacks and headlands, the
plant life is luxuriant.

Several nearby little holms,

accessible at low tide, are also
part of the reserve: a small
colony of arctic tern and an
abundant spread of oyster
plant have established
themselves on Corn Holm.
Cormorants have taken over
the Horse of Copinsay as a
nesting site, and puffins can be
seen on Black Holm as well as
Corn Holm.
Getting there: by small boat
on day trip from Skaill in
Deerness. Calm weather.
Prior arrangement necessary;
contact S. Foubister, T:085
674 252. **Access:** unrestricted
at all times. **Where to stay:**
rudimentary self-catering
accomodation in converted
farmhouse, which also serves
as RSPB Information Centre.
Further information: RSPB
Orkney Officer.

Noup Cliffs (Westray)

RSPB Reserve

Perched high on the sandstone cliffs running south from Noup Head at the north-west extremity of the island of Westray, the reserve is just a section of the 5-mile (8-km) stretch of cliffs between Noup Head and Inga Ness which house a huge number of seabirds in spectacularly overcrowded slum conditions.

In one of the largest seabird colonies in the British Isles, 60,000 pairs of kittiwake, 60,000 guillemots and many other seabirds pack the rock ledges in a state of frenzied perpetual motion. the noise, smell, personal habits and seabird expertise of these birds will never fail to astonish and amuse. Peregrine and raven hunt about the cliffs at Noup Head, arctic skua and arctic tern breed on the heathland behind, and grey seal, porpoises and dolphins can sometimes be seen.
When to go: May to July.
Getting there: by passenger ferry to Westray from Kirkwall; or on Loganair flight from Kirkwall (T:0856 2494). To get to the cliffs at Noup Head take the minor road from Pierowall to Noup Farm and then walk along the track to the lighthouse (Map Ref. HY 392500). **Access:** unrestricted to both cliffs and moorland – but please take extreme care on cliffs and close all gates behind you. No dogs. **Where to stay:** bed and breakfast, self-catering and farmhouse accommodation is available on Westray. **Further information:** RSPB Orkney Officer and Orkney Tourist Board, Kirkwall.

North Hill (Papa Westray)

RSPB Reserve

Papa Westray (known in Orkney as 'Papay') is one of the smaller, more intensively crofted islands. The reserve, situated at its uncultivated northern end, consists mainly of maritime heath, a relatively unusual habitat in Britain, of which this is the finest example in northern Scotland.

One of the three largest arctic tern colonies in Britain is located here. The terns are constantly rising from their nests in noisy commotion, sometimes because of marauding skuas, which harry the terns as they return with fish, and gobble up any undefended chicks. A substantial colony of cliff-nesting birds occupy the modest sea-cliffs at Fowl Craig on the east side of the reserve, one of the last breeding sites in Britain of the now-extinct great auk.
Getting there: by passenger ferry to Papa Westray; or on Loganair flight from Kirkwall (T:0856 2494). Enter the reserve from the northern end of the island's principal road. Contact the RSPB summer warden at Gowrie on arrival.
When to go: mid-May to July.
Access: at all times. Visits should be arranged in advance with the warden, who will escort visitors round the nesting colonies. **Where to stay:** self-catering and guest house accomodation available on the island – contact the Papa Community Co-op, Papa Westray, Orkney (T:085 74 267) for details. **Further information:** Contact RSPB Warden, c/o Gowrie, Papa Westray, Orkney KW17 2BU, or RSPB Orkney Officer.

Trumland (Rousay)

RSPB Reserve

Most of the island of Rousay is moorland, and the Trumland reserve at its southern end is no exception. The heather moor above Trumland House rises to 800ft (244m), and its otherwise monotonous expanse is enlivened by several small valleys, a lochan and a few crags. The range of birds is considerable: red-throated diver, hen harrier, short-eared owl, merlin, raven, both kinds of skua and four kinds of gull. Seabirds nest on the cliffs at the north of the island, and are easy to see: not so those other noted denizens of Rousay, the otter and the Orkney vole, who do their best to evade humankind, naturalists included.
When to go: May to July.
Getting there: by sea from Tingwall (off A966, Mainland) on Flaws Ferries, Rousay (T:985 682 203), thence by B9064 to Trumland at south end of island. **Where to stay:** some hotel and bed and breakfast accommodation available on island. **Access:** at all times. Contact the summer warden on arrival. **Further information:** RSPB Summer Warden, Trumland Mill Cottage, Rousay, or RSPB Orkney Officer.

Herma Ness in Shetland, the most
northerly land in Britain, provides
perfect sites for colonies of
gannets and puffins

Fair Isle
From the Old Norsa *Fara,*
the far isle

*National Scenic Area
Council of Europe Diploma
as a place of outstanding
natural beauty and cultural
heritage*

Situated half way between the
Orkneys and the Shetland
Islands, where the waters of
the North Sea and the Atlantic
Ocean meet, Fair Isle is 25
miles (40km) from the nearest
land, which makes it the
remotest continuously
inhabited island in Britain. It
also lies at a crossroads for
many migrant bird species in

the northern hemisphere and
has been the site of a world-
renowned bird observatory
since 1948.

Every spring and autumn
hundreds of thousands of
migrating birds use the island
as a staging post, including
exotics such as the American
kestrel, Siberian ruby throat,
Greenland redpoll and red-
flanked bluetail from as far
away as Siberia, Central Asia,
North America and Brazil, as
well as huge 'falls' of
commoner species – 65,000
redwing on one day alone.

In addition, 18 species of
seabird (including storm
petrels) breed in their
thousands on the shelves and
ledges of the majestic 600-ft
(183-km) sandstone cliffs. The
Fair Isle wren, which is larger
and darker than the mainland
version, is the only British
species listed in the *Red Data
Book of Endangered Species.*

Fair Isle also sports a wide

and luxuriant range of
flowering plants (over 238
recorded species) in habitats
as divers as heather moorland,
hill bog, sea cliff, burn side,
meadow land and cultivated
ground, and you can find
orchids growing wild here, and
Britain's smallest-flowered
plant, the allseed, as well as
arctic-alpine species like dwarf
willow and alpine bistort.

By contrast, you have only
to lift your eyes up towards
the sea to stand a fair chance
of spotting a grey seal or
basking shark, killer whale,
pilot whale or white-peaked
dolphin. Land animals, on the
other hand, are few, though
Fair Isle does produce the
largest house mice anywhere
in the world.

People have lived in Fair
Isle since earliest times. Stone
Age houses, Bronze Age sites
and an Iron Age fort can still
be seen here. The Vikings left
their place names and dialect,

the Norse colonists used it as a stepping stone on the long, hard voyage between Iceland and Scandinavia, and 300 Spanish Armada survivors of the shipwrecked *El Gran Grifon* found sanctuary here amid a populace only one-fifth their number.

Today Fair Isle's 70 residents live in the more verdant southern half of the island. It is a thriving, buoyant community – a rare thing these days on an island as remote as this – which is world-famous for its patterned knitwear and has pursued the most successful and ambitious crofting programme anywhere in Scotland.

Getting there: the *Good Shepherd* mail boat runs between Fair Isle and Shetland (Grutness) on Tuesday and Saturday May–Sep, Saturday only the rest of the year. the voyage takes about 2½ hours and costs 40p. It is essential to book in advance: contact Mr G.W. Stout, Fair Isle, Shetland, T:03512 222.

Loganair run flights between Fair Isle and Shetland (Tingwall) on Monday, Friday and Saturday from May–Oct, Monday and Friday only the rest of the year. Bookings from Loganair, Tingwall, T:059584 246, or Loganair Edinburgh, T:031 344 3341. **When to go:** May and Sep–Oct for bird migrations: May–Jul for breeding birds. **Access:** unrestricted access all year. **Where to stay:** full board at Fair Isle Lodge and Bird Observatory mid–Mar to late Oct. Apply Booking Dept, Fair Isle Lodge and Bird Observatory, Fair Isle, Shetland 2EZ 9JU, T:03512 258. **Further information:** Fair Isle Bird Observatory Trust, 21 Regent Terrace, Edinburgh EH7 5BT.

SHETLAND

Only six degrees south of the Arctic Circle, the Shetland Islands are further north than Leningrad or Labrador. In these latitudes, you can read a book at midnight in summer, when the sun shines for nearly 19 hours in the 24; but in winter there are barely five and a half hours of light a day, and conditions can be stark.

The highly fragmented Shetland archipelago is made up of 117 islands, of which only 13 are inhabited. The islands of Mainland, Yell and Unst form the core of the Shetlands; the coastline is a labyrinthine complex of peninsulas and voes (or long sea-channels) with tremendous cliffs more than a thousand feet high in places. The seabirds are reason enough to visit Britain's northernmost islands: so are the marvellous cliff landscapes and oceanic moods, the sense of standing at one of wild Europe's most dramatic ocean frontiers.

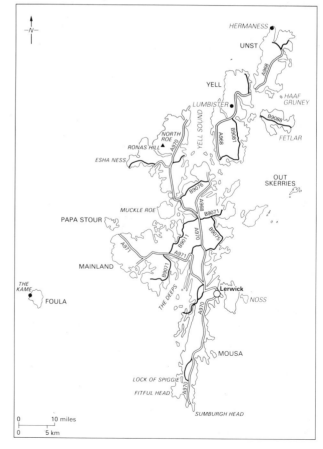

Mainland

Mainland is the largest of the Shetland Isles, its port of Lerwick the first landfall for most visitors. The island's coastline is labyrinthine, a complex jigsaw of peninsulas and voes (or long sea-channels). The stretch of coastline between Fitful Head and the Deeps, and the peninsulas of Muckle Roe, Esha Ness and North Roe have been designated National Scenic Areas.

The island has been inhabited since prehistoric times. On the seashore at Jarlshof near Sumburgh Head – the island's southernmost tip – excavations have revealed Bronze Age, Iron Age and Viking settlements. The Shetlanders of today are a hardy folk of Norse origin who have traditionally earned their livelihood from fishing and crofting, now substantially augmented by North Sea oil.

Ronas Hill in north Mainland is the most extensive wilderness area in Shetland, and at 1,475ft (450m) the highest. The country is very rough, with great sea cliffs extending 15 miles (24km) around Esha Ness to the west, and arctic-alpine habitats on the higher ground. Snowy owls, snow buntings and dotterel can be seen here. The area has been little explored, so now is your chance.

The RSPB have a reserve at Loch of Spiggie in southern Mainland. These 284 acres (115ha) of freshwater loch and marshland near the sea are the most important freshwater site in Shetland for wintering wildfowl. Some 300 whooper swans regularly spend their winters here and a variety of seabirds (skuas and arctic

terns), wildfowl and waders variously breed, moult, display or merely bathe – including 50 long-tailed duck who come each spring to moult prior to migration.
Before you go: OS Landranger Series Map Nos. 1, 2, 3, 4. The Shetland Tourist Organization, Lerwick, Shetland ZE1 OLU stocks a wide range of books, maps and guides available by post.
Getting there: BA operates frequent direct flights to Shetland's Sumburgh airport from Aberdeen, Glasgow and Edinburgh. Convenient connections from most UK airports as well as from Bergen, Oslo, Copenhagen, Paris, Amsterdam and Dublin. Loganair runs a daily service from Edinburgh to Tingwall airport, near Lerwick: flight time 2hrs.

P&O car ferries operate thrice weekly between Aberdeen and Lerwick throughout the year: journey time 14hrs. A Shetland services brochure is available from P&O Ferries, PO Box 5, Jamieson's Quay, Aberdeen AB9 8DL, T:0224 572615.
Where to stay: the Shetland Tourist Organization's *Accommodation and Travel Guide* lists all ranges of accommodation. Youth hostel at Islesburgh House, Lerwick ZE1 0EQ, T:0595 2114.
Further information: Information Centre, Lerwick (T:0595 3434). For information on Loch of Spiggie reserve, contact RSPB Shetland Officer, Peter Ellis, 'Seaview', Sandwick, Shetland ZE2 9HP, T:09505 506 or Summer Warden (by the boat shed at the northern end of the loch).

Foula

From the local dialect meaning 'fowl island'

One of the most spectacular islands in Shetland, 3,540 acres (1,430ha) in extent, Foula is situated 14 miles (22km) west of Mainland. Its precipitous cliffs rise sheer out of the ocean to a height of 1,220ft (372m) at Kame. A seabird island of international importance, it has one of the biggest breeding populations in the North Atlantic.

Altogether 16 species of seabird nest on the island's prodigious rock faces – some 125,000 pairs in all, including nearly one third of all the great skuas breeding in the northern hemisphere, as well as Manx shearwater and Leach's and storm petrel. The interior of the island is high, peat-covered ground sloping down to the scattering of crofts on the east coast.
Getting there: by passenger ferry from Walls in west Mainland every Tuesday and Friday, weather permitting; by plane once a week in summer from Lerwick. **When to go:** May to July for breeding birds. **Access:** at all times. **Where to stay:** Foula has a population of 40 people, but there is no hotel, nor pub, nor accommodation of any sort for casual visitors.

Mousa

A low grassy, uninhabited 450-acre (182-ha) island half a mile off the east coast of Mainland, with the best preserved Pictish broch (or fort) in Britain. It has withstood a thousand years of winter storms and storm

petrels nesting within its walls. Other breeding seabirds include great and arctic skua, arctic terns and black guillemots. Common and grey seals frequent the shore, the former breeding here in good numbers.
Getting there: by small boat from Sand Lodge, Sandwick (on Mainland). **When to go:** May to July. **Access:** unrestricted, except by weather. **Where to stay:** to see the storm petrels you have to stay overnight: contact Lerwick Tourist Office.
Further information: Lerwick Tourist Office.

Noss

From the old Norse *Nøs*, 'a point of rock'

NCC NNR

Noss is basically a wedge of Old Red Sandstone separated from the inhabited island of Bressay by a narrow channel. It is small, green and uninhabited, covers 774 acres (313ha) and rises to nearly 600ft (183m) at the Noup sea cliffs. When a south wind sends rollers crashing on to the island's rocky shore, making landing impossible, Noss is cut off from the world.

Noss was permanently inhabited for over 1,000 years until the last islanders left in 1939. It is still grazed by sheep, but its main claim to fame is its bird population. The towering sandstone cliffs to the east and south of the island house a vertical bird city containing more than 100,000 breeding birds of 12 different species, including nearly 7,000 pairs of gannet, 65,000 guillemots, 10,000 fulmar and 20,000 kittiwakes. Arctic and great skuas, known
210

here by their Shetland name of 'bonxie', breed on the moorland interior.

Noss is overrun by rabbits which not even the feral cats can keep down. Otters are relatively common and come ashore to sleep and breed, and seals, mostly grey Atlantic ones, can often be seen in the water hauled out on to the rocks to bask. Porpoises are often sighted in Noss Sound.
Getting there: by car ferry from Lerwick to Bressay, then by NCC inflatable dinghy across Noss Sound 10am–5pm every day except Mondays and Thursdays, mid–May to end Aug. Check with Lerwick Tourist Office before setting out in case Noss ferry has been cancelled due to fog or rough seas. A red flag is flown on Noss if island is closed.
When to go: May to July.
Access: unrestricted 10am–5pm mid–May to last week in August. Please keep to cliff path so as not to disturb inland skua grounds. No dogs or other pets allowed. Small visitor centre open in summer. **Where to stay:** on Bressay you can try Maryfield House, (T:0595 82 207) or Shalder Brae Guest House (T:0599 82 263). **Further information:** leaflet from NCC Lerwick or Aberdeen, or Lerwick Tourist Office.

Papa Stour

A small island off the west coast of Mainland, with spectacular seabird cliffs and enormous sea caves. The largest arctic tern colony in Shetland is to be found here, as well as arctic skuas and a variety of wildfowl and waders on the small inland lochs. The wild flowers are so abundant that sailors were said to have

taken bearings by their scent.
Getting there: by passenger ferry from West Burrafirth, weather permitting.
Access: unrestricted. **Further information:** Lerwick Tourist Office.

Yell Sound

RSPB reserve comprising 6 small uninhabited bird islands in the sound between Yell and Mainland – Gruney, Ramma Stacks, Unyarey, Fish Holm, Muckle Holm and Samphrey. Some 15 species of seabird are found on these islands, as well as both species of British seals and otters.
When to go: May to July.
Getting there: small boat by special arrangement.
Access: permit only.
Further information: RSPB Shetland Officer.

Lumbister (Yell)

RSPB Reserve

The reserve at Lumbister occupies 4,000 acres (1619ha) of peat moors, lochans and sea cliffs in the south-west corner of Yell, the second largest island in Shetland.

The low hills of Yell are covered in blanket bog and are not wildly beautiful to look at, though they make fine walking. But there are plenty of birds to be seen: red-throated diver, red-breasted merganser and eider breed on the lochs, arctic and great skuas and golden plover, curlew, dunlin and twite breed on the moorland and raven, rock dove, puffin and black guillemot.

Lumbister is one of the few

places in Britain where otters can legitimately be described as common: common and grey seals are common too.
When to go: May to mid-July.
Getting there: car ferry from Mainland to Yell. The reserve is best entered from the lay-by 4 miles (6km) north of Mid Yell on the B968. **Access:** unrestricted, but please take care not to disturb the divers and other breeding birds.
Further information: from Warden (if present) in summer, or RSPB Shetland.

Fetlar

The smallest of the three inhabited northern islands of Shetland, with an RSPB reserve and statutory bird sanctuary of 1,727 acres (699ha) in the northern part –

an area of grassy moorland interspersed with lochans and marshes. A breeding bird population of international importance and the only place in Britain where snowy owls are known to have bred (between 1967 and 1975). Female snowy owls can still be seen on the island, as can Fetlar specialities like whimbrel and red-necked phalarope.
When to go: May to July for breeding birds, September for migrants. **Getting there:** by car ferry from Yell Unst. By air on Loganair daily flights from Lerwick (not Sundays). Report to RSPB Warden at Bealance. **Access:** unrestricted access to the island all year, but the reserve and sanctuary may only be entered in summer (mid-May to late July) by arrangement.
Where to stay: cottage.
Further information: leaflet

The vertiginous bird cliffs of St Kilda, the most far-flung island of Britain, soar out of the Atlantic

and permit from Warden at Bealance, Fetlar, Shetlands ZE2 9OJ, T:095783 246, between April and September. Otherwise enquiries to RSPB Shetland Officer.

Haaf Gruney

NCC NNR

Small, low, uninhabited inshore island off south-east coast of Unst. Storm petrel and black guillemot breed on the boulder beach, and common and grey seals haul out on the rocks.
When to go: May to July.
Getting there: by small boat in calm weather only. **Access:** unrestricted except by

211

weather. **Further information:** leaflet from NCC Lerwick or Aberdeen.

Out Skerries

A group of very small and very rocky islands at the easternmost point of Shetland, beyond which there is no land till Norway. Because of their remote position the Out Skerries attract a remarkable number of rare birds, looking for dry land on which to rest up during passage – more species than in any other part of Shetland except Fair Isle.
Getting there: by passenger ferry from Lerwick on Tuesdays and Fridays, or from Whalsay on Sundays if booked. By air from Lerwick once a week in summer by arrangement.
Further information: Lerwick Tourist Office.

Herma Ness (Unst)

NCC NRR

The reserve on the Herma Ness peninsula of Unst is the most northerly tip of Britain. Beyond the off-shore rocks of Muckle Flugga and Out Stack there is no more land till you reach Siberia on the other side of the North Pole.

Herma Ness is one of the principal bird stations in Europe: 14 species of seabird breed here, including 10,000 pairs of gannets which you can look down on from the top of the cliffs, tens of thousnds of puffins in burrows on the grass slopes and a sizeable population of great and arctic skuas on the moorland.
When to go: May to July.
Getting there: by car ferry to Yell and Unst. By air from

Lerwick on daily Loganair flights (not Sundays). By car to the northern end of the B9086 and thence on foot across the peninsula.
Access: unrestricted except breeding season, when visitors are asked to keep to marked paths and the cliff tops in order to minimize disturbance to birds. **Where to stay:** in private homes locally – check with Lerwick Tourist Office.
Further information: NCC Lerwick or Aberdeen.

THE OUTLIERS

Off the North-West Highland and Hebridean coasts lie a small number of remote islands and rocks. None are very large, but because of their oceanic location they have a wildlife importance out of all proportion to their size. Many of them teem with unbelievable numbers of seabirds; and in their island isolation, some of them have evolved into forms found nowhere else in the world.

They are exciting and romantic places, these wave wrapped outliers of the North Atlantic and Hebridean Sea. A few of them, like St Kilda, are as fabulous as any wild place in the world; some are very difficult to get to or land on; all provide an unforgettable adventure in island-going.

St Kilda

A corruption of the Old Norse *Hirtir* meaning 'Stags'

NTS-NCC Reserve World Heritage Site

To say that St Kilda is spectacular is to clutch at verbal straws; it has a stark grandeur, an awesome magic almost without parallel in Europe. No one who has ever approached St Kilda from the sea will ever forget the first distant glimpse of the islands: massive blue shapes looming on the skyline like cathedrals towed out to sea, then nearer to hand the dizzying whirl of the seabirds, drowning all thought. If I were to be rationed to one wild part of

Britain, it would, I think, be this one.

This isolated group of 7 wild and precipitous islands and stacks lie 45 miles (72km) west of Griminish Point, North Uist, the last gigantic rock paroxysm of the continent of Europe. Hirta, the main island, is the remotest inhabited island in British waters, and its sea cliffs, which at Conachair, on Hirta, leap vertically out of the sea to the prodigious height of 1,397ft (426km) are the highest in Great Britain. Stac an Armin, where the last great auk in Britain was killed in 1840, boasts the highest rock stack in Britain, 627ft (191m) above the thundering sea.

St Kilda is the leading seabird station in Britain, with the largest gannetry in the world, the largest and oldest fulmar colony in Britain and nationally important colonies of puffins and petrels. It is also home to 3 unique sub-species: a wren, a field mouse and the wild Soay sheep, and over 130 species of flowering plants (but not a single tree or shrub). At Village Bay on the southern shore of Hirta – virtually the only place on St Kilda suitable for human habitation – lie the poignant remains of a curving line of cottages known as the Street. These were once the homes of a remarkable community; well into the age of intercontinental flight these secluded citizens of the United Kingdom eked out a living by harvesting the birds from St Kilda's terrifying cliffs. Tragically the St Kildans were forced by recurrent epidemics, successive crop failures and the demoralisation that set in when they realized they were impoverished anachronisms in the modern world, to evacuate the island in 1930.

In 1957 the National Trust for Scotland became owners of the island. The Trust then leased the entire archipelago to the Nature Conservancy as a National Nature Reserve, and the Conservancy in turn sub-leased a small area of Hirta to the Ministry of Defence as an Army rocket-tracking station. For some years annual groups of volunteers have been restoring the remains of the unique settlement in Village Bay. This is still almost the only way the ordinary civilian can get to stay for any period of time on this loneliest, stormiest, most spectacular and unforgettable of all the British Isles. **Getting there:** the Army runs regular helicopter flights out from the mainland, but you would need to have a *very* good reason to persuade them to take you. The NTS run cruises and circumnavigations

round the islands which may provide a few hours ashore. Several charter companies run short excursions to St Kilda, but you sleep on board, not on the island. Private charters are expensive. For details of working holidays on Hirta – the best way to spend a fortnight there if you don't mind working a 24 hour week doing restoration work – contact NTS Edinburgh. For small boat sailings to St Kilda, North Rona (see p.203), the Shiants (p.202) and other outliers, contact Grace Mitchell, 25 Glasgow Street, Hillhead, Glasgow G12 8JW, T:061 339 0297. **Access:** anyone wishing to stay on Hirta must first obtain permission from the NTS. Please inform the NTS even if you only propose a temporary landing. Landing on other islands or stacks is virtually impossible. **Where to stay:** if you are visiting by boat, you normally sleep on the boat anchored in Village Bay, Hirta. Accommodation on land at Village Bay is available for members of NTS work parties. There is also a camp site. Apply NTS or NCC Inverness. **Further information:** NTS Edinburgh (T:031 226 5922) or contact NCC Summer Warden, David Miller, Village Bay, Hirta, on arrival. **Further reading:** Alan Small (Ed.): *A St Kilda Handbook* (NTS 1979; K. Williamson and J.M. Boyd: *St Kilda Summer* (1960); T. Steel: *The Life and Death of St Kilda* (1965).

Sule Skerry

A flat reef some 40 miles (64km) north of Loch Eriboll on the north coast of Scotland, half a mile (1km) long, 35

acres (14ha) in extent, 45ft (14m) at its highest point. Home to one of Britain's largest puffin colonies. Lighthouse.

Sule Stack

Small islet, a few miles south-west of Sule Skerry, 6 acres (2.5ha) in extent, 130ft (40m) high. Small gannetry. Rather steep, exposed and inaccessible – only 4 naturalists have been able to get ashore in 50 years.

Rockall

A 70-ft high (21-m), 83-ft (25-m) wide rock far out in the North Atlantic, 191 miles (305km) due west of St Kilda, Rockall is the remotest part of Great Britain and the only British land beyond the continental shelf. Rockall was landed on in 1810, 1887, 1888, 1921, 1955 and 1985, on the last occasion by ex-SAS officer and transatlantic oarsman Tom McClean, who survived alone on the rock for 40 days – a record. **Getting there:** no known means. **Accommodation:** none. **Further information:** none.

'Yet three score miles – rocks – surge – uninhabited – uncouth landing places: how to get to it, and upon it – that is a question!'

T. S. Muir
Ecclesiological Notes on the Islands of Scotland

USEFUL ADDRESSES

The following organizations provide useful information and assistance for those interested in exploring Wild Britain and in learning about its flora and fauna. Several of them are mentioned throughout this book, often in abbreviated form. Where this is the case, the abbreviations used are given in brackets.

British Travel Centre, 12 Lower Regent Street, London WC1, T:01-730 3400.

Wales Tourist Board, 3 Castle Street, Cardiff CF1 2RD, T:0222 27281.

Scottish Tourist Board, 23 Ravelston Terrace, Edinburgh EH4 3EU, T:031-332 2433 and 137 Knightsbridge, London SW1 7PN, T:01-930 8661/8662.

Highland and Island Development Board, Bridge House, 27 Bank Street, Inverness IV1 1QR.

Countryside Commission, John Dower House, Crescent Place, Cheltenham, Gloucestershire GL50 3RA, T:0242 21381.

Countryside Commission for Scotland, Battleby House, Ridgorton, Perth PH1 3EW.

The Council for National Parks, 45 Shelton Street, London WC2H 9HJ, T:01-240 3603/4.

National Trust (NT), 42 Queen Anne's Gate, London SW1H 9AS.

National Trust for Scotland (NTS), 15 Queen Anne's Gate, London SW1, T:01-222 4856.

Nature Conservancy Council (NCC) – Great Britain HQ (Peterborough), T:0733 40345.

Forestry Commission (FC), 231 Corstorphine Road, Edinburgh, T:031-334 0303.

Council for the Protection of Rural England, 4 Hobart Place, London SW1, T:01-235 9481.

Council for the Protection of Rural Wales, 14 Broad Street, Welshpool, Powys SY21 7SD, T:0938 2525.

Royal Society for Nature Conservation (RSNC), The Green, Nettleham, Lincoln LN2 2NR. *(The RSNC is an umbrella organization with*

44 associated trusts throughout Britain. Those which own reserves covered in this book are listed below.)

Cumbria Trust for Nature Conservation (CTNC), Church Street, Ambleside LA22 0BU.

Devon Trust for Nature Conservation (DTNC), 35 New Bridge Street, Exeter EX3 4AH.

Kent Trust for Nature Conservation (KTNC), 125 High Street, Rainham, Kent ME8 8AN.

Norfolk Naturalists' Trust (NNT), 72 Cathedral Close, Norwich NR1 4DF.

Suffolk Trust for Nature Conservation (STNC), St Edmund House, Ropewalk, Ipswich IP4 1LZ.

West Wales Naturalists' Trust (WWNT), 7 Market Street, Haverfordwest, Dyfed.

Scottish Wildlife Trust (SWT), 25 Johnston Terrace, Edinburgh EH1 2NH.

Yorkshire Naturalists' Trust (YNT), 20 Castlegate, York YO1 1RP.

Royal Society for the Protection of Birds (RSPB), The Lodge, Sandy, Bedfordshire SG19 2DL, T:0767 80551.

RSPB Wales Office, Bryn Isel, The Bank, Newtown, Powys ZY16 2AB, T:0686 26678.

RSPB Scottish Office, 17 Regent Terrace, Edinburgh EH7 5BN, T:031-556 5624.

RSPB Orkney Officer, Smyril, Stenness, Stromness, Orkney KW16 3JX.

RSPB Shetland Officer, Seaview, Sandwick, Shetland ZE2 9HP.

Wildfowl Trust, Slimbridge, Gloucester GL2 7BT.

Youth Hostels Association (YHA), Trevelyan House, 8 St Stephen's Hill, St Albans, Hertfordshire AL1 2DY.

Scottish Youth Hostels Association, 7 Glebe Crescent, Stirling FK8 2JA, T:0786 2821.

Long Distance Walkers Association, Sue Coles (Secretary), 8 Upton Grey Close, Winchester SO22 6NE.

Ramblers Association, 1-5 Wandsworth Road, London SW8 2JL, T:01-235 9481.

British Mountaineering Council, Crawford House, Precinct Centre, Booth Street East, Manchester M12 9RZ, T:061-273 5835.

Field Studies Council, 62 Wilson Street, London EC2, T:01-247 4651.

FURTHER READING

The following books are particularly helpful at a national level. Regional or local books are mentioned in the text where appropriate.

Countryside Commission (various authors): *The National Parks Of England And Wales* (Webb and Bower 1987).

Crawford, Peter: *The Living Isles – A Natural History Of Britain And Ireland* (BBC 1985).

Hywel-Davies, Jeremy and Thom, Valerie: *The Macmillan Guide To Britain's Nature Reserves* (Macmillan 1986).

Long Distance Walkers Association: *Long Distance Walkers Handbook* (published annually).

Redman, Nigel and Harrap, Simon: *Birdwatching In Britain – A Site By Site Guide* (Christopher Helm 1987).

Scottish Mountaineering Trust: *Mountain Guides To The Scottish Highlands And Islands*.

Smith, Roland: *Wildest Britain – The National Parks Of England And Wales* (Blandford Press 1983).

Wilson, Ken and Gilbert, Richard: *The Big Walks – Challenging Mountain Walks And Scrambles In The British Isles* (Diadem Books 1981).

Wilson, Ken and Gilbert Richard: *Classic Walks – Mountain And Moorland Walks In Britain And Ireland* (Diadem Books 1986).

INDEX

Species are indexed only where information is provided in addition to location, and where they are illustrated; page references in *italics* refer to illustrations.

PICTURE CREDITS

Jacket Front Cover – John Cleare/Mountain Camera, Jacket Back Cover – Harry Williams. 10,11 – Colin Molyneux. 19, 22 – John Cleare/Mountain Camera. 27 – Dr. Alan Beaumont. 31 – Colin Molyneux. 35 – John Cleare/Mountain Camera. 38 – Dr. Alan Beaumont. 42, 43 – Michael Freeman, 47, 50, 51, 54, 55 – Dr. Alan Beaumont. 59 – Michael Freeman. 62, 63 – John Cleare/Mountain Camera. 70 – John Heseltine. 75 – Simon Warner. 78, 83 – John Cleare/Mountain Camera. 87 – Simon Warner. 90, 91 – Douglas Botting. 98 – Roger Scruton. 103 – John Cleare/Mountain Camera. 107 – Dr. Alan Beaumont. 110, 111 – Colin Molyneux. 119 – Kim Taylor, Bruce Coleman Ltd. 122 – John Cleare/Mountain Camera. 127 – Colin Molyneux. 130 – John Cleare/ Mountain Camera. 134, 135 – Colin Molyneux. 138, 139, 142, 143 – John Cleare/ Mountain Camera. 147 – Derek G. Widdicombe. 151 – Jeremy Young, Landscape Only. 155, 158, 159 – John Cleare/Mountain Camera. 175 – Colin Molyneux. 178, 179 – Archie Miles. 183 – Alastair Scott. 187 – John Cleare/ Mountain Camera. 191 – Douglas Botting. 194 – Gordon Langsbury, Bruce Coleman Ltd. 199 – Michael Feeman. 203 – Alastair Scott. 207 – Robert Burton, Bruce Coleman Ltd. 211 – John Cleare/Mountain Camera.

ACKNOWLEDGEMENTS

The author and editors wish to extend special thanks to James Millar Watt for his hospitality at Sandaig, Wester Ross; Anthony Smith of Bamburgh, Northumberland for hospitality and facilities; and to Bud Young for hospitality and facilities on Dartmoor and in the New Forest.

Grateful thanks are also due to: Kevin Baverstock; Dr David Boddington; Kit Boddington; Roger Boulanger; Louise Brown; Valerie Chandler; Franky Eynon; Verena Gnatzy; Tony Hare; Judith Harte; Debbi Loth; Anthony Mason; Rob Mitchell; Christine Noble; Sonal Patel; Tracey Stead; Lee Toomey.